Suddenly Single

Heartbreak in Paradise
(inspired by real life events)

Written By:
M. Sherrer

Suddenly Single: Heartbreak in Paradise

Copyright © 2015 by M Sherrer

www.darkdiamondbooks.com/author_msherrer.html

Dark Diamond Publishing, LLC.

All rights reserved. No part of this book may be reproduced, scanned, or distributed in any printed or electronic form without permission. Please do not participate in or encourage piracy of copyrighted materials in violation of the author's rights. Purchase only authorized editions.

Book Cover Art by Darien Pitts
Edited by Dark Diamond Publishing, LLC.

ISBN: 9780989578028

www.darkdiamondbooks.com

Printed in the United States of America

PUBLISHER'S NOTE
This is a work of fiction. Names, characters, places, and incidents either are the product of the author's imagination or are used factitiously, and any resemblance to actual persons, living or dead, business establishments, events, or locales is entirely coincidental.

To the Kia's of the world:
Love will come. ♥

Prologue

Little did Kia know, her fate started when Jordyn purchased her timeshare.......

"Hello?"

"What's up whoadie? How is your brother? I know he just had the heart attack." Kia says to Jordyn when she answers the phone.

"He's doing better. He is at home getting stronger each day. What's up with you?"

"Listen, when are you going to Barbados again?" Kia inquires.

"Week 50, dawg....week 50. December 15 – December 21. Well, the 15th starts my timeshare but I was thinking of going a couple of days early if the airline ticket is cheaper. Why? You coming?"

"Yea. I want to come this year. I need a vacation!!!...I'm tired of this same ole shit every day. They are driving me crazy. Hell, I need a cigarette and I don't even smoke!!!"

"It took you 7 years to decide you want to come with me!!! Come on!! Shiiid, I'm ready to go now... We gon' have fun. Dawg, wait until you see the sea turtles!! They are big hell! Shiiid Allison was scared of them," Jordyn says enthusiastically.

"Whaaat?"

"Yea dawg, 'cause they will just swim up to you."

"Umm where were y'all at where the sea turtles were just swimming up to you?" Kia asks with one eyebrow raised.

"We went out on the catamaran and we were on a snorkeling stop. Allison can't swim so one of the crew members took us out. Babay, that turtle came up to us and I looked around and Allison was back on the boat!!!" Jordyn laughs as she recalls the story.

Both ladies burst out in uncontrollable laughter.

"Let's look up tickets. Gone and bust out that ole laptop," Jordyn says once they compose themselves.

"Yea dawg. I need to get away. I decided this year I'm going to treat myself. It just feels like it is the right time for me to go. I figured out where I can get some extra money, so I'm good!!...OOOOH I can't wait!!!"

For the next two hours, Jordyn and Kia look up ticket prices to see which one is the best deal. Even though they were looking at the same website, they were getting two different prices. Eventually, they decide on the flights they would take. Incidentally, leaving on the 13th was the best deal so they would have 2 extra days, and each book their ticket. Since Jordyn lives in Dallas and Kia lives in Houston, they will meet in Miami then catch American Airlines flight #1995 to Barbados departing at 6:30PM. Jordyn relays this information to her friend Haileigh who also said she wanted to go this year. Haileigh books her ticket as well and the three ladies were ready to get their vacation started!!!

Chapter 1

<u>December 13, 2012</u>

Dear Lord, thank you for waking me up this morning and allowing me to see another day. Thank you for letting me be able to take this vacation and get away. Thank you in advance for letting me have the time of my life. Lord, I ask if this plane is not going to land safely, please don't let it take off. Hold it on the ground until it is going to land safely. Please let the airplane mechanics not have malice in their hearts and sabotage the safety of the plane and its passengers. Please let the pilots be well rested and give them guidance should they encounter any trouble. Lord, please let Jordyn and Haileigh arrive safely and have a good flight. And Lord, please forgive me for anything that I may have done that has not been pleasing to you. Help me to recall those things to my memory and not do them again. Help me to be quick to forgive others as you are quick to forgive me. Lord, I love and I need you. These things I ask in your son Jesus Christ name I pray. Amen.

"Ladies and Gentlemen, the front doors of the plane have been closed. Please turn off and stow all portable electronic devices. Anything with an on/off switch needs to be powered completely down and stowed. Please make sure your seat backs and tray tables are in their full upright position as we prepare for takeoff..."

Here we go! Kia thinks to herself trying to contain her excitement. Before she knew it they were getting ready to land in Miami.

"Ladies and Gentleman, as we prepare for landing, we will be arriving at gate D4. If you have a connecting flight to Barbados you will depart from Gate D5, connecting on to Bogota, Gate D9, and Montego Bay, Gate D10. Local time is 5:25PM, and it is a cool 72 degrees. Welcome to Miami."

Oh good, I only have to go one gate over. Thank you Lord!! Kia thinks to herself. As she disembarks the plane, she makes a beeline for the bathroom before having to board the flight to Barbados because she hates using the bathroom on the plane. When coming out she looks around for any sign of Jordyn and Haileigh for their flight is scheduled to arrive from Dallas any minute now.

"American Airlines Flight #1995 is now boarding Group 2. All passengers with a Group 1 or Group 2 Boarding Pass, please proceed to gate D5 at this time and be sure to have your passports in hand."

Oh shit that's me. Still not seeing any sign of Jordyn and Haileigh, Kia proceeds on to Gate D5 to board the plane and hands the gate attendant her passport.

"Ma'am, you did not check in at the desk. Amy she needs to check in," she yells over to the other gate attendant.

"Ma'am let me see your passport. Ok hun. You are all checked in."

"Ummm, let me ask you something. If a connecting flight does not arrive on time, will you all hold the plane?" Kia asks with a sinking feeling in her stomach, still not seeing any sign of Jordyn or Haileigh.

"Where is it coming from?"

"Dallas."

"Oh, they are not going to make it."

Kia's heart drops down to her feet. "What do you mean they are not going to make it?!?!"

"The flight was delayed coming out of Dallas."

Suddenly Single

Kia stands frozen, wanting to cry, in between the counter and the door to the jet way and thinks to herself, *What am I supposed to do? I have never been this far out of the country before, it is going to be nighttime when I get there and....*

The gate attendant breaks her train of thought by asking, "What's wrong, honey?"

"My friends are not going to make this flight and I don't know what to do, I have never been to Barbados before."

"Go on anyway. Do something for yourself. You will be fine."

With that, Kia reluctantly boards flight #1995 by herself still clinging to the hope that she will see some sign of Jordyn and Haileigh. She stows her CPAP machine and carry-on bag and sinks down into her seat by the window. Jordyn is supposed to have the seat right in front of her, but oddly enough there is already somebody else sitting in that seat. *Hmmph. That's strange,* she thinks to herself. As people are still boarding, she pulls out her phone and calls Jordyn, but it goes straight to voicemail. "Damn. They haven't landed."

She quickly sends a text message: `Dawg, I am on this plane and was told y'all were not going to make it. Can you please call the place where we are staying and let them know I'm coming? Try and call me as soon as you land.`

The phone starts announcing: Incoming coming call from Jord---.

Kia answers the phone before it could finish announcing who it was. "Dawg, where are you?

"Whoadie, we just landed, but we are not going to make it."

"What do you mean you are not going to make it? We are still sitting here at the gate, and the doors are still open."

"Dawg, we are at Gate D35 on the other side of the airport and Haileigh can't run because she hurt her ankle."

"Damn. Okay."

"Listen, I will call them. The name of the place where we are staying is called Divi Southwinds Resort. Take a cab from the airport. You will be okay. It is safe."

"Damn, okay...Y'all still try and make it because the doors are still open."

"We trying, dawg....we trying."

"Okay, well if you don't make it I will text you when I get there."

"Okay. Bye."

Not knowing if her phone will even work in Barbados, Kia quickly dials the number to Verizon customer service where they explain that her phone will work over there and the roaming charges ($1.99/minute for incoming and outgoing calls; $.25 for sent texts and $.05 for incoming texts). She thanks the lady on the other end of the phone but rushes her off as the flight attendant is telling her she has to turn off her phone now.

Before she could power off the phone, it starts announcing: Incoming coming call from Jord---.

"Whoadie, did y'all make it?"

"We are at the gate but they won't let us on!!!"

"Why not?!?!"

"They say the door is already closed."

"Dawg, no it's not!! The door is still open!!!" Kia tells her trying not to yell to loudly.

"Dawg, they won't let us on. Ain't this a bitch?!?!"

"Damn, Dawg!!"

"Listen, I'm going to call the hotel and tell them you are coming. Just take a cab when you get there."

"Okay...SHIT!!! Bye."

"Bye."

"Ladies and Gentleman, this is your pilot, Captain Michael Pitts. We are checking the weights and balances on the plane. Once that is complete we will push away from the gate...." Kia does not hear anything he says after that because she is lost in her own thoughts of what the hell just happened. She tells herself, *You are grown; you have traveled before, put on your big girls panties and do this.*

"Are you okay?" asks the rather nice looking man that has taken a seat next to her on the plane.

She doesn't even notice him sitting there with all that had occurred. *Mmmm....When did he get here?* she thinks to herself.

"Not really," she dismally states.

"What's wrong?" he asks.

"I have never been to Barbados, and I was supposed to meet my two friends here, but their connecting flight was late. They made it to the gate, but they won't let them on the plane."

"What?? That's crazy," he says.

"The worst part about it is this is the first time I have traveled this far alone, I have no idea where I'm going and..." She begins to shake her head and choke back tears. "...and everything is in my friend's name."

"You will be fine." He half chuckles and tells her reassuringly. "Where are you staying?"

"Divi Southwinds."

"Oh yea. You will be fine. Divi is in a good location next to restaurants and clubs. It's on The Gap. They should let you check in. Just explain what happened, and you should be good to go. Don't worry about it. Just relax and enjoy yourself."

"Thank you," she says. "How do you know so much about Barbados?"

"I'm from there. I'm going home to see my family for the holidays. I live and work in St. Louis."

Oh, she thinks to herself. She would have never guessed he was from there, as he did not speak with any kind of accent. He was about 6'0" tall, very fair-skinned complexion, and looked as if he was a cross between Puerto Rican and White. Not to mention he had the longest, prettiest, wavy hair that was pulled up into a very masculine ponytail. She just wants to rub her hands all through it. He kind of reminds her of Fabio from the romance novels.

Over the next three and a half hours, Kia and "Fabio" talk candidly about life, travels and relationships. As it turns out, he is single with no kids (*plus*), works as an actuary (*plus*), and makes this trip at least twice a year (*likes to travel - plus*). It seemed as if the rocky start to her trip has taken a turn for the better.

"Ladies and Gentleman, as we prepare for landing, we will be arriving at gate 11. Local time here in Barbados is 11:05PM, and it is a nice 78 degrees. As always, we know you have a choice when flying. Thank you for choosing American Airlines. Welcome to Barbados. "

"So, what is your name?" she asks as she is gathering her belongings.

"Steven. Steven Edington, nice to meet you. What is your name?" he asks.

"Kia, nice to meet you as well. So do you think I will get to speak with you again?" she bravely asks.

"Probably not," he says just as calm.

She has to catch her bottom jaw from hitting her lap. *What the hell does he mean 'probably not'?!?! Is he serious??!!!*

"After you sat here and talked to me for three and a half hours, reassured me I was going to be okay, and even joked with me when I had to get up and use the bathroom?" She stares at him searching for any sign of "I'm just playing" or something of the sort to fall from his lips but it never did.

Instead he says, "Yea. Probably not, I stay busy."

"Ok," she says dryly as she politely rolls her eyes and looks out the window into the darkness of the unknown and unfamiliar airport. All she could see was a glow of lights about 50 yards away. *Why does the gate area look so far away?* she thinks to herself. She then sees the passengers walking down the stairs, off the plane OUTSIDE and then into the airport. *This is different.*

Once inside the airport, she was able to use the bathroom once more and make her way through Customs, which fortunately, at that time of night, did not take very long. She makes her way over to the luggage carousel to claim her bag and she notices the "last bag" suitcase is circling on the belt. She continues to wait and look for her bag with about 25 other people who are still waiting themselves. After about 5 minutes, she comes to the realization that all the bags are off the plane and have been sent out already. Her bag is not there. *This can't be happening,* she thinks. She and the 25 other people then join about 30 other passengers from her flight, including Mr. Actuary and his friends, to make a claim for their bags that have not arrived.

It is close to 2:00AM when Kia finally leaves Bridgetown Grantley Adams Airport. As she is walking through the doors of the airport, she is a little anxious because she does not know what to expect. She spots a taxi sign and walks towards the gentleman who greets her warmly. He asks where she is going, and she tells him. He loads up her luggage and instructs her to get in the car on the left side. She forgot they do drive on the left over there so the steering wheel and such is on the right side of the car. *This will take some getting used to.*

As they are making their way along the road to the hotel, Kia can't help but take in the sights, well what she can see at 2:00 in the morning anyway. She can feel the warm breeze on her skin as they drive along. She can't see the water because of the darkness but she can hear the waves crashing in the distance. She also hears a very loud, unidentifiable noise.

"What is that noise?" she asks the cab driver.

"Frogs," he replies. "They are very small, and you can barely see them."

"Frogs? Wow. Our frogs don't sound like that at home," she says amazed.

"Where are you from?" he asks.

"Houston, Texas."

"Ah the States. Is this your first time to Barbados?" he asks inquisitively.

"Yes it is, and I'm excited about it. Is there anything open to eat?" She asks because she has not eaten all day and her hungry alter ego "Agatha" was on the verge of showing herself especially given the rocky start to her trip.

"Umm, most of the restaurants are closed. There is a place doing a talent show that may have some chicken. Do you want that?"

"No. I guess I will just go on to the hotel and see what they may have," she tells him. Right about then they are passing a Shell petro station. She should tell him to stop, but she opts to keep going. Another 30 seconds further, and they are pulling into Divi Southwinds Resort. She pays him the fare, in US Dollars because that is all she has, and thanks him. As she walks up to the desk, she gives the lady her name and starts explaining the story and the lady stops her mid-sentence and tells her it is okay because her friend called and explained the situation. Relieved to hear that, Kia asks her do they have room service and she says no. She asks do they have a vending machine and she says no. The lady does tell her that there is a Shell petro station right up the street that she can get something to eat but she would have to walk. Kia wasn't walking anywhere at that hour in a country that she had never been in before. The lady does tell her that the breakfast will be served in the restaurant from 7:00AM-11:00AM in the morning. Kia says "okay", took the key and thanked her for the information. She heads to the room where she could finally exhale.

The room is nice. It has a full kitchen to the right as you walk in the door, a living room area further ahead, and a bedroom and bathroom to the left as you come in the door. *This is nice.* She thinks to herself. She looks through the kitchen for any sign of nourishment but can find none. She goes into the bedroom and takes her carry-on bag and CPAP machine and places them on the bed. Thankfully, Kia had sense enough to pack her toiletries, an outfit, a swimsuit, some flip flops, and some underwear in her carry-on bag just in case something like this happened. She takes a shower in the lukewarm water, and tries to suppress the hunger she is feeling. At least she can drink a glass of water and go to sleep and will not have to think about it.

After she gets out of the shower, she puts on a t-shirt she had in the carry-on and she pulls out her phone to call Jordyn and it goes to voicemail. She leaves a message. She turns on the TV and searches for something interesting to watch, but all she can find is Family Feud. She looks out the sliding glass door that was in the living room to try and see what kind of view she has, but all she could see was the front of the hotel. She comes back in and drinks that glass of water and goes back into the bedroom to try and watch TV and unwind from her long day of travels.

The phone starts announcing: Incoming coming call from Jordyn.

"Hello?"

"Whoadie, you will never guess where we are."

"Where?"

"New York City..."

"New York?!?!?" Kia says bewildered.

"I said New York City."

"What the hell are you doing in New York?"

"It was about 30 people on our Dallas flight that were supposed to get on the Barbados flight. Flight 1089 that leaves in the morning from Miami to Barbados was oversold so we would've had to fly stand by. So they flew us to New York because the flight to Barbados from New York was not sold out. So we leave at 8:00 in the morning and get to Barbados around 2:30 tomorrow."

"Dawg, so ya'll flew from Dallas to Miami, Miami to New York and then will go from New York to Barbados?!? I know you are sick of flying!!"

"Dawg, right about now, I am ready for my head to hit the pillow!!" Jordyn says.

"I feel you, dawg. I'm sorry you had to go through all of that, but you will be here tomorrow and can rest and relax. Dawg, guess what? They left my luggage in Miami!! Thank goodness I packed some clothes and stuff in my carry-on."

"Whaaaat whoadie? I know you are tired too. When is your bag coming? "

"It will be here sometime tomorrow. They are going to deliver it. That's probably why they were checking the weights and balances on the plane. When I was waiting in line to make my claim, I did notice that there were these huge and I mean huge black bags that made it on the plane. They were probably too heavy and that is why so many bags were left. I don't know. I'm just happy to be here."

"How many bags were left?"

"Dawg, it was at least 50 people or so in that line. It was like they left a whole tram full of luggage in Miami. And the worst part about it is, they did not even call ahead to BGI to let them know so it was only ONE girl working. She finally got some help from the dude that probably unloaded the plane. But dang….. I have only been here at the hotel for about 30 minutes."

"Well damn. Ok, whoadie, well I am going to hit the pillow. I will see you tomorrow."

"Ok, dawg, well y'all be safe. See you tomorrow, bye."

"Bye." With that, Kia put on her CPAP mask, turned on the machine, and went to sleep.

The next morning, she wakes up around 9:45AM. She jumps out of bed anxious to see the beauty she missed the night before. She walks outside on the balcony and still all she can see is the front of the hotel. At least this time, she can see some houses in the distance and a huge odd looking tree on the hotel grounds. Still no water in sight, but she can hear it. She brushes her teeth, pulls her braids back in a ponytail and puts on her swimsuit under the sundress she had in her bag. By now it is a little after

10:00AM and she gathers the things she needs puts them in her beach bag and heads for the restaurant to get some breakfast.

As she leaves out the door to the hotel room, she catches a glimpse of the water from the opening at the end of the hallway. She is mesmerized by the different shades of blue she sees in the distance. She stands there for a minute and takes it all in before heading down to the restaurant. She even snaps a couple of photos to capture the moment.

When she arrives at the restaurant, the waiter tells her the restaurant is closed and that it closes at 10:00AM. Her heart sinks because she is so hungry not having eaten at all the day before and not knowing where else she can go. She tells him that the lady at the front desk overnight told her it would be open until 11:00AM. He tells her okay and lets her come on in because it is still some food left on the buffet. He asks her does she want some eggs because they are made to order. She tells him no thank you on the eggs and proceeds to make her way to where the food is located. She picks up her plate and fills it with hash browns, bacon, fish cakes (which she never had but is willing to try), pineapples, strawberries and a biscuit, and to drink she has pineapple juice and hot tea.

She tries not to inhale the food but does eat it rather quickly because she is so hungry. When she finishes eating, she tells the waiter thank you for letting her eat and asks which way was the beach. He tells her she is welcome and pointed her in the way of the water. As she is walking to the beach, which is across the street out the back gate of the hotel, she feels humbled in a way because she never thought she would have to ask somebody to let her eat.

As she gets closer and closer to the beach, she tries not to cry as she has become a little overwhelmed with emotion with all she has been through the day before and she is taken aback with all of the breathtaking beauty of the surroundings; white sand and turquoise blue water is all she could see for what seemed like miles. She spots an empty lounge chair under a tree and puts her things down. She takes off her sundress that was serving as a cover up and situates herself on the lounge chair. She pulls out her iPod, and her favorite song *Saravah* by Les Nubians is already queued. She relaxes on the lounge chair and takes in the scenery and lets her food digest before taking a dip in the beautiful water.

After about 30 minutes of listening to music and looking at people from all different walks of life on the beach, she decides to go for her first swim in the Caribbean Sea. As she walks down into the water, she feels eyes on her watching her every move. She pays them no mind. *Perhaps they have never seen all this lusciousness in a swimsuit before,* she thinks to herself. Whatever they were thinking it didn't matter. She is determined to immerse herself in that turquoise goodness that she has waited this long to do and she struts right into the water. It is nice and warm and does not take long to "get used to". The waves are very mild and the sea is almost still.

I could get used to this, she thinks out loud. She goes out only about waist deep because she is out there by herself and from what she could see there are not any lifeguards on this beach. She is amazed that she can look down and see her feet clearly. This is the total opposite of the beaches back home. She wouldn't even go ankle deep in that doo-doo brown, nasty water and she doesn't even like going to the beach at home.

She splashes around in the water and watches the people on the shore and even catches a school of fish swimming by every so often. At one point she turns and looks out on the horizon and is captivated by the endless shades of blue. She is snapped out of her barrage of thoughts, some good, some X-rated, with the sight of something sticking its head out of the surface of the water. She hurriedly makes her way back to the shore, because after her experience in Florida 3 years earlier, she does not want to take a chance. After she gets back to land she realizes that it was a sea turtle. It was hard for her to see while in the water because she didn't have on her glasses, but she wasn't risking it.

She settles back in her lounge chair and fires up the iPod again. She decides to whip out her cell phone and take a few shots of the scenery and herself to post to Facebook. When she finishes her "photo shoot", she sinks in the chair and absorbs the relaxing atmosphere while looking out over the white sand and blue water. Oh how she longs to be in a relationship, and how she wishes she could be here with the man of her dreams. Her thoughts seem to be as vast as the sea she was looking at.

"Excuse me." Her concentration is broken by a man standing to her right in some sort of uniform.

"Yes?" she says rather sarcastically. She is a tad bit upset that her daydream is interrupted.

"I'm sorry to bother you, but I was watching you in the water earlier and I wanted to tell you, you are a very pretty lady."

She smiles shyly, embarrassed by her sarcastic tone moments ago, and tells him, "Thank you."

"Where are you from?" he asks.

"Houston, Texas," she responds.

"Oh okay. You are from the States. Is this your first time to Barbados?" he asks.

"Yes it is," she says.

"Well welcome to the island," he boasts.

"Thank you. So what do you do? I see the uniform."

"I'm a Beach Ranger. I patrol up and down the beach and make sure nobody is getting into trouble," he says proudly.

"Kind of like the beach police then?"

"Yes kind of like that," he laughs. "So are you here by yourself?"

"No. My two friends are on their way."

"I see. Okay. That's good. Would it be okay if I gave you my number? I would love to take you out," he says.

Not quite knowing how to politely decline, Kia takes his number. "What is your name?" she asks not wanting to just take a number from a stranger.

"Devon, what's yours?"

"My name is Kia, nice to meet you."

"I'm off on Sunday. Maybe I can take you down to the boardwalk for a drink."

"That sounds like a plan," she tells him.

"Perfect. I will see you later. Enjoy your afternoon."

"I will. Thank you."

He walks on down the beach doing what she assumes is his normal patrol. She wonders how many other tourists he hits on each day, what if he is the one and she doesn't like him, and what if she goes out with him anyway and she ends up liking him. But the thoughts flee as she refuses to be consumed with the "what if's". She is trying to enjoy the sereneness of lying out at the beach, under a tree, enjoying a nice warm breeze while gazing at the waves that gently crash on the shore.

She picks up her phone and notices that is about 2:20PM. Jordyn and Haileigh should be arriving soon. She keeps looking towards the sky because she has seen planes fly over all morning. Sure enough right about 2:25PM, an American Airlines plane flies overhead. She figures this has to be Jordyn and Haileigh's flight, and she even manages to snap a pic as it flew past. She figures she will give them about an hour or so to get to the hotel at which time she will head back. For now she continues to do what she is doing: enjoying her vacation!! *Crown Royal* by Jill Scott is playing in her ears and images of her and her dream man are playing in her head.

Kia heads back to the room about 3:45PM to wait for Jordyn and Haileigh as they should be there at any moment. When she gets there, she turns on the TV and opens the curtains to let some sunlight in. Before she can settle in good, she hears voices outside and the front door starts to open.

"What's happening, whoadie?!?!? We made it," Jordyn announces. She walks over and the two exchange hugs.

"How ya doin' girl?" Haileigh says as she walks in, and they exchange hugs.

"I'm fine," Kia says. "I'm glad y'all made it!!"

"Hello. How are you?" says the gentleman that has brought up the luggage.

"I'm fine. Thank you. And you?" Kia asks him.

"I'm doing fine now that I have seen you," he says boldly.

Caught off guard, Kia does not quite know what to say so she smiles and tells him that his remark is sweet. He unloads the luggage and heads out the door. As he was leaving, Kia does notice that he smells quite good. There is nothing she loves more than a good smelling man.

"Girl, guess what?" says Haileigh, "American Airlines lost my bag too!!"

"Aww naw. They lost it or they left it?" Kia asks.

"They lost it. I talked to them at the gate and she couldn't locate it," Haileigh exclaims.

"I bet it is in Miami," Jordyn pipes in. "I can't stand Miami airport. They are always losing shit. That's why I carry on my bags."

"Damn. At least they knew mine was in Miami. It should be arriving any minute now because it was on flight 1089," Kia says.

Over the next hour or so, Haileigh tries feverishly to speak with someone at American Airlines in the US to see if her bag can be located. Jordyn takes a shower and changes clothes and Kia catches a little TV while waiting for them to get settled in. She can't shower yet because her bag has not yet arrived and she is out of clean clothes to put on.

"Whoadie, what did you do today?" Jordyn asks Kia.

"Dawg, I got up, ate breakfast, and then went to the beach which is where I have been until a few minutes ago."

Jordyn laughs as she understands all too well how easy it is to get caught up in the spell of the Caribbean Sea. She has owned a timeshare here for 7 years. "I understand, whoadie. I understand. So, tonight is Friday and they have a big fish fry down at Oistins. Y'all want to do that tonight?" She asks both of them.

"That's fine with me," Kia and Haileigh chime in almost in unison.

"Cool. I'm hungry now though so maybe we can get some lunch or something to hold us over until tonight," Jordyn says.

"That is fine with me. I haven't eaten lunch and I need to keep Agatha at bay," Kia chuckles.

"I just want my damn bag!" exclaims Haileigh, "but yes we can go eat."

Before leaving Haileigh is finally able to talk to an American Airlines rep who states her bag never left Dallas. It will arrive on Saturday and they will deliver it to the hotel. The ladies decide they will go eat somewhere along

St. Lawrence Gap which is the strip right outside the back gate of their hotel. They choose a little restaurant that serves all types of food from hamburgers to seafood to breakfast, but most of all there was a bar. Jordyn remembers the bartender from last year and they strike up a short conversation.

Kia orders a grilled chicken sandwich and fries; Haileigh orders a fish sandwich and a salad; and Jordyn orders a cheeseburger and fries. They all order a round of shots as they need something to help soothe their travel woes. After three rounds of shots and a plate full of food, the ladies are feeling better and more relaxed. They are busy laughing and talking and catching up on old times and don't even realize it is after 7:00PM and it has gotten dark. They decide to head back to the hotel to rest a little and let their food digest before going to Oistins.

As they arrive at the hotel, they stop by the front desk to see if Kia's bag has arrived and much to her dismay, it has not. The bellman that brought up the luggage earlier is there and reassures her he will bring it up to her room as soon as it arrives. She thanks him and the three girlfriends head off to the room. *He sure does smell good.* Kia thinks to herself. She glances back at him as they walk off and he is looking at her intently and smiling.

Once back in the room, they all find a spot in the living room to sit and begin to discuss some activities they would like to do while there in Barbados. They decide that tomorrow they would like to go snorkeling so they will wake up and go to the Activities desk first thing to get it set up. They also say they would like to go do some shopping and sightseeing since this is Kia and Haileigh's first time on the island. After about two hours of talking, the effects of the Tequila shots had worn off and they were ready to head to Oistins. They did not want to arrive too late and miss the party, so they head out towards their destination.

As they pass the front desk, Kia notices the bellman is looking at her and smiling. "Good night. Ladies, are you all headed out this evening?" he asks.

Suddenly Single

"Yes we are going to Oistins," says Jordyn.

"That's the place to go on a Friday night. You all will have fun. Just cross the street in the front of the hotel and take a bus or a van down there." He instructs with a nice Bajan accent.

"What is your name?" Kia asks.

"Phillip, and what's yours?" he asks.

"Kia, nice to meet you Phillip. Listen, I just want to tell you that you smell good!!"

He smiles from ear to ear and even blushes a little when she compliments his scent. "Thank you," he says shyly, "I will see you when you get back. Have fun."

"Okay. Have a good evening," she says as she is walking towards the street with her friends.

They cross the street in front of the hotel and decide they will take a bus down to Oistins. Kia only having been on public transportation once in the last 22 years is a little averse to doing that but she gets over it. *Hey when in Rome do as the Romans,* she thinks.

Luckily they do not have to wait too long for a bus to arrive. They board the bus and immediately Kia feels uncomfortable because she feels as if all eyes are on her. She thinks, *I know my butt is big but gosh.* This may be all in her imagination, but it feels very real. She shakes it off and looks outside the windows and takes in all the sights while waiting for Jordyn to signal them that it is time to get off.

The entire bus trip takes about 15 minutes. *That wasn't so bad.* Kia thought. They get off a block or so from where they are actually going and as they are walking towards the mall of outdoor restaurants, Kia is looking around trying to be very conscience of her surroundings, after all this is a foreign country.

"Which one do you all want to go to?" Jordyn asks.

"It doesn't matter to me," Kia says.

"I want to go to one where they have Red Snapper," says Haileigh.

"Okay well let's take a look at some of the menus," Jordyn says.

"Good night ladies, we have Red Snapper, Tuna, Dolphin, Flying Fish, Grouper whatever you want. Come, we will cook it up right for you." The lady boasts trying to get them to eat at her place.

They take a look at her menu and decide to look at a few other places before making a decision. As they are approaching the rest of the restaurants, the aroma of hot charcoal and succulent goodness just hits your nose like a sucker punch. All you hear is the sizzle of whatever is cooking on the grill, the buzz of people laughing and talking and festive island music playing. *This is vacation,* Kia thinks. This is unlike anywhere she has ever been. She is enthralled with everything that is going on around her yet slightly irritated that Haileigh and Jordyn have not made a decision on where they will eat. By now, they have looked at the menus of at least 5 other places searching for reasonably priced Red Snapper. They finally decide on Mo's Grill.

They take their seats at a long table in some plastic lawn chairs directly in front of where the chefs are doing the grilling. Kia can feel the heat from the fire on her back. As they are looking at the menu, Kia becomes a little concerned because she is a finicky eater, you wouldn't know it by looking at her though. The girls talk her into trying some Red Snapper, but she has to have it fried. Haileigh and Jordyn of course get theirs grilled.

"Umm I have a question," Kia states, "This says Dolphin on here…"

"Not Flipper, whoadie. They don't eat Flipper here. That is Mahi Mahi. They just call it Dolphin," Jordyn explains while she is laughing at Kia for thinking they ate real Dolphins.

"Whew. Okay. I was a little worried for a minute there," Kia says relieved.

"So Kia, what do you think about Phillip? I think he likes you," Haileigh says with that side eye smirk.

"I think he smells good," she says laughing. "He seems sweet. He is just too short. I would crush him. I am a big girl, so I need to stand next to you and feel small not like I'm going to smother you. You need to be this tall to ride this ride," and she raises her hand high above her head.

They all burst out laughing. By that time the waitress brings them out their drinks. Jordyn orders water, Kia has a ginger ale and Haileigh orders a Coconut Cooler which she promises is the bomb. They sip on their drinks while waiting for their food. Kia orders some fried chicken wings for an appetizer because she is not sure about the Red Snapper and she does not want to be hungry.

The trio is having a good time enjoying the sights and sounds of the land and engaging in small talk. The waitress interrupts their flow when she brings them their food. As she is sitting each plate in front of their prospective takers, Kia tries to unsnarl her face. It seems that when they cook red snapper over there, it is the WHOLE fish...head and eyeballs and all. Kia is not quite sure how to approach this fish as she has only eaten filets and never a whole fish. Haileigh gives her a quick lesson on how to eat the whole fish and they all dig in.

"MMMM, this is good!" Kia exclaims. It is not quite what she expected but it was very flavorful. It is rare that Kia will try new food. She normally sticks to what she knows. Her friends back home tease her and ask her how she got so voluptuous because she does not eat anything.

"Girl, if that fried snapper is good, you need to try this grilled snapper. You will love it," Haileigh says trying to convince her to try it.

"Ok let me taste a little piece," Kia says reluctantly and she gets a little piece off of Haileigh's plate. "Girl, this is good. I should've gotten mine grilled."

"Girl, I'm telling you this is good!! We can't get fresh fish like this at home. They have to fly it in from somewhere. I'm sure this was swimming in the ocean this morning!"

"Hell naw, we can't get this at home." Jordyn chimes in between bites.

The ladies finish their meal leaving nothing but fish bones on their plate. They sit there for a while and enjoy the tunes the DJ is playing and they watch people of all ages get up and dance as they are sitting right next to the stage. They would get up and dance themselves but they are too stuffed. They decide to head back towards the hotel because it is getting late and they have had a long day. On the way to catch the bus back, they decide to stop by the market to pick up some items for the room, since they do have a full kitchen.

Once back on the hotel grounds, they stop by the front desk to see if Kia's bag has arrived and they are greeted by Phillip who seems to be at work rather late but none of them know what time he is scheduled to get off.

"I have something for you," Phillip says to Kia as the ladies are walking in the outdoor lobby.

"Do you now? What do you have for me?" She asks hoping it was her suitcase.

He goes in the back behind the desk and a couple of minutes later, he emerges with her suitcase. Sweet Jesus! She could've shed a tear right then. Never in her life has she been so happy to see one piece of luggage.

She tries to take her bag from him, but he holds on to it and states that he will bring it up.

"Kia, I am a man. Let me bring this up for you," he says.

Seeing that she really didn't have any other option, she says, "Okay come on."

The four of them head up the elevator to their room.

"Did you all have a good time tonight?" Phillip asks.

"Yes we did," they all remark.

"What time do you get off, if you don't mind me asking?" Kia asks as they are making their way to the room. She knows it is well after midnight.

"Eleven," he responds.

"Why are you here so late then?" She asks bewildered because if it were her she would've been gone.

"I was waiting for you to give you your bag," he says with a smile.

"Awww that's sweet. Thank you," she says but she feels bad because she doesn't have any change left to give him a tip and embarrassed she explains she will give him a tip tomorrow when she gets some change. He tells her no worries. He did not do it for the tip. He wanted to make good on his promise of making sure she got her bag. He tells them all good night and leaves.

"Girl, that man likes you," Haileigh quips.

"Mmm hmm, dawg, he sure does," Jordyn adds in.

"No, he doesn't," Kia says while laughing because deep down she knows it is probably true. "I'm about to take a shower now that I can put on some clean clothes. I have been in this swimsuit all day."

"At least you can put on some clean clothes, I have to wash out my clothes on my hands and hope they dry by morning," Haileigh says.

"Y'all gone learn. Don't check your luggage. Carry it on. This right here is exactly why I carry my stuff on," Jordyn remarks.

Chapter 2

The next morning, the ladies get up and start moving around about 10:00AM. It is close to 11:00AM by the time everyone is dressed and walking out the door. Kia is dolled up in her black on white sundress, with the matching earrings and hat. She loves wearing this dress because she gets nothing but compliments from men and women whenever she wears it. This dress shows off all her curves in a nice way and it "calls all the boys to yard".

The first stop is the Activities Desk so they can get their snorkeling trip scheduled and hopefully be able to get some breakfast before they go. When they get there, they meet the activities coordinator, Helena who is very helpful in suggesting excursions and things for them to do. Unfortunately, it is too late to go snorkeling that day, but she sets them up to go on that Monday on the Jammin' Catamaran. They step outside to discuss what other things they will do so Helena can make the necessary calls and get them set up. They decide that Sunday, they will go to Harrison's Cave, Monday is snorkeling on the Jammin' Catamaran of course, and Tuesday they will go on the Island Safari. Since they can't do as they had hoped for that day, they decide to get something to eat and go into Bridgetown to do some sightseeing and shopping.

They take a bus up to Bridgetown and get off at the last stop because the bus has to go into the terminal. They stop and look at some of the fruits and vegetables from some of the street vendors and Haileigh decides to purchase a couple of banana's and plums to have for later. They ask for directions to Cave Shepard which is the major department store there. They get directions from one gentleman who must have been turned around himself because the directions he gave were just the opposite of where they need to go. They head back towards the main street and ask an older woman. She points them in the direction they need to go. As it turns out, they are only about 4 blocks from where the store is located.

Bridgetown is considered the "downtown" of Barbados and it has a canal that runs through it. The ladies stop and pose for pictures in front of some of the landmarks and some of the boats as they make their way towards Cave Shepard for some duty free shopping. After the picture taking session is done, they press their way further and the area by Cave Shepard is reminiscent of downtown New Orleans.

"What is this place Chefette?" Kia asks, "I see them on almost every corner, well that and KFC."

"It is like their McDonald's," Jordyn answers.

"I think this is the place Mr. Actuary told me to go for late night eating," Kia says

"Ok if you want to go there we can, but not right now," Jordyn says.

The ladies finally arrive at Cave Shepard and the first stop is the swimsuit department so Haileigh can find her a swimsuit to have on hand since her luggage has not arrived. They start browsing through the racks and are surprised at cost of swimsuits.

"Girl, look at this one. It is gorgeous," Haileigh says as she is looking at the tag. "Umm hell no, not for $95.00 Duty Free. They must be crazy!! It's not that cute."

"I think I need a hat so I can cover up from the sun," Jordyn says as she is looking through the racks also. "Dawg, this shit is expensive."

"I see," says Kia looking for something, anything in her size. She gives up trying to find some clothes in her size and starts trying to help Jordyn find a hat while Haileigh is feverishly looking at swimsuits.

"How does this hat look?" Jordyn asks.

"It looks fine. Do you like it?" Kia asks.

"Yea, I like it. I will probably get it. It seems reasonable," Jordyn says. "Haileigh are you having any luck?"

"No, not really. All this stuff is too high. I think I will hold off and if my bag does not get here today then I will come back."

"Ok. I can understand that. I think I'm going to get this hat."

"It's cute you should get it. We all can't be fly like you and Kia," she laughs. "Let's look upstairs and see what they have."

"Okay, let me pay for this hat first because you have to pay for it on this floor. You can't walk around with it," Jordyn says.

"What kind of shit is that? I mean it's not like you are leaving the store with it," says Kia in somewhat disbelief.

"Calm down, dawg, it's okay."

"I'm calm. Just shocked that's all."

Jordyn pays for her hat and they head upstairs to the second floor. They have to make a pit stop by the ladies room where there is a sign outside the door that reads: *In our efforts to maintain a high standard of service in our washrooms we have implemented a nominal fee of $0.25 for their use. Your co-operation is appreciated.*

Are they serious?!?!? Kia thinks to herself. She opts to sit on a bench outside the bathroom and wait for the other two to come out. She doesn't really have to use it anyway. When Jordyn comes out she asks her what does it look like in there and she states, "A mess."

Obviously, charging the $0.25 is not working. She did state they just ask that you contribute but it's not like the bathroom door is not going to open or you won't get any toilet paper if you don't pay the coin.

Haileigh joins them and they look around on that floor and Kia finds a really cute swimsuit that she wants, but she talks herself out of it. She brought 4 swimsuits with her anyway. She didn't need another one. When they finish looking on the second floor, they head to the third floor to do some souvenir shopping. Kia picks out a little purse she thinks her sister may like because it has blue in it and blue is her favorite color. Jordyn does not buy any souvenirs because she says they are too high and her people got stuff the very first time she came anyway. Haileigh looks around but does not find anything. Kia pays for her item and the three of them decide it is time to head back to hotel.

"So, let me get this straight we have to go to the bus terminal to catch the bus back?" Kia asks Jordyn as they are walking down the street.

"Yes, Dawg. There are two buses we can take either Silver Sands or the other one," Jordyn says.

"What's the other one?"

"I forgot but I know it when I see it," she laughs.

Haileigh sucks her teeth at her and laughs as well.

The three women head off toward the bus terminal and when they reach that block they get pulled in by a street vendor trying to sell them some more produce. Haileigh talks to the vendor while Kia and Jordyn are standing off to the side.

"I'm about to sit on this bench because my feet hurt," Kia says as she makes her way to sit in the empty space on the bench.

As soon as she sits for one second the older man next to her tells her," You can't sit there."

"Why not?" she inquires.

"Because you did not ask me," the man says jokingly. "I'm just kidding," he says. "You can sit anywhere you would like. Where are you from?"

"Houston, Texas."

"The States ok. Is this your first time here?" he asks.

"Yes it is," Kia responds.

"I want to marry you. You are one sexy woman," he says confidently and is looking at her with lust in his eyes.

Kia's jaw drops as she is caught off guard with his comments. She is not used to getting this kind of attention at home. Not quite sure what to say she smiles and says, "Thank you."

He scoots a little closer to her and asks, "Are you going to let me take you out?"

Not wanting to stand up but not wanting this man in her personal space Kia scoots over and turns slightly on the bench and says to him, "I don't know if I will have time this trip."

Just about then Haileigh finishes talking to the vendor and is ready to head into the bus terminal. The old man says, "Your friends are ready to go. Go ahead and get up so I can see your beautiful body."

At this point Kia just wants away from this man, and the younger man sitting on the turned over bucket in front of them sees the frustration on Kia's face and tell the man to behave himself and stop hassling the lady.

As the three women walk off into the terminal, Kia hears the old man tell the other men in the area "look at the ass on that one in the white dress..."

Kia turns looking at them once more, gives them a smirk then walks off.

As they are walking into the bus terminal Kia is looking at this crowd of people and wondering how in the hell they are going to make it. It reminded her of a Greyhound Bus Station inside the terminal. They locate the lines for the two buses that they can take. They opt for the bus with the shorter line. It is three people in that line as opposed to the thirty-five or so that is in the other line.

They are waiting for seems like hours and Kia is growing uncomfortable because her feet are hurting and they are standing, and because she feels as if EVERYBODY is looking at them. They wait for about thirty minutes and the bus that had the longer line comes and goes and the line has gotten long again. Tired of waiting for their bus, they agree that if the other bus comes first then they will get on that bus. Sure enough, it comes a few minutes later, so they get on that bus. They leave the short line and get in the other line before it gets too long as people start coming from everywhere.

They board the bus and take their seats and before they could pull off, the other bus, that had the shorter line, pulls in. It's too late at this point to change because they are already on this bus. Every seat on this bus is filled and there are even a couple of people standing. The first couple of stops the bus make, more people get on but nobody gets off, so this bus is really crowded. Kia and Haileigh have never been here before so they do not know the landmark to look for to ring the bell to get off and Jordyn's view is blocked by somebody standing over her. They do not see their hotel until they are passing it and they scramble to pull the string to ring the bell. By the time they get off the bus, it is down the street and around the corner. Kia wants to take a van back to the hotel because it seems far, but Haileigh and Jordyn don't mind walking, so Kia gives in and walks with them.

They decide to stop at the Shell petro station to get more drinks and snacks for the room. After they make their selections and are standing in line to check out, Jordyn says to Kia, "That man behind you just looked at you and mouthed the word 'wow' ". So Kia turns to look and see who she is talking about and her heart almost stops beating but something else instantly starts throbbing. Behind her is this gorgeous, dark chocolate man who stood about 5'8" tall. He is the very epitome of tall, dark and handsome, minus being tall. Obviously he was coming from work, which was something in construction or something with his hands; you can tell by the way he is dressed.

Kia catches her breath and manages to ask him if he said "wow" when he looked at her and he replied, "Yes I did."

Kia being Kia says, "Well do you like what you see?"

"Yes I do," he says. "What is your name?"

"Kia, what's yours?"

"Levy."

"That is different. I like that," she says.

"Are you visiting?"

"Yes I am."

By this time Jordyn and Haileigh have moved to another line that has opened up and have paid for their things. The line Kia is in has not moved, but she stays in it so she can continue to talk to this man that has caught her attention.

"Where are you staying?" he asks.

"Divi Southwinds," Kia tells him.

"Oh okay. That is right around the corner. Let me put my things in the car when we check out, and I will walk you back."

Kia turns to Jordyn and Haileigh who are waiting off to the side and tells them, "Levy is going to walk us back to the hotel."

Jordyn says, "Levy is walking YOU back to the hotel. He doesn't care about us," she chuckled.

By this time the line starts to move and Kia and Levy check out their items. They all walk out of the gas station and Levy put his things in the car and starts to walk with the ladies back to the hotel. Jordyn and Haileigh are already a few steps ahead of the two of them.

"Can I carry something for you?" Levy asks Kia.

"Here you can carry this bag, because it is heavy." She gives him the bag with the water and ginger ale, and Coconut Cooler in it.

He takes the bag from her and moves to the outside of her so she will not have to walk along the street. "So where are you from?" he asks her.

"Houston, Texas," she responds.

"I see. So how long have you been here?" he asks.

"Since late Thursday night, early Friday morning," she responds.

"When are you leaving?"

"Next Friday, but I won't get home until Saturday," she says. "I have an overnight layover in Miami on the way back."

"I see. So we only have six days left," he says.

Suddenly Single

"Yes, I will only be here six more days."

"Can I call you?" he asks.

"Yes you can call me, but can you call me at the hotel, because it will cost too much for me to talk to you from my cell phone?"

"Of course I can do that. Do you have the number to the hotel?"

"I don't, but you can get it from the front desk."

By this time they made it on to the hotel grounds. Jordyn turns back and gives Kia a look and she knows exactly what that look means.

"What does that mean?" Levy asks.

"You see that guy standing at the front desk?"

"Yes."

"I think he likes me," she says shyly.

"Don't worry, I won't ask him for the number to the hotel. I will ask the other lady."

They both laugh and continue to walk towards the front desk. He gets the number to the hotel from the lady and walks back over to Kia.

"What is your room number?"

"Penthouse 12," she tells him. Before they left for Bridgetown they changed rooms because they paid for an upgrade so everybody would have their own bed.

"Penthouse 12," he repeats. "Okay, so I will call you tomorrow if that is okay with you."

"That is fine with me. I look forward to it," she says with a big smile on her face.

He gives her the bag and tells her goodbye, and he walks off back towards the gas station and the three women head to the room, Haileigh now with her suitcase that has arrived while they were out.

"Girl he was cute!!" says Haileigh as they were getting on the elevator, "but you have to watch those island men honey. They are something else. Trust me. I know." Haileigh is from Jamaica so she would have some insight into island men.

"Yea, he is handsome," Jordyn states, "just don't get caught up."

"I'm not. He is cute though." She couldn't help but smile.

They make it back into the room, unload their snacks, and are getting ready to decide what they want for dinner when the phone rings. "Who could that be?" says Jordyn as the room is in her name.

"Hello?" Jordyn answers. "Hold on please. Kia, it's for you."

Could it be him? she thought. "Hello?"

"Good night, this is Levy."

Stumbling for what to say, she says, "Hey."

"I just wanted to make sure you made it back into your room safely."

"I did. Thank you very much. Did you make it back to the car okay?"

"Yes, I did. What are you getting ready to do?"

"We are getting ready to decide what we are going to eat for dinner. We will probably go somewhere on The Gap."

"Okay. Okay. Well perhaps I can call you a little later then."

"I would like that," she states smiling from ear to ear. Could he be the one? She quickly banishes the thought because she did not want to fall for someone who lived so far away. She would just have fun these next six days then go home.

"Okay cool. I will talk to you later then," he says.

"Bye," she says as she is hanging up the phone. She thinks *Hmm, it is going to be difficult to understand him with that heavy accent. But damn it is sexy.*

Chapter 3

The next morning, the ladies wake up and prepare for their excursion to Harrison's Cave. The driver will be there to pick them up at 10:00AM so they need to hurry if they wish to get breakfast as it is already after 8:30AM. As they are walking out, the phone rings.

"Hello?" Kia answers the phone because she is closest to it.

"Hi, good morning. This is Levy."

"Good morning Levy. How are you?" she waves Jordyn and Haileigh on and tells them she will catch up with them.

"I'm doing fine today. How are you?"

"I'm doing okay, happy to be on vacation."

"What are you doing today?" he asks.

"We were just leaving to get breakfast then go to Harrison's Cave. We are going snorkeling on the Jammin' Catamaran tomorrow and the Island Safari Tuesday." She figured she would just go ahead and give him the run-down of her itinerary.

"Okay. Can I come and see you this evening when you get back?"

Kia's face lights up and she can't help but smile from ear to ear. This gorgeous man wants to come and see her. *Hell yeah he can come visit, but I must lay down some rules for myself and him as well,* she thinks to herself. "Sure you can come and see me. I don't think that will be a problem. We can chill on the balcony or something depending on what time you come."

"Cool. Well, I won't hold you because I know you have to go. I just wanted to tell you good morning and that I am thinking about you. I will call you later this afternoon. What time do you think you will be back?"

"We should be back by about 4:00PM I guess. I really don't know."

"What time do you want to come over?" she asks. She needs to prepare and know how much time she will have.

"What about 7:00? Will that work for you?"

"That will be fine. We should be back way before then."

"I will call you when I think you have made it back to the room and if you are not there, I will just try back. Take care and have fun today," he says before they hang up.

Kia hangs up the phone with a smile on her face. This man has called her to see if she made it in. He called to say good morning, and he wants to see her later today. He seems to be doing all the right things at this point. She will let him come over, but she is not leaving the hotel with him. "Stay strong Kia...Stay strong," she whispers to herself.

She catches up with Jordyn and Haileigh in the restaurant and they grab a quick bite before proceeding to the front to wait for the driver to come and pick them up. As they are walking to the lobby, they spot Phillip and wave at him. He waves back and asks them where they are going but keeps his eyes fixed on Kia.

"We are going to Harrison's Cave," Jordyn answers.

"Oh okay. You will like that. It is pretty interesting," he says. "Are you all waiting on the driver now?"

"Yes we are," Kia tells him as they are taking a seat in the lobby chairs.

"Did you have a good night?" he asks Kia.

"I did," she answers just as their van is pulling up.

"You ladies going to Harrison's Cave?" asks the driver.

"Yes," Haileigh replied.

"Right this way," he says extending his hand towards the open van door.

"That's my ride. I have to go. Have a good day," she tells Phillip as they all get up and walk over to the van.

"I will. Same to you."

As the ladies get in, they speak to the other lady that was already seated on the front row of the van. The driver gets in and they are off.

"So where are you ladies from?" he asks as they are driving off.

"Texas," Jordyn says.

"I've been to Texas once," he says. "What part are you from?"

"We are from Dallas, and she is from Houston," Haileigh says pointing to Kia.

"Where are you originally from? I hear the accent," he asks.

"Jamaica," Haileigh replies.

"Ahh...an island woman," he says with a smirk.

"What is that supposed to mean?" she says with a little sass in her voice.

"Nothing...It doesn't mean nothing, and where are you from?" he asks the other lady.

"I'm from Dominica, but I live in Illinois," she says.

"Oh okay, Dominica, I haven't been there yet, but I know it is beautiful," he tells her.

"What are your names?" he asks each one of them.

"Kia"
"Natasha"
"Jordyn"
"Haileigh"

"Well nice to meet you ladies. My name is Jamal."

"Nice to meet you, Jamal," the ladies all say to him.

As they were driving along, Jamal gives them a tour of sorts. He points out different landmarks and gives some history of each area they pass through. Before heading to the cave, they have to make a stop over by the port. Jamal tells them that there are 2 more people scheduled to join them that he has to pick up. He opens the door to the van and tells the ladies they can get out and look around because they have about 20 minutes to wait.

All four ladies do just that. They get out of the van and take in the lush scenery. The area they are in is lined with big boulders overlooking the ocean. Then there is a sidewalk that has benches that run parallel to the boulders and the grassy area that is in the middle. As the ladies are busy snapping pictures of each other with the beautiful water as the backdrop, all Kia can do is think about Levy. She wonders what he is doing and how his day is coming along. She is snapped out of her trance by these two nice looking men in uniform that have stopped to talk to Haileigh. As it turns out, they are police officers walking their beat. The ladies ask if they can pose for pictures with them, and they graciously oblige, unbeknownst to them that in Barbados you have to get permission to take a picture with an officer.

After the picture taking is done Jamal tells them to come on because the other two people are not coming. They all get back in the van, and they head off to Harrison's Cave. The view on the way to Harrison's Cave is beautiful. It seems that if you get on the slightest of hills, you can look out and see water no matter which direction you turn.

As they are driving along, Jamal tells them that in Barbados, there is a rum shop for every church. They start to notice that there are a lot of churches and a lot of rum shops.

So Haileigh asks Jamal, "Where's our rum? You didn't bring us any?"

"I didn't think you ladies drink," he says.

"Why would you say that?" Jordyn asks.

"You all don't look like the drinking type," he says playfully.

He feels they are about to let loose on him for giving him a hard time, and luckily they pull into the parking lot at that very moment.

"Ladies, we have arrived here at Harrison's Cave. Give me just a minute to get your tickets, and then you may go in."

He returns with the tickets a few minutes later, and he instructs the ladies that he will be back here in two hours to pick them up. He shows them the way into the building where they are greeted by one of the staff who shows them where to go next.

While they are waiting for the start of the tour, they take the elevator down to ground level and they mill around in the outdoor waiting area which is very picturesque. It is a small open area that is in between 2 tree covered cliffs. They are able to spot a monkey high up in one of the trees overhead. That is the highlight of the trip so far for Haileigh because she heard about the monkeys in Barbados, and she wanted desperately to see one. After about 15 minutes, they are signaled into what is the public entrance to the cave. They watch a brief 10 minute video that gives instructions before loading onto the tram they will take through the cave.

Once inside the cave, they are able to see magnificent stalactite and stalagmite formations and natural pools of water. They stop and take pictures along the route as well as snapping some as they are passing in the tram. Kia can't help but think of what it would be like to come here with Levy. They could get cuddled up and steal kisses while snapping pictures. *Get a grip!* she tells herself. *You just met this guy.* But it was just something about him.

When the tour is over and they are exiting, they notice Jamal waiting for them in the outdoor waiting area.

"Hey ladies are you all ready to go?" he asks all excited.

"Whenever you are," Natasha says.

"I have something for you all," he says.

"What is it?" asks Haileigh.

"Let's go see."

So they get back into the van and Jamal pulls out a brown paper bag with a bottle of Old Brigand Rum in it.

"I got you ladies some rum!!" he says proudly. "There are cups and Coke in this bag and some ice in the cooler. Help yourselves."

"That's what I'm talking about!" Kia exclaims "free liquor."

They all laugh and pour up a cup of rum and Coke except Natasha. Hers was mostly Coke because she does not really drink. On the way back to the hotels, all 4 ladies converse and somewhat get to know one another as Jamal takes them the scenic route back, again giving them a history lesson along the way.

They arrive back at Natasha's hotel first. They exchange numbers with her and agree to meet up later for dinner because she is in Barbados by herself. She stopped through there on her way back to the US from her home in Dominica. When they arrive at Divi, Jamal gives the bottle of rum to Haileigh as the ladies are exiting and they are greeted by Phillip.

"Good afternoon ladies. Did you have a good time?" he asks.

"We did. It was very interesting," says Kia. "I have never been inside a cave before so it was interesting to see the different formations."

"Well I am glad you had a good time," he says before they get on the elevator to go the room.

"Thank you," she says and smiles before the doors close on the elevator.

Once back in the room, the ladies relax and pour another rum and Coke. They discuss their adventures of the day and where they may want to go for dinner later that evening. They decide to go to Pablo Dante's which is on The Gap. Natasha's hotel is at the start of The Gap so they will meet in the middle then walk on to the restaurant. The phone rings, and they tell Kia she may as well get it because it is probably for her.

"Hello?" Kia answers.

"Hi good afternoon. This is Levy."

"Good afternoon. How are you?" she says with a huge smile on her face. He can probably hear her smiling through the phone.

"How was Harrison's Cave?" he asks inquisitively.

"It was fun. I have never been inside of a cave before so it was interesting to see the different formations."

"I see. Well it was good you got to experience that here in Barbados. So are we still on for this evening?"

"Absolutely; what time are you coming?"

"I should be there by 7:00."

"Ok cool. Well just tell them you are coming to penthouse 12 when you get to the gate and they should let you in."

"I will do dat. I will see you then. Bye," he says with that sexy ass accent.

Kia's heart is just beating hard with anticipation of seeing him again. She can hardly stand it.

"Umm I'm sorry, but I will not be joining you ladies for dinner tonight. Levy is coming over. I thought maybe we would be back before he came but he wants to come at 7:00."

"That's okay, whoadie. We figured as much," says Jordyn. "The way you over there cheesing and shit. We can count all your teeth!!"

They burst out laughing.

"Shut up!!" Kia insists.

"Well that works out perfect because that is the time we were going to meet Natasha," Haileigh adds. "Where are y'all going?"

"I don't know. I will probably tell him let's just get something to eat back here on The Gap. I'm not leaving with him in a car. I don't know him like that. That would be all I need is to leave with him, and he chop my ass up and throw me in the Caribbean Sea and nobody would ever know. I mean I don't think he would do that but still. Please believe I am going to leave his number up here on the bar."

The ladies rest and relax for the rest of the afternoon. Kia runs down to the beach to take a quick dip before her "date". It is her goal to go to the beach every day, even if it is only for a few minutes. She did not come all this way to not go to the beach.

As she is taking her dip, she goes over the rules she made for herself in her head: 1) Be strong. Don't let him kiss you. Kissing leads to sex. 2) NO SEX. You will not have an island fling…you did not come here for that; remember you are done with men and their shit. You want more than just sex… Plus you fall too quick, especially if the dick is good, and you would be crazy being this far apart. 3) Be strong and refer to rules 1 and 2.

She stays down at the beach for about an hour before heading back to the room to get ready for her "date". After Kia makes it back to the room, she takes a shower and decides which sundress she will put on for this evening. She wants something that will show off her curves but not too revealing. She settles on her black maxi sundress with the braided halter straps and the colorful paisley print at the bottom of the dress. Jordyn and Haileigh give their approval as they leave to go meet Natasha for dinner.

"Alright now," says Jordyn. "Don't hurt him tonight."

"I'm not going to," Kia says laughing. "I don't know what we are going to do, but we will probably just go get something to eat back here along The Gap. I'm not leaving with him in a car. At least we can walk somewhere or maybe chill on the balcony or something."

"Alright girl, well have fun tonight," Haileigh adds.

"Will do."

As Jordyn and Haileigh leave, Kia becomes a bit anxious. *What if he doesn't come? What if he pressures me for sex? What if he tries to kiss me? What if I'm not strong?* She thinks to herself becoming lost in the "what if's". The phone ringing breaks her train of thought. Instantly, her stomach sinks a little and she becomes filled with nervous energy. *OMG,* she thinks. *Is this him?* All of a sudden she has to go to the bathroom.

"Hello?"

"Hi, this is the front desk. I have a Levy here to see you."

"Yes, please send him up to penthouse 12."

"Will do."

"Thank you!!"

AAAHHH, Kia silently screams to herself. *He is here. Don't fuck this up*, she tells herself just as she paces the floor. About two minutes later, there is a knock at the door.

Kia looks out of the peephole just to make sure it is him before opening the door.

"Hi," she says to this beautiful man that stands before her. He is dressed in work jeans and a work t-shirt and some slide-in sandals. Not quite what she thought he would wear on a date, but who cares.

"Good evening," he says as he enters. "I'm sorry for the way I'm dressed, but I just came from work, and I did not have time to go home and change clothes and get back here on time."

"It's no problem. Have a seat."

Kia decides to sit next to him on the couch. "So how are you this evening?" she asks.

"I'm doing fine and you."

"I'm okay. So how was your day?"

"It was not too bad. I did some work on a house today in Speightstown."

"Oh okay. What kind of work do you do?" Kia inquires. She already figured it was some type of construction or something.

"I do masonry work, mainly on pools. But I do construction also."

This confirmed what she already thought.

"Oh okay. Did you go to school for that?"

"Not exactly."

"Not exactly?"

"I didn't go to college," he states.

"Oh okay. Well that's okay. College is not for everybody. So how old are you?"

"31. I will be 32 in May."

"May what?"

"May 1. How old are you?"

"I'm 38. So when did you graduate from high school?" Kia tries to do the math in her head but doesn't feel like thinking that hard.

"I didn't. I stopped going in the 10th grade."

"What happened, if you don't mind me asking?"

"It's no problem with you asking. My mother could not afford the supplies I needed to stay in school, so I had to drop out."

"Ok. Have you ever thought about going back?"

"No. I haven't."

"Oh okay. Well look, I was thinking we could go and get something to eat on The Gap and hang out. I haven't had dinner yet."

"Ok listen. I feel bad and ashamed to say, but I don't have money to buy you dinner."

"I'm not asking you to buy me dinner."

"Oh. Ok then, let's go."

Levy stops Kia as they get to the door and asks her to let him go out first. "I did not grow up with my father, but I am learning what I should do to be a man. Let me go out first to make sure it is safe before you come out. This older gentleman friend told me that is what a man is supposed to do."

Stunned, Kia looks at him in disbelief because no one has ever done this for her before. "No problem, go ahead."

The two leave out of the room and are conversing as they are walking out the back of the hotel. Once they get to the street, they walk right into Jordyn, Haileigh and Natasha.

"Hey, look who it is," Jordyn says.

"Hey. Imagine running into y'all. Levy, you remember Jordyn and Haileigh."

"Yes. How are you?"

"Levy, this is Natasha. Natasha, this is Levy," Kia introduces them.

"Nice to meet you Levy." Natasha says.

"Well we are going to walk on and go get something to eat. See y'all later," Kia says as they walk off from each other.

"The other girl came with you all?" Levy asked.

"No, we met her on the excursion that we did today. She is in Barbados by herself."

"Okay. I was just asking because she was not at the store with you all when we met."

"It's no harm in asking. So where should we go?"

"Do you eat Chinese food?" Levy asks.

"I do, but I don't know about Chinese food in Barbados, besides, I can get that at home. What about something different."

The restaurants along The Gap have the menus posted outside where you can review them and decide if you want to patronize them without having to go inside. Kia and Levy continue along down the road and decide on Paolo's Brazilian Steakhouse. They go in and take their seats outside with a nice view of the water. Even though it is now dark, you can still see the boats that are anchored out there. They look over the menu and Kia decides on her meal and Levy orders a Screwdriver.

"Would you like a drink?" he asks. "I can pay for that," he adds.

"Sure. Let me get a vodka and cranberry."

Suddenly Single

So Kia places her order and asks Levy if he would like something to eat because she will feel bad eating in front of him if he is hungry. He assures her that he does not want anything to eat and he will be fine. Kia orders a grilled chicken sandwich that comes with coleslaw and grilled potatoes. Levy and Kia indulge in conversation as they are waiting for the meal to arrive. Kia learns that Levy is the oldest of 6 children, he is originally from The Grenadine Islands, he is not currently in a relationship, his last relationship ended about 3 years prior at which time he came back to Barbados to work, he has never been married but has lived with a woman (his ex-girlfriend), and he does not have any children.

As the food arrives, Kia offers some of her food because she does not want to eat in front of him if he is hungry. He decides to eat the coleslaw since she does not eat coleslaw. As they are dining, they continue their conversation.

"So do you go to church?" Kia asks.

"I don't go to church, but I do believe in God," he answers. "I was thinking about being a Jehovah's Witness. Some guy I know has been telling me about it. I am really thinking about checking it out."

Kia instantly thinks to herself, *This ain't gon' work. I can't do that. I'm going to have to change his mind about that.* She practically tunes out the rest of what he has to say after that only interjecting "ok", "ah huh" and "mmm hmm" when there is a pause in him talking. She does hear him say that he is open to exploring other denominations.

When the waitress arrives with the checks, as promised, Levy pays for the drinks and Kia pays for her food. Once the bills are settled, they collect their things and set off on their walk back to the hotel.

The main street in The Gap is filled with street vendors selling everything from jewelry and souvenirs to food, in particular macaroni pie, which is very popular in the Bajan culture. Levy decides he wants to stop at one of the street vendors and get some chicken and macaroni pie. He asked Kia if she wants anything, but of course she doesn't as she has just finished eating. She asks him why he didn't get something at the restaurant. He tells her that he would not have felt right having her pay for his meal on their first "date". She almost rolls her eyes at him but catches herself because she can see the sincerity in his face.

The two walk a little further up the road and decide to sit at Jocelyn's Beachside Restaurant that is located on the backside of Divi. It is closed for business but they could still sit there and look over the water while Levy ate his meal.

"You seem like you are a very nice person, and you have yourself together. I can't believe that you don't have a man."

"Listen, men don't approach me at home. I don't know if they are intimidated or what. I have gotten more attention in the few days I have been here than I have gotten in the last 6 months at home. "

"Nooooo...that can't be true," Levy says in disbelief.

"I promise it is true. I have been told that I look mean and unapproachable, I look settled, and I look like the type of woman that you have to have yourself together before you approach me. Personally, I don't see anything wrong with the last one. I mean you do have to have your stuff together, but damn, you can at least say hi. I am a very nice person, but you wouldn't know it if you don't say anything." She has to stop herself from going off on a tangent because she is headed there fast. She chuckles to herself a little bit about her mini rant.

"I know you are nice. Men in Houston must be crazy to let all this get away," he says touching her hand softly.

"All what?"

"YOU. Look at you. You are beautiful. You are intelligent. You don't have any kids, and not to mention you are sexy as hell!!"

"That's sweet. Thank you," Kia says blushing slightly but she knows it's true. "I noticed men like voluptuous over here, and that I am for sure."

"You definitely are that, but you are more than your body."

Kia is rendered almost speechless but she manages to get out, "Thank you." At last somebody recognizes….damn. *What does he want?* she thinks to herself.

After Levy finishes eating, they walk back up the path to the hotel and Levy boldly grabs Kia's hand not knowing whether or not she is going to resist. Kia is a little taken back by his move but she doesn't let go. Instead, she starts to swing his hand with hers.

"You swing a child's hand. I am a man," he says as he lets her hand go.

Shocked by his dropping of her hand she says, "There is nothing wrong with swinging hands. It means we are happy."

He grabs her hand again and again she swings it, just having a little fun. And again, he lets her hand go. She told him she was having fun, but really this was her way of getting him to let it go. First holding hands, next kissing, and then well you know what kissing leads to and she isn't having it. She is determined to be strong.

They make it back to the room and Jordyn and Haileigh are upstairs getting ready for bed, so Levy and Kia go and sit on the balcony to talk and visit some more before calling it a night.

"Hey, let's take some pictures," Kia says, wanting to capture every moment of her trip. "I know it is dark out here, but my camera has a flash."

"Okay. Come on."

The two pose for pictures individually and together out on the balcony. They are laughing, talking and having a good time.

"Which is your favorite?" he asks her.

"I like this one," she says pointing to one of Levy leaning back on the balcony. It is something that is extra sexy about that one. "Which one do you like?"

"I like this one," he says showing her the one of the two of them together, "because it has both of us in it."

Kia smiles at him. *Is he trying to get me or what?!?!* she thinks to herself. "Now you are trying to mack me," she says laughing.

"Mack you? I'm not trying to mack you. If I was trying to mack you, I would do this..."

He slowly and delicately grabs Kia's face with his hands and lifts her chin where her lips meet his lips in a passionate embrace.

DAMN IT!! Kia exclaims in her head, *I BROKE RULE #1!!!!!*

Determined to stay strong and not end up with her dress pulled up on the balcony, she goes and sits in one of the chairs. He follows suit and sits in the other chair. He grabs her right leg and places her foot in his hands and starts massaging it.

"I like to cream feet. When next I see you I will bring the cream and cream them real good," he says to her.

She uses her context clues to figure out he is talking about massaging her feet. She is still a little thrown off by that kiss, and she is trying to regain her composure.

"Creaming feet huh?! Okay. I like that. I will definitely let you." *He likes to rub feet – plus,* she thinks to herself.

He goes on to rub both of her feet then proceeds to rubbing her shoulders and arms.

"If you were mine, I would do this for you every day."

"Would you now?"

"Of course I would. If you were mine ,I would also do this..." he says as he gets down on one knee and grabs her hand and says, "I would say 'Will you marry me?' And I would give you a diamond solitaire ring."

"Is that all you would say is, 'Will you marry me?' Shouldn't you probably say something more like 'I love you' and 'I want to spend the rest of my life with you'?"

"Listen, if I am asking you to marry me, those things are understood," he says as he gets up and kisses her on the cheek.

"I see. Well....listen," she says thinking she must say something now to prevent her from breaking rule #2 because she is getting weaker by the moment, "...we are not having sex this week while I am here. So if that's all you want then I'm sorry but it ain't happening. I did not come here for that."

"Kia listen, I would be lying to you if I told you I did not want to see you naked and have sex with you. Any man would be lying if he said that. But listen, you are a classy woman, and I respect your wishes."

"Ok. Good as long as we have that understanding that it is not going to happen."

"You don't have to do anything you don't want to do," he says reassuringly.

Something in Kia told her that this man is serious about getting with her. I need to tell him..., she thinks to herself, *but how? What will he say? Will he still like me? What difference does it make anyway? I mean I don't like him anyway...right?*

"Levy, I have something to tell you," she starts nervously, "I......I...umm....I have herpes. I was diagnosed a little while ago and I have been dealing with it...so if you don't want to talk to me anymore, I understand. From what I can trace, I got it from an ex-'hook up' when the condom broke. I take 1 pill every day to manage it. It won't kill me and I can have kids." She is a bit relieved she told him but at the same time scared that he won't accept her with this news.

"Okay." He sits back in the chair taking in what she has just told him and looks at her in disbelief, for what seems like forever, as if he just saw a ghost. He was rendered somewhat speechless, but tells her, "It's okay. I can handle that," and he gives her a hug.

"Are you sure?" she asks while still hugging him.

"Yes. I'm sure." Then he kisses her on the forehead.

What the hell just happened? Kia says to herself in her head. This is something she reveals on a need to know basis and not everyone needs to know.....only certain people. *Is he one of them?*

Chapter 4

After talking for a little while longer, Kia walks Levy to the door and gives him a hug and tells him to be careful going home and let her know when he makes it in. He agrees and tells her he will talk with her later. She sincerely hopes this is true. She locks the door and retreats upstairs to catch up to Haileigh and Jordyn who are indulging in conversation about politics.

They both look at her smiling when she walks in the room where she and Haileigh are sleeping.

"How was it?" Jordyn asks.

Kia can't help but smile as she thinks over her evening with Levy. "It was nice. He seems cool. The only thing is that is he was thinking about being a Jehovah's Witness."

"Nope...don't do it. He's crazy," says Haileigh.

"He was just thinking about it. He's not one yet and if I can help it, he won't be."

"That's too bad because I had y'all married with a little girl with 2 afro puffs," Haileigh says.

"Dawg, don't count him out because of that. Just help him to see Christianity," Jordyn adds.

"I will. He is cool though. He wants to cook for me, build me a sand castle and rub my feet, and I will let him do all three," Kia laughs.

"Dawg, don't get caught up. Just be careful."

"I won't," Kia says as she goes to take a shower.

The next morning (7:30AM), the ladies are awakened by the phone ringing. Jordyn answers the phone because it is in her room.

"Hello? Hold on.....KIA!!" she yells.

Kia gets out of bed and goes downstairs to talk on the phone in the kitchen so she won't further disturb the "house".

"Hello?" she says in her 'I just woke up voice'.

"Good morning. Were you sleeping?"

"Good morning, Levy," she says instantly perking up. *Yes!! He called!!!* she screamed silently to herself.

"How are you today?"

"I'm doing okay. I am just waking up. How are you?"

"I'm doing better now that I have heard your voice. I figured I would call you on my way to do some work."

"Now you are trying to mack me again."

"I'm not macking," he laughs, "so you are going snorkeling today right?"

"Yea, they are picking us up at 8:30, so it's actually good you called when you did."

"I see. Well, have fun out there today."

"I will. Can you swim?"

"No, not really."

"How is that possible and you are surrounded by this BEAUTIFUL water?!?!?"

"To tell you the truth, I don't really go to the beach."

"WHAAAT? That's crazy. You know that, right?"

"I know," he laughs.

"I just don't have time with work and all."

"I guess I can understand, but not really," Kia laughs. "If the beaches at home looked like this, I would go all the time."

"I'm sure you would," he laughs. "So listen, I was thinking I could cook for you tomorrow, and we can go down to the beach so I can build you that sand castle."

"Ooh okay. I would like that. What are you going to cook? You know I'm picky."

"I know. I was thinking some fish, you eat fish right?"

"Yes."

"...and broccoli and potatoes."

"Perfect!! I'm looking forward to that."

"Me too. Well listen, I know you have to get ready to go snorkeling, so I will let you go. Have fun and call me when you get in. Ok?"

"Ok. I will do that. Thank you. Talk to you later. Have a good day."

"I will. You too. Bye."

"Bye."

Kia is beaming when she gets off the phone with Levy. This could not have been a more perfect start to the day. She uses the downstairs bathroom to wash her face and brush her teeth before heading back upstairs to prepare for her day of snorkeling.

"Dawg, why does Levy have to call so early in the morning? Doesn't he know we are on vacation?" Jordyn asks jokingly but seriously.

"I know. I'm sorry. He is on his way to work and he wanted to hear my voice. I thought it was sweet." Kia says as she is smiling from ear to ear.

"Girl, that man likes you!!" Haileigh screams from the bathroom upstairs.

"I know huh?" she says.

"Girl just be careful with them island men. They ain't nothing nice." Haileigh says. It sounds like she is speaking from experience. Well she is from Jamaica so she would know.

Kia can't help but laugh. This type of stuff doesn't happen to her. She is enjoying the attention and it does not hurt that Levy is easy on the eyes.

"What time is it?" Kia yells not wanting to be late to be picked up for the trip.

"7:52" Jordyn responds.

"Thank you."

Since everyone is awake and moving around, Kia decides to turn on some music. So she grabs her phone and scrolls through the 314 songs she has downloaded. She decides on *Apache* by The Sugarhill Gang to get their morning started with some energy. When it gets to the chorus, they all stop what they were doing in their varying stages of getting ready, to do the dance where you put your hands on your hips and move them to each side in a circle before hopping around in a circle. You know the dance.

This really wakes them up and gets the blood rushing. Kia does not dance too many times as she feels like she is starting to cramp. She hopes her "friend" holds out until at least the end of the day because she is getting in the water....

Kia decides to wear her turquoise one piece swimsuit with the keyhole neckline. It's kind of too big because she ordered it from Old Navy on-line and was not able to try it on, but it is still cute. She opts for her short black dress as a cover up and her matching black flip flops. You can't tell her that she isn't cute. She smiles to herself as she looks in the mirror before her and Haileigh head to the lobby to wait to be picked up. Jordyn left a few minutes earlier to meet Natasha, who they talked into coming with them on the excursion.

"Good morning ladies," Phillip says as they are approaching the chairs.

"Good morning," they chime in unison.

"Where are you all headed today?" he asks.

"We are going on the Jammin' Catamaran," Haileigh tells him.

"Oh that sounds like fun. Too bad I have to work or I would join you all. So how are you?" he asks Kia as he sits on the arm of her chair.

"I'm doing great!!" she says. *Damn, he smells good!* she thinks to herself as his scent is tickling her nostrils.

"Great huh? I see..."

"What is that you have on?" Kia asks, "You smell delightful."

"Mambo," he says.

"Well, it goes with your body chemistry nicely."

"Thank you. So do you need anything this morning? Is there anything I can do for you?"

"Aww that's sweet. But no, I'm fine. Thank you for asking though. I really appreciate it."

"No problem sweetheart. I'm going to get back to work. You ladies take care and have fun today. I will see you when you get back."

"Ok Phillip. Thank you. You too!!" Kia says.

Right about then Jordyn and Natasha walk up and join them in the lobby. The ladies wait about another fifteen minutes or so before the bus arrives to pick them up. There is another couple on the bus when they all get on and take their seats. They make three more stops before heading to the dock where they will board the boat.

The boat leaves from a port in Bridgetown. As the passengers are boarding, one of the crew members takes their shoes from them and puts them in a tub. Kia is hesitant to give up her shoes because she does not walk around barefoot, not even in her own home, but she obliges and boards the boat. It is unlike anything she has ever been on. The ladies decide to take a seat below deck to stay out of the sun that is beaming full on this morning. As soon as they are settled, crew member Josh comes by and offers them some Jammin' Punch. Kia wants some but it is too early in the morning to start drinking…even if she is on vacation, besides she hasn't had breakfast and she doesn't want to have to go to the bathroom on the boat.

Suddenly Single

It is about 20 people on the boat including the four ladies and the crew. After the passengers are given information about what to expect for the day and how to flush the toilet on the boat, they are told they are free to move about and most of them move to the top of the boat to get a better view as they start sailing out to sea. The boat uses the motor to get out of the port and when it is in open water the crew members hoist the sails and turn off the motor and it is all wind power from there.

The ladies decide to move above deck so they can take pictures and have an unobstructed view of the coastline.

As they head North up the West coast of Barbados, Kia is mesmerized by the stunningly beautiful turquoise blue water. It almost matches her swimsuit. It turns a darker shade of blue the farther out they go. The coastline is absolutely amazing as well. As they are sailing along, they pass a yacht that is unbelievable. It is probably the length of a football field or longer. It is a multi-level floating mansion complete with a helicopter pad on the back of it. "I would take the maids quarters" Kia says.

"Girl me too!!" Natasha agrees.

Further up the coast they pass areas where it is difficult to discern whether the structures are houses or apartment complexes or buildings because they are quite sizeable.

Crew member Melvin comes around and offers the passengers breakfast. It consists of fish cakes and a pastry and as much Jammin' Punch or any other alcoholic or non-alcoholic beverage of your choice. The catamaran is equipped with a fully stocked bar.

As they are sailing along, Kia can't help but think about what it would be like to be here with Levy. She imagines they would take pictures with the picturesque coastline as the background, and steal kisses along the way. She also imagines they could spend some alone time in the bathroom while the other passengers are above deck...*Snap out if it Kia!* She tells herself.

After sailing for about 30 minutes, they reach their first snorkeling stop at Payne's Bay where they will see the sea turtles. The crew tells them that they will feed them so they can come up to the surface of the water so they can interact with them. They also instruct the passengers not to chase the turtles, but to have fun.

Jordyn, Haileigh, and Natasha jump off the boat into the water with their personal lifeguard (crew member Josh) and Kia hesitates just for a split second because as she is looking at the water, she can see it is deep and she has on nothing but a swimsuit, a snorkel and a mask and no personal lifeguard because she can swim. She stands there for about 5 seconds then dives in feet first. After she surfaces from the initial dive, she checks her mask to make sure it is not leaking, she positions the mouthpiece correctly in her mouth and she is ready.

As she sticks her head under the water, almost immediately she sees 4 large sea turtles a little ways in the distance. She swims a little closer and manages to grab the underwater camera she has strapped to her wrist and starts snapping pictures. The turtles are all around her. They swim up to where crew member Fabian is sitting on the float feeding them leftovers from breakfast. Kia swims around him so she can get a different view. She is constantly snapping pictures and even manages to get a selfie underwater. She surfaces for just a minute and she sees the other ladies not too far away from where she is in the water. Natasha looks as if she is about ready to get back on the boat.

Kia continues to swim in the beautiful blue abyss and before she knows it the crew is telling them it is time to return to the boat and head to the next stop.

"Man, it's no way that was 40 minutes," Kia tells Jordyn as they were getting back on the boat.

"Yes it was, dawg. It felt like it to me. You didn't feel like it because you were out there swimming like it was nothing."

Both women laugh as they return to their spots on the boat before leaving for the next stop.

As they approach the second stop on the excursion, the crew tells them they will need to wear fins on their feet because they have quite a ways to swim and the fins will help them swim faster. Kia is excited about this but knows the fins will take some getting used to. Jordyn, Haileigh and Natasha are apprehensive because they are not that comfortable in the water but Josh reassures them he will be there with them every stroke of the way.

They arrive at the next stop at Colony Grove and all the ladies once again put on their gear and get into the water. They swim over to the site of the shipwreck and then over to the reef which is about 150 yards away, and there they see all kinds of colorful schools of fish. They stay out for 30 minutes before heading back in to the boat. The third and final stop is lunch, and Kia can't wait because she did not eat too much breakfast.

"This is fun!!" Natasha says to them as they are boarding the boat.

"It is more fun than what I expected," Haileigh says.

"I know I am absolutely having a great time," says Kia "I just wish I had a man to do these things with. I mean don't get me wrong, y'all are cool and all, but ummm……" They all start laughing.

"Girl I hear you, me too."

"Me three."

"Me four."

They all laugh…

"Ladies, how are you all doing this afternoon? Would you like something to drink?" asks Melvin.

"I think I will try some of that Jammin' Punch now, Melvin," says Kia.

"Nothing for me," Jordyn and Natasha say.

"Let me have a coke," Haileigh orders.

"Coming right up."

He returns a few minutes later with the Jammin' Punch for Kia and the Coke for Haileigh.

"Here you go ladies," he says as he is handing them their drinks.

"Thank you," they chime.

"My pleasure. Let me know if you need anything else. We are almost to our lunch stop where we will dock for about an hour and a half and eat, and you all can get off the boat and spend some time in the water if you want to."

"Cool. I am looking forward to it," Kia says. "Mmmmm. This is what's up!!" she says as she takes a sip of the Jammin' punch. She really does not want to have to use the bathroom on the boat so she sips cautiously.

As the catamaran pulls into Sandy Lane Bay for lunch, the ladies snap a few more pictures of the scenery before getting their plates to eat. Kia looks at her cup and notices all of the Jammin' Punch is just about gone so she flags down Melvin who graciously refills her cup.

After dining on grilled Flying Fish, fish cakes, grilled chicken, pasta salad, garden salad, green beans and dinner rolls, the girls refill their cups (Jordyn and Natasha decided to try the Jammin' Punch) before retreating into the water to lounge a bit. Once in the water, Kia decides to go jet skiing. Once on the back of the Jet Ski, the local she is with hangs on for dear life because she drives it as if she is racing against time. She punches it as they take on waves head first in the craft causing them to go airborne before hitting each wave. She is loving it!!

Their adventure lasts for 45 minutes and they make their way back over to the boat where Haileigh has snapped some good photos of Kia doing her thing on the Jet Ski.

"Girl you were gone out there." Haileigh quips.

"I know. It was fun too. I figure hell I'm on vacation so why not set it out."

"You right. I would've been a wreck out there going so fast."

"Nonsense; you are on vacation. Enjoy yourself!!"

The ladies are lounging in the water chatting with some of the other passengers and crew members. Kia is floating close to the landing of the boat where you enter/exit the water and Crew Member Fabian is showering off with the water hose and he accidentally splashes her with the water.

"Alright now you better stop before you get me wet," Kia laughs.

"But you are already in the water. How can I get you wet?" he asks.

"It's not but one way that you can make me wet if I'm already in the water." She smirks as she climbs aboard so he can get a full view.

He chuckles and tells her, "Girl, don't have me take you in the bathroom. It's big enough for the both of us."

"Really now? What would you do with me in the bathroom?"

"I would take you and bend you over let you feel all of this." He says as he walks up right behind her so close that she feels all of his manhood tapping her on the butt cheek.

"Ooh well shit. Umm..." Kia is a little speechless because what she feels on her backside is massive.

Fabian takes her hand and places it on the bulge in his shorts and she can't help but grab at what feels like a great time.

"How many women have you taken in the bathroom?" She asks somewhat seductively as she moves in closer to his face.

"None as sexy as you," he replies as he gets so close to her she can almost taste the pineapple juice he sipped earlier.

At that moment, she is saved from making a decision driven by the throbbing between her thighs because another passenger gets back on the boat. Kia tells Fabian she will speak with him later and she retreats back in the water to cool off and enjoy every minute of her ocean adventure.

They stay in the water for another 20 minutes before the crew calls everybody back on the boat. Kia gets on and dries off as much as she can before taking her place above deck. On the way back to the dock she chooses to sit on the platform by the sails. Haileigh joins her up there while Jordyn and Natasha stay on the deck.

Once they get going, Melvin comes around and asks the ladies if they would like something to drink as he gives them a cupcake as an afternoon snack. Kia orders some more Jammin' Punch because it is really tasty. She figures she can drink a little more now because they are on the way back in, and she should be okay in not having to use the bathroom. Melvin brings her back her drink and she takes a sip.

"Melvin, this is good but I can't taste the alcohol. Can you put some more alcohol in this please?" she asks as she bats her eyelashes.

"I can do anything you would like but are you sure you want more alcohol because it is plenty alcohol in there?"

Suddenly Single

"Yes, I am sure. I want to taste it."

"Ok. Coming up," he obliges and returns a short while later with her topped off drink. "Here you go Madam. Is this better?"

Kia takes a sip and raises her cup to him as a sign of "this is on point". It tastes like he added some coconut rum or something to it. She hopes it doesn't sneak up on her.

Kia is enjoying the sail back; the ladies are conversing with the crew members, taking pictures and jamming on the Jammin' Catamaran. They all start dancing and singing when *Dancing Queen* by Abba comes on over the speakers on the boat. Melvin and Josh look at them and laugh before joining them in chorus.

Five cups of Jammin' Punch and a shot of rum later, Kia can barely do the line dance they do around the boat as they are pulling back into the dock. It is tradition that everyone on the boat dances as it is pulling up to the dock. Kia manages to slowly gather her things but has to use the bathroom before getting off the boat because she is not going to make it until they get back to the hotel.

She walks into the bathroom, closes the door, looks at the toilet, then opens the door and yells for Jordyn because she can't figure out or remember how they said to flush the toilet. Jordyn motions to her that she has to pump the handle up and down. She says okay and proceeds to do her business. *This is big enough for two,* she thinks to herself as she is washing her hands.

"Dawg, come on!! We have to get off." Jordyn yells.

"I'm coming." Kia yells as she opens the door, but she can't move too fast because the Jammin Punch has indeed snuck up on her.

Once back at the hotel, Kia sits on her bed and falls backwards. She manages to put on her CPAP mask a few minutes later, and she is down for the count. She sleeps for about three hours before waking up. Once she is awake, she calls Levy because she hasn't spoken with him since earlier that morning.

"Hello?" He answers on the second ring.

"Hey. This is Kia. How are you?"

"I know who you are. I recognize your voice. I'm doing better now that I know you are safe from snorkeling. Did you have a good time?"

"I did!! I really did. It was amazing. I took some pics of the sea turtles with the underwater camera. I hope they come out. I think I had one too many Jammin' Punches though. We have been back for a while but I have been sleep. I am worn out."

"Mmmm hmmm, I see. So you drank like a fish since you were swimming with the fish, huh?" He laughs. "I'm just teasing. I'm glad you had a good time. I wish I could've been there with you."

"I did, and I wish you could've been there with me as well."

"So what are you doing for the evening?" he asks.

"We are going to meet Natasha and get something to eat. We probably will get something on The Gap."

"Ok. Well, I need to finish up this work. Maybe I can come take you for ice cream later. I will call you a little later when I finish."

"Sounds like a plan. I will talk to you later."

"Ok. Bye."

"Bye."

Kia is smiling from ear to ear and her heartbeat has sped up just a little bit as she walks up the seemingly steep stairs to take a shower and get ready for dinner. When she gets up there, she finds Jordyn and Haileigh sitting in the master bedroom talking.

"Well look who it is...sleeping beauty," Jordyn teases.

"I know huh. That damn Jammin' Punch snuck up on my ass and gave me a punch alright. Woooo. I have never been that to'e up before in my life. Thank God it didn't make me sick though. I'm about to take a shower and get ready for dinner. Where are we going by the way?"

"We decided we would try Cafe' Sol around there by Natasha," Haileigh replies.

"Okay cool. I will be ready in a few minutes."

As Kia is soaping up her body trying to wash off all the saltwater, she notices she is feeling a little woozy. *Am I still fucked up?* She thinks out loud. She looks around as if there is someone there to confirm her realization but there is no one of course. *I'm still fucked up!* She declares in her head. "Oh shit!! What am I supposed to do now???" she says as she finishes her shower and steps out. All of a sudden she really wants to just go back to sleep but she knows she needs to eat something to soak up the rest of this liquor. *Damn, what did Melvin put in that drink?* she thinks to herself.

She puts on her lime green halter dress and pulls her braids into a high ponytail and as she is waiting for Jordyn and Haileigh to finish getting ready. She fights the urge to lie down in the bed upstairs because she knows if she lies down, it is over.

"Y'all, I am still fucked up," Kia yells to Jordyn and Haileigh.

"What?? Girl, Melvin got you with that drink. I'm glad I didn't have that many," Jordyn says as she is putting hair combs in her hair. "Girl, he told you the punch had plenty of alcohol in it to start with, but no...somebody wanted him to keep adding more," she laughs.

"That's alright. I know now," Kia laughs as she rubs her head hoping she will not have a hangover.

Once everyone is dressed and ready, the ladies leave for dinner. Kia is walking a step or two behind them and as they are walking past the swimming pool located on the property a rock comes barreling past Kia and almost hit her in the head. Kia turns around and yells, "Hey!!!" Jordyn and Haileigh turn around and look and Kia tells them somebody threw a rock at her.

"Dawg, that dude up there ran as soon as we turned around. He probably threw it," Jordyn says.

"I mean damn, why would he throw a rock?!?! That's crazy!! I'm glad he didn't hit me, shit."

"I know, right!" Jordyn exclaims.

The ladies press their way on towards the restaurant only stopping to look at the big, bright Hibiscus flowers that line the back sidewalk of the hotel. Kia likes to look at flowers however, she is ready to sit down because she is still feeling the effects of the Jammin' Punch and it just so happens Café Sol is the farthest restaurant away.

Once the ladies arrive at Café Sol, they have to climb the stairs to get to the entrance of the restaurant. "Damn, more stairs," Kia mumbles to herself. She is hoping she does not stumble or fall because there are some people standing along the railing.

"Good night, ladies. How are you this evening?" says one of the gentlemen standing at the top of the stairs.

"Fine," Jordyn, Haileigh and Natasha respond in unison.

Kia does not bother to respond because she is focusing too hard on staying upright and getting to a table. The four women are shown to a table at the back of the restaurant where they take their seats. *What is it with everything being so far away?* Kia thinks to herself. She normally wouldn't mind but being that the Jammin' Punch is still running rampant in her bloodstream she just wants to sit and be still and be quiet, but that is hard to do in the company of three other people.

The ladies finish dinner and make their way back to the hotel. Kia is feeling a little better since she has eaten something, but she is still very much under the influence. Divi Southwinds seems so far away but she tries to keep a steady pace because she is ready to be horizontal again watching the back of her eyelids.

As they are approaching the elevator, they see Phillip. "Good night, ladies."

"Good night, Phillip. How are you this evening?" Jordyn asks.

"I am doing well; even better now that I have seen you ladies. You know you all are my favorite guests," he says with confidence. "And how are you doing?" he asks Kia directly.

"I'm a little tipsy from earlier, but otherwise ok," she half chuckles.

"Too much Jammin' Punch, huh?" he asks as he winks at her.

"How did you know?" Kia asks shyly as she drops her head in shame.

"I just know. Go on and get you some rest. You will be fine."

"I'm going right now," she smiles. "Good night."

"Good night."

And with that the ladies hit the elevator button that is going to take them to Penthouse 12. They get to the room and Jordyn and Haileigh go up to their rooms and Kia stays downstairs, puts the ceiling fan on, takes her dress off and puts on a t-shirt, puts that CPAP mask on and is down for the count. She is so out of it that she doesn't even realize Levy has not called her.

Chapter 5

The sun peeking through the crack in the curtain hits Kia's eyes at about 7:25 the next morning. She decides to go ahead and get up and opens the curtains and steps out onto the balcony. While there is not a direct view of the water she can see it in the distance. Any view is better than the view she has from her bedroom back home. She is standing out there when it hits her that she did not hear from Levy last night. *Aww hell, here we go.* She thinks to herself. She tries to remain optimistic giving him the benefit of the doubt. Anything could have happened.

She goes back in the room and completes her morning routine of washing her face and brushing her teeth and seeing how many braids have come out. They seem to come out by the handful each day. She makes a mental note not to use human hair for braids again. She goes in the kitchen and gets a guava juice box from the refrigerator and sips on it. As she stands there in the kitchen, she looks at the phone and looks at the clock then back at the phone. She wants to call Levy, but she hesitates because it is before 8:00AM, and she has a rule that she does not call people before 8:00AM unless it is absolutely necessary. Really she shouldn't even be thinking about calling him because he didn't call her, but Kia operates on the principal of - if you want to talk to somebody, then call them. Besides, better she call him before he calls her disturbing the others so early in the morning. So, after having rationalized it in her head, she picks up the phone dials his number.

"Hello?" he answers on the first ring.

"Good morning. How are you?" she asks trying to sound stoic.

"I'm doing fine, how about yourself?"

"I'm doing okay, waiting for some ice cream," she says sarcastically.

"I know. I am sorry about that. I am glad you called me because I was trying to wait to call you because I didn't want to bother your friends so early, but I wanted to apologize for last night. I did not finish work until after midnight and I wasn't going to call you that late."

"Mmmm Hmmm...okay," she says trying not to be accusatory in her thoughts. *Really what difference does it make Kia? He is not your man and y'all just met. Get a grip.* She reminds herself in her head and she smiles anyway.

"I know you probably don't believe me, but I have no reason to lie to you," he tells her.

She hopes he is not lying. She is about tired of men and their lies. "It's okay," she tells him. "I was sleep anyway."

"Did you sleep well?"

"I did, and I am feeling good today. I woke up early and was out on the balcony for a little while before calling you."

"Enjoying some of the Caribbean fresh air, huh? I wish I were out there with you."

"Do you now?"

"Yes, I do."

"Well, if we are going to be out on the balcony early in the morning then it has to be a good reason why. I'm just saying," she says as she laughs.

"Well, if we are out on the balcony early in the morning, it could be several reasons why," he says with a naughty laugh. "I will just say if we were on the balcony early in the morning you would be enjoying yourself."

"Levy!!!! Stop being bad!" Kia yells but grins as she is yelling. The thought of his smooth dark chocolate body up against her golden honey skin sent a wave of electricity down her spine right to the warm place at the base of her torso.

"What?" he says as he tries to sound innocent. "Okay, let me stop picking with you. So you are doing the Island Safari today, right?"

"Wow. I'm impressed that you remembered. Yes we are. They are going to pick us up at 9:00 AM."

"Why are you impressed that I remembered? I remember everything about someone I care about."

Did he just say care about?

"You just remember that I said I want to cook for you today and build a sand castle for you when you get back," he reminds her.

"I remember. What time do you want to get together tonight?"

"I will call you about 6:00 and then go from there. It really depends on what time I get in from fishing."

"Fishing?"

"Yes, I need to catch dinner."

Catch dinner? Kia tried to process this quickly in her mind.

"So what if you don't catch anything? Will we be hungry?" She laughs but is serious.

"No," he laughs, "I will buy some fish if that is the case."

"Ok. I was just checking," she chuckles.

"Well, I will let you go and get ready for your day. Enjoy yourself today."

"I will. You do the same. I look forward to the dinner and the sand castle," she tells him.

"Me too. Talk to you later."

"Bye."

Kia tips upstairs because she is not sure if Jordyn and Haileigh are awake. They should be because it is a little after 8:00 and they are getting picked up at 9:00.

"Dawg, was that Levy you were talking to?" Jordyn asks.

"Who else is it gon' be?" Kia laughs.

"Did he call because I didn't hear the phone ring?"

"I beat him to the punch this morning. I figured I should because I didn't want y'all to be mad at me," she laughs but knows it's true.

"Okay? Good. I'm glad you know!" Jordyn laughs as she makes her way out of bed.

Haileigh is already out of bed and is doing her morning routine in the bathroom.

"Dawg, you know Levy is supposed to be cooking for me tonight right, but he has to catch it first!!" Kia boasts.

"Say what?" Jordyn asked to make sure she heard correctly.

"He said he is going fishing today to catch dinner," Kia repeated.

"What y'all talking about?" Haileigh interrupts.

"When Levy told Kia he was going to cook for her, he meant he is going to catch it and cook it for her," Jordyn tells Haileigh.

"Girl, that's that island man!! He knows how to build things and catch fish and cook what he catches. He may just be a keeper after all," Haileigh laughs.

The ladies finished getting dressed for the day and go downstairs to wait for the safari company to pick them up. Kia is looking fly as usual, so she thinks anyway, with her black maxi tube dress and her black and white hat to match. While they are waiting, they decide to take some pictures in front of this very large unusual looking tree that is located in the front of the hotel property. After waiting for about 20 minutes, they get concerned because it is after 9:00, and they should have gotten picked up by now. Kia pulls out her confirmation and discovers their pick up time is 9:30AM.

The ladies laugh, but are a little disappointed because they did not eat breakfast. It is too late to get something now, but if they would have realized sooner, they could've grabbed something at the restaurant.

"Hey it's my favorite ladies," says Phillip as he is walking up from the back of the lobby. "How are you all this morning?"

"Fine," the say in unison.

"How are you?" Kia asks.

"I'm doing well this morning. No complaints here other than you look like you are about to leave me," he says.

Kia smiles. She is flattered by the attention she is getting from him. He really seems to be a nice person, but her sights are set on Levy.

"What adventure awaits you today?" he asks.

"We are going on the Island Safari today," Kia answers.

"Oh okay. That should be fun. I think they go all over the island."

"They are supposed to. At least that is what the brochure says. They better!!" she laughs.

Just as she is saying that, the Jeep to pick them up drives up. It is open in the back with a canopy on top. The plastic sides are rolled up and can be let down if need be. That is a good thing because it looks like rain today.

"Ladies, are you waiting for the Island Safari?" the driver asks.

"Yes, we are," Haileigh says.

"Right this way," he instructs them.

"Well, I will see you later. Have a good day," Kia says to Phillip as she turns to head toward the Jeep.

"Will do, you have a good day as well," he says back to her.

The ladies climb into the Jeep and take their seats which are not "big girl friendly" because they are not as wide as they should be for someone with a large posterior and they are hard. Kia struggles with sitting on something hard because "her friend" has come to visit for a couple of days, and the cramps have kicked in full force. She has already taken some Ibuprofen this morning. The seats are lined up next to each other with six on each side. She hopes they do not have to pick up too many more people because she does not want somebody sitting all up on her like that. It was already one couple on there when they were picked up so hopefully this was the last stop.

As they are driving off, the driver introduces himself. He is talking through a headset which is projected through a speaker in the back. He states that we will have to make a stop down the road and transfer to another Jeep because he has to pick up another group. They drive to the gas station 5 minutes down the road to make the transfer. The new Jeep is a little different. Same concept but a little more spacious and the seats were bigger. *Yes,* Kia thinks as she climbs aboard.

There is already one couple waiting when they all get on. "Hopefully this is it." Kia accidentally says out loud. And it is.

The new driver introduces himself, and gives a brief synopsis of the itinerary for the day. He says they will go through all of the parishes on the island with the exception of one. They will start in Christ Church where they were and travel towards the East Coast of Barbados and stop at key scenic points and landmarks along the way. They will stop for lunch at a restaurant that is at a quaint hotel that is located on the North Eastern side of the island. Kia is pleased to hear this because she forgot it came with lunch.

They start off driving through a residential area that seems to lead toward the middle of the island. Kia is excited because she gets to see the rest of this beautiful island. They drive past Gunhill Signal Station and stop for pictures with the Gunhill Lion. This looks familiar because Jamal drove them through here on the way back from Harrison's Cave. As they continue along the road and are passing the Anderson Mill Sugar Cane Factory, it starts to rain so they have to pull over to the side of the road and pull down the sides to the Jeep. While this keeps them dry, it cuts off the air circulation so it gets hot. They drive a little further along getting a full historical tour. It is very informative. Kia did not realize that sugar cane is their main export.

Their first scenic lookout point where they could get out is called Edge Cliff and it is on the East Coast of the island. It is at the top of a high cliff overlooking the Atlantic Ocean. The driver tells them not to step too far out to take pictures because they will fall and there is no way to save them. The ladies cautiously step about 2 feet out and take panoramic pictures of the view. It looks like something off of a post card. Kia notices that on this side of the island the waves are stronger and you can see more whitecaps. The driver tells them that this side of the island is known for its surfing. It is not safe to swim, but you can surf there.

In the last few minutes of that stop, the driver offers the passengers some Rum Punch.

"No thank you. Not right now," Kia tells him. Kia politely declines for 2 reasons: 1) She did not want to have to go to the bathroom and 2) She had quite enough the night before.

They drive further along heading to Bathsheba passing by some landmarks known in Barbados. Their next stop is at what looks like a rock shaped kind of like a mushroom. It is called Parlour Rock. Jordyn says this area was used in the intro to one of the soap operas she used to watch. The driver again offers some Rum Punch and chips. This time Kia takes him up on it because she is a little parched. As she expected it is delicious. She will definitely not over indulge today. She has to stay ready for her evening with Levy. She is looking forward to it. This will be the first time in a long time that a man has cooked for her, and then to think he is going to catch their dinner first. She is impressed, but she dare not let him know that.

There are restroom facilities at this stop so the ladies take advantage whether or not they feel like they have to go. They wash up and then pose for pics in front of this rock and some of the other rocks in the area. They stay about 20 minutes at this stop before moving on. Kia gets one more cup of Rum Punch before they climb back in the Jeep and head off to the next stop.

"Dawg, this is good. You should get some," she says to Jordyn.

"I'm going to try some but I feel like I am coming down with a cold or something."

"A couple of cups of this and any cold you may be getting should be knocked right out," she tells her friend.

They both laugh but Jordyn knows Kia is right. They all return to the Jeep and head off to their next stop which the driver tells them is the "jungle". As they are driving along the way, they can see a rock formation in the distance which resembles a man lying on his back sleeping. If you look at for a few seconds the image will jump out at you. The ladies all snap pictures of this as they drive by.

When they arrive at the "jungle", the driver tells them to keep their hands inside the vehicle because they are going to drive past some trees that could injure them if they were to touch them. The first interesting thing they see is a tree that looks as if it has long vines hanging from it. The guide tells them this is a Banyan Tree and Banyan means "the bearded one". These trees are all over the island. Kia realizes this is what is out in front of Divi. Then they see a Spiked Palm Tree. This tree looks just like a palm tree only the trunk has these very large spikes coming out if it that look as if it your fingers will surely be a bloody mess if you touch it. They hope to see a monkey or two since they are in the jungle but no luck.

As they leave out of the jungle, Kia wonders if Levy has ever been in here with anybody. While it is not the kind of place where people go and hang out, it did have a couple of duck offs where people could go and make out. She tries desperately to get him off her mind but she is unsuccessful.

A short while later they arrive at the hotel where they will have lunch. They catch up with the other tour group they had seen earlier at a couple of the stops. Jordyn and Haileigh use the bathroom before joining Kia in line for lunch.

"Girl, this looks good," Haileigh announces.

"It does doesn't it," Kia replies. "Hopefully they will have something that I eat."

"They have some chicken so you will be fine," Jordyn laughs.

"Fuck you. I eat more than chicken!" Kia laughs. She is relieved though.

The ladies get their food and Kia has Garden Salad, barbequed chicken, some kind of grilled fish, a dinner roll and a slice of cake for dessert. Kia is looking around for where to get her drink and she notices a very nice looking gentleman behind the bar area.

"Hello. May I get you something to drink?" he asks her very politely.

"What do you have?" she asks him.

"Juice, soda, diet soda, and fruit punch," he tells her.

"I want a fruit punch," she orders. She looks at both her hands and wonders for a split second how she will carry her cup because both of her hands are full.

He sees her looking and tells her don't worry about it because he will bring it out to her. She joins Jordyn and Haileigh at the table outside and the guy is in her shadow with her drink.

"How you get table service? We had to bring our own drinks out," Jordyn teases.

"My hands were full and he offered." Kia laughs because she knows where this is coming from.

Haileigh sucks her teeth at the both of them and dives in her plate. "This fish is pretty good."

"Mmmm it is," Jordyn co-signs.

Kia takes a bite also. "Yea it is good. I should've gotten more of this and less of the chicken," she laughs.

Suddenly Single

The trio enjoys their Bajan Buffet lunch and makes small talk with the other couple sitting next to them who is also on their tour. Come to find out they are from Dallas and are on vacation as well. Kia looks up and the guy that brought her drink out is walking towards their table.

"Would you like some more fruit punch?" he asks Kia noticing her glass is half empty.

"Yes, please. Thank you," she tells him.

Jordyn and Haileigh look in disbelief because their glasses are empty and he did not ask them if they would like a refill also.

"You want me to get your refills for you?" Kia asks them.

"No it's ok. I will just go in there myself and get it," Jordyn answers. "You can't come with us anymore. We don't get any attention when you are around," she says jokingly.

"Well, I'm sorry these dudes can't get past my ass," she laughs as she bats her eyelashes. She knows it is all they see but she really wished men would understand that she is more than a big, round booty.

When the guy returned with the fruit punch he notices Jordyn and Haileigh's empty glasses and offers to refill those as well.

They continue their lunch for about another 20 minutes or so before getting back in the Jeep and making their way back to their prospective hotels. There will be no more stops but they do definitely take a scenic route back. They pass through Speightstown, Holetown, Lime Grove, Bridgetown and then back to the hotel where they are greeted by Phillip.

"Ladies, you made it back I see."

"We did...we did," Kia tells him.

"Did you all enjoy yourself? Did you get to see a lot of the island?" he asks them.

"We did. It was very enjoyable. I did not realize that the Atlantic Side is so different from the Caribbean Sea side. It is all very beautiful indeed."

"Yes, the water on the Atlantic side has a stronger current and is not really safe for swimming. That's why it is not really any hotels on that side of the island."

"That makes sense. I'm sure people come here to swim and enjoy the water and if they can't do it on that side of the island then it is no point in building hotels over there. I get it," Kia tells him.

"Yep, exactly," he agrees. "So what are you all going to do now?" he asks.

"Well I'm going to the beach. I don't know what they are going to do," Kia answers looking over at Haileigh and Jordyn.

"I will come with you," Haileigh responds.

"Me too," Jordyn says.

"Cool, so it looks like we are going to the beach."

"Well enjoy yourself down there," Phillip tells them as the elevator door opens.

"We will," they say as the doors close, and they head up to Penthouse 12.

Suddenly Single

Chapter 6

The ladies look like they are a part of the cast from the Real Housewives of Anywhere when they arrive at the beach. Each woman has on a swimsuit that looks as if it were tailor-made for her body. Kia is the medium height "size sexy" one and has on a black and white two-piece that has a tribal design halter top and boy short bottoms that show off her curves nicely; although it is two pieces, it is very flattering. She also has on a black chiffon sarong tied around her waist, her black and white hat on her head and her new Prada sunglasses on her face. Haileigh is the tall, slender one in the group. She has on a solid turquoise two-piece with a bikini top and bottoms that has some embellishments at the cleavage line and on the sides of the bottoms. She has her white sarong tied as a dress, her hat that matches the sarong and her white sunglasses. Jordyn is the short curvy one in the group. She has on a soft yellow one piece swim dress that has a halter top neckline and ruffles along the bottom of the suit. Kia really likes this one and wishes she could fit it. Jordyn also has on the hat she bought at Cave Shepard and her sunglasses that perfectly match her swimsuit. They walk up to the beach as if they own it.

They locate three lounge chairs under a nearby tree and head over to claim their spot. Almost immediately, the Beach Ranger Devon spots Kia and decides to walk over and speak as if staking some imaginary claim.

"Good afternoon. How are you doing?" he asks.

"Hey, look who it is. I'm doing well this afternoon. How are you?" Kia responds enthusiastically.

"I'm doing well. I see your friends made it in."

"Yes, they did. This is Jordyn and Haileigh," she says as she introduces each one of them.

Suddenly Single

"Hello," they both say.

"Nice to meet you; I am Devon," he says extending his hand to both of them. "You didn't call me," he says turning his attention back to Kia.

"I know. I'm sorry. We got busy going on different excursions," she says apologetically. She really had no intention of calling him anyway even though he did seem like a nice guy. He just is not her type. He is short and slim. Kia likes her men tall with some meat on their bones, like a football player build. It would be ideal if they could pick her up. Since she is 5'6 ½" and size sexy, she wants to stand next to him and feel small, not big.

"It's okay. I figured you would get busy once your friends got here. So what have you done so far?"

"We went to Bridgetown, and Harrison's Cave, then snorkeling on the Jammin' Catamaran, and today we went on the Island Safari."

"Wow, you guys have done a lot. Are you having a good time?"

"I definitely am," Kia smiles as she reflects on meeting Levy.

"Do you have plans for this evening if you don't mind me asking?" he asks her.

"I do."

"That's too bad. I wanted to take you for that drink."

"Well, I will be here a few more days. You never know what may happen," she tells him not quite knowing how to just tell him it probably wasn't going to happen.

"Ok, cool. Well you ladies enjoy your time out here today."

"We will. Thank you," Kia says.

"Girl, who was that?" Jordyn asks.

"That was the Beach Ranger Devon. I met him on Friday when I was out here waiting for y'all. He wants to take me out for a drink, but I don't want to. He isn't my type. I mean he seems nice and all but ummm no. I will talk to him out here though. Besides, I don't want him thinking that I want to do it with him. You know how men think. If you accept a date with them they think you are down to fuck, or at least they hope so anyway."

"Tell me about it," Haileigh says as she sucks her teeth.

"I told Levy we were not going to do it this week and he was okay with that. He did say that he wanted to but he respects my wishes. I don't know. They get on my nerves, shit," Kia laughs but she is serious in what she is saying.

"Fuck 'em hell," Jordyn says.

"Dawg, you sound a little bitter or something. You okay?" Kia asks.

"Dawg, I am fine. I just don't have time for men and their shit. I need to spend my time on other things such as figuring out how in the hell to move here!!!"

"Okay! Right! I would love to move to paradise," Kia agrees.

The ladies stay out on Dover Beach for about 3 hours enjoying the water and the sun and looking at the people and making up stories about each of them. They even see Frajile' and her man, they met earlier that day on the Island Safari, enjoying the sun. When the ladies get back to the room it is a little after 6:00PM and Kia does not see the light on the phone blinking indicating any messages. She figures Levy will have to build her a sand castle on another day because it is getting dark. She takes a shower and decides that she will put on her white linen pants and her lime green print tunic for her dinner this evening with Levy.

When she finishes getting dressed and all gussied up, it is almost 7:30, and Levy still has not called. Kia is starting to get a little worried hoping something has not happened to him or that he has not changed his mind. Against her better judgment, she decides to call him, but there is no answer. She does not leave a message but decides to try again in a little while. She makes up in her mind that if she does not hear from him by the time Jordyn and Haileigh leave for dinner, that she is going with them and will have to get with Levy later.

While she is waiting for them to finish getting ready, she pulls out her cell phone and turns on *Rainforest* by Paul Hardcastle. She needs to distract herself from thinking the worst which is always what she does. By the time Jordyn and Haileigh are ready, it is close to 8:20 and Kia still has not heard from Levy. She has listened to most of her "Get Crunk" playlist on her phone and her stomach is now talking to her. She tries Levy one last time before leaving with her girls. She can't believe this shit. If it is one thing she cannot stand, it is this: TNS (Typical Nigga Shit). This right here is TNS!!!

Later that night, Kia is awakened when the phone rings, but she does not answer it. She lies still in her bed and hears Jordyn say, "She's sleep right now, but I will tell her you called."

She is secretly hoping it is Levy calling, and it is. Not wanting to appear too desperate, she continued to lay there, not move, and see if Jordyn was going to come and tell her he called or was she going to have to fake going to the bathroom so she could "get up". Just then Jordyn stuck her head in the room and told her that Levy called. Kia said okay. She decided to get up and call him back so that he would not call and disturb them in the morning.

"Hello?" he answers on the first ring.

"Hey, you just called me?" Kia asks with the best 'I'm sleep and you woke me up' voice she can give.

"Yes, I did. I am sorry about tonight. I am just getting off of work…"

Kia glances at the clock and it is 11:45.

"…My phone died and I was not able to charge it until my brother reached there so I couldn't call and tell you that I had to work late."

TNS at its finest, Kia thinks to herself. This whole episode snaps her out of the lala land she has been in. She does not have time for TNS this day or any day for that matter.

"Ok Levy. I went on and had dinner. I wasn't going to sit around and wait."

"I didn't expect you too. I'm sorry. I am so upset. I was supposed to cook for you and build you a sandcastle. What are you doing tomorrow?"

"I don't know. Haileigh is leaving tomorrow so after she leaves, we will probably go to the beach and then do some souvenir shopping."

"Ok. I see. If it is okay, I will come and see you tomorrow."

"That should be okay. I will call you when I get back in from dinner tomorrow then."

"Ok. That will work. I will cream your feet tomorrow and give you a good rub down if that is okay with you."

"I will let you know about that, but it should be okay as long as you don't try and make me do something I don't want to do." Really she wanted to and that was the problem.

"I would never make you do anything you didn't want to do. What kind of man do you think I am?"

Typical, she thinks to herself but does not say it out loud because she does not want to have to go into that with him right now. Besides she is leaving in 3 days.

"I know you wouldn't," she tells him.

"Good. Well I will let you go so you can go back to sleep. I'm sorry again. But I will see you tomorrow, I promise."

"Ok Levy. Good night."

"Good night."

When they hang up the phone, Kia is relieved to have talked to him and know that he is okay. At this point, it didn't matter what happened; he was alive, and that is all that mattered. This is important to her because she is still affected by the death of two of her friends that occurred sixteen years earlier. They were on their way home and were hit by a drunk driver. Kia worked with one of them at the time and had just seen him the day before he was killed. So, in her mind, as long as you are alive, she can deal with the rest.

The next morning, she and Jordyn bid their farewells to Haileigh, and they decide to get some breakfast down on The Gap. As they are walking to the restaurant, they stop at one of the gift shops along the way to look for some souvenirs and to get a hit of the A/C. It seems to have gotten hotter outside or something because Kia is just about to break a sweat.

"Good morning ladies," says the gentleman who is working at the shop.

"Good morning," they each tell him.

"Can I help you find something?" he asks both of them.

"She's looking for some stuff," Jordyn tells him while pointing to Kia.

"Ok. Can I help you find something?" he says turning his sights on Kia.

"I'm just going to look around and see what I see. I am looking for things for a few people," she says.

"Ok, no problem. I will let you look around. Let me know if I can help you. My name is Sheldon."

"Will do Sheldon. Thank you," Kia tells him.

In the meantime, he walks over to Jordyn, and they strike up a conversation. As it turns out, Haileigh had come in here earlier in the week, and he remembered her. When Kia gets through looking around, she decides on a blue and white decorative plate for her mother, as this will match some things in her living room, and a t-shirt for Rylan, who is her youngest unofficial godbaby. As she is paying for her things, the conversation takes a turn that Kia is not expecting. They start talking about men and relationships and porn. Sheldon pulls out his iPad and shares some of his favorite free porn sites with them. He then asks them have they been getting a lot of attention since being on the island, and he is looking right at Kia when he asks the question. Kia chuckles as Jordyn throws her hands up in disgust like, *what the hell*, as he did not even look her way. Jordyn redirects his attention to her and says, "Yes, she has been getting all of the attention," as she points to Kia, "I told her she could not come back with me."

His eyes get big, but Kia laughs because she knows she is only kidding about not coming back with her.

Looking back at Kia he says, "So you have been getting a lot of attention, eh? I'm sure you have because look at how big your ass is. I mean wow. Excuse my frankness."

Suddenly Single

Oh hell, here we go, thinks Kia. "Well, thank you Sheldon. I know my ass is big, but that is all the men here seem to notice. I am more than my ass you know."

"I know you are. I would hope so anyway, but you know how we men are. We see something we like, and we can't help ourselves. Men are visual creatures."

"Apparently so. I ain't gon' lie. I have gotten more attention in these last few days than I have gotten in the last few months at home."

"You're kidding," he says in disbelief.

"Not at all. Back home I am not the stereotypical image of beauty. I am considered 'big' or 'fat'. The men want the 'light and fluffy' video hoes. Well I am not that. Here they like voluptuous, and that is definitely me. I have also been told that I look mean and unapproachable, I looked settled (however that looks), and I look like you have to have your shit together before approaching me…"

"Whaaat?" he interjects.

"Yep, that is what I have heard. Personally, I feel like I may intimidate some men. If I look mean, ask me what you can do to put a smile on my face. If I look settled, ask me am I involved with anyone especially since I do not have on a wedding ring and if you don't have your shit together, don't even bother….Just kidding, holler anyway, hell you never know. I may not have mine together. I do, but I'm just saying…Don't be afraid. Be confident."

"Yep that is true," he agrees, "I think most men may be afraid of being rejected."

"I'm sure that is true but damn nobody wants to be rejected," Kia says.

"True, true," he says.

The three of them talk for a few more minutes before Jordyn and Kia leave out to go to breakfast. They tell Sheldon they will stop back in to chat with him before they leave on that Friday.

After breakfast, the ladies hit up a few more of the shops that are along their walk. Kia seems to be finding the things that she is looking for and has even bought a thing or two for herself. As they are entering the hotel grounds, they see Phillip who is talking with the guard at the back gate.

"Ladies how are you this morning?" he asks.

"Fine," they say in unison.

"Where is your friend?" he asks looking for Haileigh.

"She left this morning," Jordyn tells him, "she told me to tell you goodbye and thank you for everything."

"Awww, I hate I missed her. Well, be sure to tell her hello for me and that she is welcome."

"I definitely will." Jordyn tells him.

"Where are you all coming from?"

"We went to breakfast and then we did some souvenir shopping," Kia tells him.

"Oh okay. Did you buy me anything?" he laughs.

"Not this go 'round," Kia jokes with him.

"So what are you going to do for the rest of the day?"

"Umm I don't know. Go to the beach for sure. I'm determined to get in the water every day," Kia tells him.

"I will probably take a nap. I am starting to feel bad again," Jordyn tells him.

"What's wrong?" he asks her.

"I don't know. I feel like I am coming down with an ear infection or something," she tells him.

"Well, if you decide you want to go to the doctor, there is one not too far from here. Let me know and I can arrange a ride for you," he tells her.

"Thank you. I will let you know."

"Ok ladies. Well I will let you go so that you can get on with your day. It was nice chatting with you."

"Nice chatting with you as well," Kia says to him, "see you later."

The ladies head up the path leading to elevator and Kia wonders what Levy is doing. It was right along in here where he first boldly grabbed her hand. She knows she told him she would call him after dinner, but she wants to talk to him now.

Chapter 7

Since Jordyn isn't feeling well and wants to rest, Kia makes her way down to the beach as she had done what seems like so many times before. She is grateful to be able to spend some time by the water alone with her thoughts and her music. This time she decides to sit a little further down the beach off to the right. She locates a lounge chair under an umbrella and sets her things out. As she is getting situated, she pulls out her iPod and phone unable to decide at that moment which she will listen to. Eventually, she opts for her phone because it has more songs and playlists that are already created.

Since she wants to relax and enjoy the sun and the water and the sea of endless relaxation, she decides to play *70's Love Groove* by Janet Jackson. As soon it starts, she quickly hits next because this song will send her mind straight to the gutter, and this is not where it needs to be especially since she will hopefully be seeing Levy that night. *Bed* by J Holiday came on next. She couldn't do it; next, *Naked* by Marques Houston. "Damn what are you trying to tell me phone?" she mumbled to herself. She decides to just scroll through her library instead of leaving it up to the phone. *Genius of Love* by the Tom Tom Club is what she landed on. This was perfect, something upbeat and old school.

As she is enjoying being able to relax, her mind drifts into thoughts of Levy and the "what if's" start up again. *What if he is the one? What if he wants to get married? Where would we live? What if he doesn't want to move to the US? Could I live here? Hell yea!! I would miss my family though and my friends and my babies. What if he can't fuck? Even worse what if his dick is little?*

Her thoughts are interrupted by the man she had seen jogging back and forth down the beach standing in front of her.

Suddenly Single

"Excuse me?"

"Yes?" she asks him.

"I don't mean to be intrusive, but I couldn't help but notice how beautiful you are."

"Thank you," Kia says to him trying not to roll her eyes at him in disgust for interrupting her daydream. "You are too kind."

"What's your name?" he asks.

"Kia, what's yours?"

"Michael. So where are you from?"

"Houston, TX," she answers.

"Ok from the States. How long are you here for?"

"I will be here until Friday." She answers trying not to seem interested.

"Oh okay, cool. Have you been able to go out and sightsee? Have you been on any excursions?"

"Mmmm hmmm. We went to Harrison's Cave, out on the Jammin' Catamaran and on the Island Safari."

"We? Who is we? Are you here with someone?"

"Yes, I am here with one of my friends. Our other friend left this morning."

"Oh ok. It sounds like you ladies have done a lot."

"You assume I am here with a lady. You know what they say about assuming."

"You are right. My apologies, it's just that if you were here with a man, he would be crazy not to be out here next to you."

"Touché. I'm just giving you a hard time. My friend that is still here is a lady, and we have done a lot."

"Well if you all want to go snorkeling again, I have a small catamaran."

"Do you?" Kia says all perked up because now he is speaking her language.

"I do. I go out whenever I have at least 3 people."

"How long do you go out for?" she asks showing some interest because her curiosity is peaked and the wheels in her head are turning about how she can convince Jordyn to go out with her again on this boat.

"I go out for 4 hours. I go in an area where the sea turtles live and feed. So you are guaranteed to see some sea turtles."

"Oh okay, cool. How much do you charge?"

"For someone as beautiful as you, I would do it for free," he tells Kia.

Score!!! Kia thinks to herself. "Awww, you are flattering me," she says to him coyly.

"I'm serious," he says "I would love to just have you in my presence. Somebody as sexy as you, how could I charge you when I would be the one getting the treat?"

"So what you're saying is you make money off all the ugly people?" Kia laughs. She laughs, but she knows she most certainly cannot go out with him on the catamaran even if she could convince Jordyn to go with her.

He laughs at her statement but responds, "All I'm saying is that you are beautiful, and I would love to take you and your friend out snorkeling if you would like to go."

"Well, I appreciate the offer. I will let you know if I can convince her to go," Kia tells him knowing she would not even really try to convince Jordyn. Besides, she is sick anyway.

He gives her his number and tells her to be sure to call him, and as quick as he jogged up, he jogged off back down Dover Beach.

Kia goes back to enjoying her music and getting caught up in her thoughts. She stays out there for about 3 hours soaking up the Caribbean sun and dipping in the warm water of the sea before heading back in to check on Jordyn.

"Dawg, how are you feeling?" Kia asks when she returns to the room.

"I'm okay. I have an ear infection."

"How do you know?"

"I went on down there to the Elcourt clinic that is around the corner, and dawg, that Dr. Jenson is fine! I could hardly contain myself when he was checking me out. Shit, you know they like thick around here."

"Whaaat? What did he look like?"

"Girl he was tall, one of the few 6 footers I have seen around these parts, nice chocolate brown, and oooh wee...just handsome. He looked good."

"So did he give you any medicine?"

"Yea he gave me some antibiotics and some drops to put in my ears after swimming if I get back in the water."

"Oh ok. Well that's cool."

"He told me to come back in a couple of days for a follow up if I didn't feel better but we will be gone. I may have to slide on back over there tomorrow just because….," she said laughing.

"Dawg, I hear ya shiiid. Do it. You don't have anything to lose," Kia laughs.

Jordyn retreats upstairs to take her medicine and rest for a while. Kia decides to call Levy just to make sure they were still on for tonight. She does not want a repeat of last night.

"Hello?" he answers on the first ring.

"Hey. Good afternoon," she says to him relieved to hear his voice. She can't help but smile.

"How are you today?" he asks her.

"I'm doing okay. I thought I would just confirm for tonight and make sure we are still on."

"Of course we are. I really want to see you. I'm just worried that once you leave I will not hear from you again, and I don't want that."

"Why would you say that Levy? Of course you will hear from me, but let's just focus on the time we have left." Kia is delighted to hear that Levy wants to keep in touch with her, and truth be told she wants to keep in touch with him as well.

"Ok good. We can do that. I will bring the cream to cream your feet tonight. What time will you be free?"

"What time do you want to come?"

"What about 8:00PM?"

"Then I will be free at 8:00." Kia smiles as she tells him.

"Now you are trying to mack me," he teases.

"Me?" Kia says trying to sound innocent. "Nooooooo never that. I'm not trying to mack you. Did it work?" Kia asks as if she was seriously trying to mack him.

"You had me at hello," he tells her.

Kia almost melted. "Ok, you win," she laughs.

"I know I have won. I met you. I will win bigger if you end up being mine." He says taking on a serious tone.

At a loss for words, Kia is not quite sure what to say. She has longed to hear someone say something of the sort to her for a long time. "Oh Levy. You have macked me for sure." Kia tells him not really wanting to get caught up but feeling some kind of way about this for sure.

"Good," he says with a more confident tone. "I will see you tonight at 8:00."

"Yes I will see you tonight. Don't pull a repeat of last night." Kia tells him with a hint of sarcasm in her voice.

"Tonight....8:00," he tells her firmly.

"Tonight...talk to you later."

They hang up the phone, and Kia goes upstairs and takes a look at her clothes wondering what she will wear tonight. While going through her clothes, she starts to fold and repack her suitcase, which feels like too soon, because they will be leaving this magical place in two days. She decides to wear her burnt orange maxi dress, with her matching shoes and silver jewelry.

After the ladies return from dinner, Jordyn goes upstairs and gets ready for bed so she can rest and feel better. Kia freshens up and waits for Levy to call her. Right on queue at 8:00 PM, the phone rings, and it is the front desk saying that Levy has arrived. Kia instructs them to send him up. She does one last mirror check before he knocks on the door.

"Hey, good evening," she says with enthusiasm as she opens the door and invites him in.

"Good night. How are you?" he says giving her a hug and a kiss on the cheek.

"I'm doing well. I'm full from dinner."

"Where did you eat?"

"We went to Pablo Donte's. I had a steak and baked potato. It was pretty good." She tells him thinking about the char on the steak and how it was cooked perfectly.

"Oh ok. That's good you had something that you enjoyed. Where is your friend?" .He asks not seeing Jordyn anywhere around.

"She's upstairs getting ready for bed because she is not feeling well, so we have to keep it down or go outside on the balcony."

"I see. We can go wherever you are comfortable."

"Let's go out on the balcony and enjoy the breeze."

"Lead the way," he tells her.

"Follow me," she smiles as she looks at him shyly.

She sits in one of the chairs, and he moves the other chair directly in front of her about two feet away. As soon as he sits, he pulls out the tube of Avon lotion from the bag he carried in with him. He grabs Kia's right leg and places it in his lap where he starts to rub her foot with the lotion he has brought.

"Wow you give a good foot massage," she tells him as he continues to send waves of electricity up her leg with each stroke.

"Thank you," he says as he looks at her and flashes his sexy smile showing off his pearly whites.

"Have you ever thought about being a professional masseuse?"

"No I haven't. I don't think I'm that good at it."

"Please. You should think about it. You could make a killing." She tells him. "You could work at one of these hotels around here giving massages to the tourists or set you up something on the beach or something. There is money to be made out there, and you could definitely get your piece of the pie with this."

"There are people at hotels that do this already, besides don't you have to have some sort of certification or something?"

"I don't know about over here, but in the US, there are certifications that you can get. You really should look into it."

"I may consider it. So you like how this feels?" he asks her with a hint of seduction in his voice.

"I do. It feels really good."

"If we were together, I would do this for you every day after you get in from work before you eat the dinner I have prepared."

"Would you now?"

"Yes I would."

"And I would let you." Kia tells him thinking to herself that she could see this happening but she is still trying to be cautious because she doesn't want to fall for someone who lives so far away.

The two of them sit out on the balcony for another two hours or so getting lost in conversation and losing track of time. Levy massages Kia's other foot, her calves and her shoulders. Kia is feeling very relaxed, and all of sudden, sleep has hit her. They make their way back inside and sit on the couch to continue their conversation. While Kia is enjoying her time with Levy, she is really sleepy and wants to go to sleep. She hopes Levy is not trying to spend the night on the sly because he also has underwear and a toothbrush in the bag he brought with him.

"So how are you getting home?" she asks him knowing he does not have a car.

"I will probably catch a van. My brother dropped me off, but I don't think he is going to come and get me."

"Oh ok, well what time do the vans stop running?"

"Not until two or three in the morning. Why? Are you ready for me to go?" he asks her not wanting to wear out his welcome.

"Yes and no." Kia responds.

"Explain please."

"Yes, I am only because I am sleepy and I want to go to bed, but no because I am enjoying our time together."

"I see. No problem. Let me gather my things and then I will be out of your hair. I don't want to stay anywhere where I am not welcome," he says sarcastically.

"Good. You get the point!" Kia laughs. If he wants to play she can play too.

He gathers his things and walks over to the door. When he gets there, he turns around and gives her a hug and a kiss before opening the door. She feels herself starting to fall for him, but she has to catch herself before it is too late.

"I will call you tomorrow," he tells her.

"Okay, and thank you for the massage," she tells him.

"You are most welcome," he says as he kisses her on the nose.

Kia shuts the door behind him and goes upstairs to prepare for bed and for what her last full day in Barbados may bring.

Chapter 8

The ladies wake up to the sound of the phone ringing as they had become accustomed to.

"Hello?" Kia answers the phone.

"Good morning. How are you doing this morning?" Levy greets Kia.

"I am good; just waking up. How are you this morning?"

"I'm doing well now that I have heard your voice."

Kia smiles and chuckles. "There you go trying to mack me."

"I'm not trying to mack you, I promise. I'm just telling the truth."

"Mmm hmmm...That's what you say," she tells him trying to sound hard but she is smiling too big. "So what's up?"

"Well, I was just calling to say that I hope I can see you today before you leave tomorrow and to tell you that I am sorry."

"Sorry for what?" she interrupts.

"I am sorry because I promised you three things and I fell short on two of them and now time has run out. Time was just not on our side."

Kia almost sheds a tear because no man she has ever encountered has apologized for not doing something he said he would do. This has gone a long way with Kia. Unbeknownst to Levy, he has just gained a lot of points with Kia. She is not quite sure how to respond.

Suddenly Single

"That's okay Levy. I know time was not on our side, but at least you recognize that you did not do what you said you would do, and you are holding yourself accountable for that. That's a good thing."

"Okay. Listen, can I come see you tonight?"

"I would like that. What time?"

"What about 7:00?"

"Seven is fine with me," she says with excitement.

"Perfect, I will see you tonight. Enjoy your day, okay?"

"I will. You do the same. See you tonight."

"Yes, I will see you tonight. Bye."

Kia is excited because she will get to see him again, but she is a little sad because she will be leaving the next day and does not know if or when she will return.

Once the ladies fully wake up and get dressed, they decide to go to Happy Days for breakfast. It is a quaint little internet café located next to Pablo Dante's. Both ladies are dragging somewhat because they know this is their last day in Barbados before heading back to reality in the morning.

"Dawg, what do you want to do today?" Jordyn asks Kia.

"Go to the beach for sure. The rest does not matter to me. Levy is coming over at 7:00 so I can see him one last time before leaving."

"Ok that's cool. We can go to the beach and tonight when Levy is there I will wash my clothes so you can have some privacy."

"That's cool, but we don't need any privacy. We are not going to be doing it," Kia laughs but she is very serious.

"I hear ya dawg...I hear ya...."

"I hear my stomach growling. They need to come on with the food...shoot!" Kia exclaims.

Both ladies laugh because they share the same sentiment.

After breakfast, the ladies decide to peruse the souvenir shops along their route back to Divi, starting with the ones located across from Happy Days. Kia goes in the first shop and she sees some friendship bracelets she decides to get for her friends Danielle, Liz and Emma. She doubts that they will ever wear them but hey it's the thought that counts right? At the next shop, she sees a necklace that she decides to get for herself. This is the only thing she will have to bring back from Barbados for herself, besides maybe Levy. They walk a little further down and in the last shop she purchases the last of what she is going to get which are the pot holders her mother requested she has looked all over for some and she is thrilled to finally have found them.

"Dawg, I may be a little sad," Kia tells Jordyn as they are walking back towards the hotel to get changed for the beach.

"Why?"

"Because, I don't want to go back to reality tomorrow," Kia says sadly. "At least I am staying over in Miami and may be able to see my friend Alex. He moved to West Palm Beach a few years back. I let him know that I had an overnight layover in Miami and he said he would drive down to see me because Miami is a lot closer than Texas. That will be a pick me up because I have not seen him since before he left. I didn't get to go to his going away party."

"That's right I remember him. Y'all were really good friends back in college."

"Yea, we were."

"Well, at least you came here this year and got to experience it for yourself. Now you see why I have a timeshare here. This just feels like home to me," Jordyn says with a hint of sadness in her voice as well. "I always hate to go too!"

"I see why....I see why," Kia says shaking her head.

As the two women are approaching the back entrance to the hotel, they see Phillip walking down the path in the distance. He spots them and waves to them.

"Good afternoon ladies. How are you this afternoon?" he asks the both of them as they approach.

"Good afternoon. We are okay, just a little sad," Kia tells him.

"Why are you sad?"

"Because we have to leave and go back to reality tomorrow."

"Wow, it came up quick didn't it? Well listen, what time does your flight leave tomorrow? I don't work so I can ride with you to the airport to see you off."

"It leaves at 2 something in the afternoon I believe. We should get there probably around 12-ish," Kia informs him.

"Okay, perfect. I can be up here around 11:45 and I will get the cab for you, and I will ride with you to make sure you get there safely."

"Ok, that will be nice," Kia tells him.

"What are you ladies doing for the rest of the day today?" He asks both of them.

"We are going to the beach," Jordyn says to him.

"Well, you will enjoy it. The water is calm today," he tells them.

"It will be bittersweet," Kia says sadly, "but we will make the most of it." Kia tells him as they are getting on the elevator. "We will see you later."

Both ladies head up to Penthouse 12 to get changed for the beach and enjoy their last full day in this tropical paradise.

"How do I look?" Kia asks Jordyn.

"Dawg, you look fine. Levy will love that dress. It shows off all that ass," Jordyn laughs.

Kia gives Jordyn a blank stare then bursts out laughing. She knows Jordyn is right. This dress definitely shows off all her "ass"ets. Kia glances over at the clock on the kitchen wall and sees that it is close to 7:00. She is expecting the phone to ring any minute, and it will be the front desk saying that Levy has arrived.

"I am headed downstairs to wash my clothes so you and Levy can have some privacy, then I will probably hang out in the lobby or by the pool," Jordyn tells Kia.

"Thanks Dawg, I appreciate that although Levy and I won't really 'need' privacy. I mean it's not like we are going to be up here naked or something," Kia laughs because she hopes not anyway.

"Oh, it's no problem. If the shoe were on the other foot, I would want you to get yo' ass out," she says while laughing but Kia knows she is serious.

"You're stupid!" Kia laughs. "Bye," she tells Jordyn as she leaves out the door.

Kia can hardly catch her breath before there is a knock at the door. She looks through the peep hole and her heart sinks.

"Phillip?" she says bewildered as she opens the door.

"Good night. I'm sorry for coming up here like this but I was getting ready to get off from work in a few minutes and I wanted to see if I could take you to dinner if you didn't have plans. Damn you look good!!" he says once he finishes talking and finally looks at her up and down.

Kia is floored by his boldness and does not want to disappoint him but she already has plans.

"Phillip, that is really nice of you to offer to take me to dinner however, I already have plans for the evening."

Just as she says that, her eyes get big because Levy walks up behind Phillip at the door. Phillip sees the expression on her face change and looks behind him and sees Levy. Levy is glaring at him.

"Good night," Phillip says to Levy before turning back to Kia. "I will leave you to your plans for this evening. I will see you tomorrow. Have a good night." He turns and walks off before Kia could get a word out.

"Good night," Levy tells him as he is walking off. "Hello. How are you?" he asks Kia.

"I'm doing okay," she tells him as she closes the door behind him.

"What did he mean he will see you tomorrow?" he asks her.

"He is taking us to the airport."

"I see. What did he want tonight?"

"Honestly, he came to ask me to dinner, but I told him I already had plans," she smiles.

"Yes, you do have plans," he says as he kisses her on the cheek. "Listen, do you want to go for ice cream?"

"Go where? Is it somewhere we can walk to?" Kia was serious when she said she was not leaving the hotel with him in a car. She did not know him like that.

"My brother is downstairs and he is going to take us."

"No, I'm good. I can be lactose intolerant at times and that would be ugly," she laughs but is serious.

"Ok, well let me call him and tell him to go and come back and get me later."

After he makes the call, he tells her, "Come sit next to me and give me those feet."

Kia is a little taken aback but she obliges and sits next to him on the couch and puts her feet in his lap anxiously awaiting his tender touch.

"What are you going to do with my feet," she asks already knowing the answer.

"What do you think I am going to do with them?" he says as he takes out the tube of lotion.

"Well, I'm hoping you are going to rub them and caress them."

"Did you think I was going to do this?" he says as he gently put her toes in his mouth and begins to suck them.

"Uhhh no, I DID NOT!!!!" Kia says quite shocked. She is hoping he will stop soon because this is starting to feel real good, and she is determined not to end up upstairs naked.

"I just wanted to shock you a little before you leave," he laughs.

"Well, you did that!"

He grabs the tube of lotion and squeezes almost half of what is left in his hands and rubs them together then proceeds to rub her right foot then her left. As he is massaging her feet they start talking about all kinds of things but in particular he asks her what kind of man she likes physically. She tells him she likes a man that is 6 feet tall and above, football build, with pretty teeth and easy on her eyes.

"Three out of four is not bad," he tells her.

"What three might those be?" she asks him while smiling. She knows he is probably going to say being 6 feet tall is the one he doesn't have.

"Football build, pretty teeth and easy on the eyes."

"I thought those might be the three you had in mind. You are assuming I think you are cute," she says sarcastically. "I'm just kidding. Of course I think you are easy on the eyes."

"I know you do..." he laughs.

Kia's jaw drops.

"Close your mouth. I'm going to miss you," he tells her.

"I'm going to miss you too."

"Can I ask you something else kind of personal?" he says cautiously. "Please don't be offended."

"Of course you can," she says as she turns to sit between his legs with her back leaning on his chest.

"What size dick do you like?"

All Kia heard was the scratched record sound effect in her mind. If she was drinking something, she would've choked. *What did he just say?*

"Big," she replies trying to keep her composure and keep from laughing at her response to him.

"Like this?" he says as he is trying to get her to turn around and look.

"I'm not turning around." Kia says fearful that if she turns around, she may see his naked manhood staring her in the face. Deep down, she wants to turn around and look at the package and then go upstairs and try it out, but she has to resist the urge because if this man is serious about her, she can't give it up so soon. How would that make her look?

"Just look," he urged, "I promise it will be okay."

"I'm not going to look!" she said forcefully.

"I hope this is enough to satisfy you when the time comes," he says.

Before Kia knew it, she is touching the print of his erect penis through his pants. From what she could make out it is definitely workable. Once she realizes what she is doing she snatches her hand away quickly. *What the hell am I doing?* she asks herself. "I'm sorry for touching you," she tells Levy with a shame look on her face.

"You have nothing to be sorry for. You did nothing wrong. So is it enough for you?" he says as he gently kisses her lips.

"Yes, it is," she responds as she gets up off the couch and walks over to the refrigerator to look for anything to put out this fire that has started in her body.

"Where is Jordyn?" he asks realizing he has not seen or heard her.

"She is downstairs washing."

"Oh, okay. Can I ask you something?"

"Sure" she was a little nervous.

"What is that?" he asks pointing to her CPAP machine.

"It is my CPAP machine. I have sleep apnea. It helps me to breathe while I sleep."

"I see. Okay. Can I see what the upstairs looks like?"

"Of course you can," Kia says but she is cautious because she is trying her best not to end up indulged in his chocolate goodness.

She comes out of the kitchen and walks upstairs with him following close behind her. The upstairs is really small. It consists of a master bedroom that has a king bed and a balcony, a second bedroom that has 2 twin beds in it and a bathroom. Levy peeps in each of the rooms then takes off back down the stairs. Kia is a little surprised that he does not come up with something to try and stay upstairs so he can coax her into doing it, but she is glad he doesn't because she is so hot and bothered right now that he could get it if asks for it.

Once back downstairs, they decide to sit out on the balcony and take in the night air.

"So have you enjoyed yourself here in Barbados?" he asks her.

"Yes I have. I had a great time! Nothing else I have done in my life compares to coming here. I have been a few places in my time like the Maya Riviera in Mexico, the Bahamas, and Toronto and all over the United States, but nothing compares to this. Even though it started out rough, it ended up GREAT!!"

"Well, I am glad you had a great time, and I am even more glad you came. If you had not come, I would not have met you."

"There you go trying to mack me," she laughs.

"I'm not trying to mack you. I'm serious. I like you. I really do. I'm just scared that once you leave I will not hear from you again."

Kia takes a long look at Levy while he is talking trying to discern whether or not he is telling the truth or if she is just another tourist to him. Her gut is not giving her any indication either way.

"Listen, look at me, you will talk to me again. I promise."

"Ok. I will take your word for it. I would hate to lose you," he tells her.

"You have to get me before you can lose me."

"True. I am hoping to get you and have you forever."

Kia wants to melt, but she stays together. No one has ever told her such sweet things, not even her ex-boyfriend she was with for five years. She is definitely a sucker for somebody who is sweet to her.

The two of them stay out on the balcony for another hour or so enjoying each other's company, indulging in conversation and stealing kisses every now and then.

"Well it's getting late. I have to get up early in the morning for work. I should go."

Kia does not want him to go because she has truly enjoyed the time they have spent together.

"Ok. I will walk you out."

"No, you can walk me to the door. I don't want you to walk me out because I don't want you to walk back in by yourself."

"Ok." Kia didn't have the strength to challenge him. She is all of a sudden overcome with sadness. She knew her *"How Stella Got her Groove Back"* fairytale was coming to an end, and she doesn't want to go back to reality.

Levy gathers his things and Kia is walking in front of him to the door. They pause in front of the floor length mirror that is opposite the counter by the door. Levy stands behind her in the mirror and gazes at what they look like.

"This looks like a wedding picture or the kind of picture a married couple would have in their house," he says. "Look at us. Look at how good we look together."

"Yea, we do look good together." Kia agrees. She likes the way her golden honey complexion contrasts with his flawless dark chocolate skin. She does wish he was about six inches taller though, but oh well.

Kia takes two steps to the door and reaches for the handle then pauses. She turns around and throws her arms around Levy holding him close. She is fighting back tears because she does not want him to go. She lets him go then quickly turns back around and grabs the handle before he could see her face. She does not want him to see that a tear had managed to swell up and fall. She takes a deep breath and opens the door.

"Well I guess this is goodbye," he says to her quietly.

"Yes for now anyway. You never know what may happen in the future," Kia says as she tries to pull out a smile. She says this, but she does not know if or when she will ever return here.

"Please let me know when you reach the states tomorrow, okay?"

"I will."

He grabs her and gives her a hug and a peck on the lips. "Safe travels." He kisses her on the nose. "Until next time."

"Bye," she tells him and closes the door. She couldn't bear to watch him walk off.

Chapter 9

"Hello? Hold on. Dawg, it's Levy," Jordyn yells from the other bedroom.

Kia goes downstairs to get the phone. She is already awake. She did not sleep well because it was her last night in paradise, and she was missing Levy.

"Hello?"

"Good morning sleepy head."

Kia smiles. "Good morning. How are you?"

"I'm doing better now that I have heard your voice. Listen, can you come downstairs?"

"What?"

"I'm in a van and I'm about to pass by Divi and I want to see you for a few minutes before you go."

"Ok. Here I come." Kia hangs up the phone and quickly runs upstairs and throws on her hoodie over pajama pants and t-shirt she doesn't bother to put on a bra but she does brush her teeth because she doesn't want to offend him with her morning breath.

She takes the stairs down to the first floor; she doesn't want to wait on the elevator. She spots him walking in over by gate and she meets him halfway and gives him a big hug. They walk over to the sitting area in the atrium by the fountain on the first floor.

"Sit here in the chair," Levy tells her.

He sits in the love seat couch adjacent to the chair and grabs her right foot and starts rubbing it.

"You love to rub feet don't you?" Kia asks playfully. She is glad she got the chance to see him once more.

"Yes, I do, especially when they are yours!" he laughs.

"So what brings you over here this morning?" Kia asks but she doesn't care why he decided to come by she is just glad he did.

"I wanted to see you one more time before you leave today."

"Aww I wanted to see you too!!!" Kia exclaims.

Kia hears talking and she looks around and she sees Phillip walking by in his work uniform walking with another staff person. He sees her but does not say anything, and he keeps on walking. Levy does not seem to notice Phillip or if he does, he does not seem to care.

"What time does your flight leave today?"

"It leaves at two something. I need to look for sure."

"Ok....Ok... I am really going to miss you."

"I'm going to miss you too, Levy. Do you think you will be able to come and visit me in the States?"

"I don't know. I want to. I have a passport but I don't have a Visa to the U.S. I will have to work on getting one."

"Well, work hard."

"I will. I promise." He grabs her other foot and starts rubbing it as well. He wants to make sure it gets equal time.

"You look beautiful this morning."

"Now I know you're lying. I look a mess. I don't even have on a bra."

"It doesn't matter. You look beautiful anyway."

"You trying to mack me for sure," she laughs.

"I promise you I am not. Anyway, listen I need to get going. I just wanted to see you again." He puts his arms around her and squeezes tight. "Take care and please let me know when you get to the States."

"I will. I promise. Listen, are you on Facebook?"

"I am. Levy Brathwaite. Look me up. I have a picture of Flash as my profile pic. I don't really get on there a lot, but I will get on there so we can chat for free."

"Ok, I will look you up when I get back. I'm going to miss you."

"I'm going to miss you too."

He gives her a kiss on the cheek and turns to walk off to catch a van to work. Kia stands there a moment and watches him walk, then she heads back towards the lobby so she can get on the elevator. She sees Phillip standing by the front desk, and she stops for a minute even though she is not confident in her looks at this moment.

"Phillip? What are you doing here?" she asks him because he just told her last night that he did not have to work.

"They called me in to work, and I need the hours so I came in. This means I will not be able to ride with you to the airport, but I will still arrange the van for you."

"I see. Well it is not a problem. You have to do what you have to do. Let me get back upstairs because I look too bad to be seen in public," she laughs.

"Nonsense you look fine."

"No I don't, but thank you. I promise I clean up well," she tells him as she walks over to the elevator and punches the button.

"You look fine. I promise," he yells as she steps on the elevator.

After breakfast, the ladies return the room and do one last sweep to make sure they have not left anything. They decide on an amount of cash to leave for the housekeepers and on an amount to give to Phillip since he has been so sweet to them.

They call downstairs for help with their luggage and within 5 minutes Phillip is knocking on the door.

"Good morning Ladies. How are you today? Which bags are going on the cart?"

"Good morning Phillip. All of them are going," Jordyn responds.

"Ok. Let me get them for you please," he tells Kia as she is rolling one over to the cart.

"Ok, I will let you get it." Kia resigns and takes her hands off the bag. She is bummed about leaving this beautiful place, but she is excited to see her friend from West Palm Beach, her family, and of course her beloved dog Sisi.

Phillip gathers all of the luggage on the cart and takes it downstairs. He tells them he will see them in a few minutes. Jordyn walks through the entire penthouse one last time while Kia steps out onto the balcony to take in the view before having to say goodbye to it. She looks around the balcony and smiles reminiscing about the moments she and Levy shared out here. She hopes to make it back to this place because maybe just maybe she might like Levy.

Once downstairs, the ladies step to the front desk and settle their bill including getting the list of phone calls. Kia has racked up quite a bill calling Levy. It was only $30 BDS ($15 US Dollars) but it is still more than she expected to pay. Once the bill is settled, she and Jordyn walk towards the van in which Phillip has already placed their luggage. Jordyn gives him a hug goodbye and then gets in.

"Well, I guess this is goodbye," he tells Kia.

"It is for now. Hopefully, I will make it back here."

"Remember, you have two men in Barbados that want your heart. You are a really sweet person and I really like you."

"Thank you. You are really sweet to Phillip. Thank you for everything that you have done for me. I really appreciate it."

"You are more than welcome. I enjoyed you staying here. It made me look forward to coming to work."

Kia smiles at him. "Listen, what is your phone number so we can keep in touch?" She grabs a piece of paper and a pen out of her purse and gives it to him to write down his information.

He writes it down for her, and then gives her a big hug before she gets in the van. He shuts the door behind her then sticks his head through the window and gives her a kiss on the cheek.

"Be careful. Call me," he tells her. "Goodbye Jordyn. Safe travels."

"Bye Phillip. Thank you for everything." Jordyn tells him.

"You're welcome."

Kia hands him the cash that she and Jordyn are giving him for a tip and tells him thank you again for everything.

"Thank you," he tells them.

"You're welcome." Kia says as the van is pulling off to take them back to reality.

Once on the plane, Kia has to choke back tears as she sits in her seat thinking about Levy and the time she spent with him. She really does not want to go. She wonders if she will ever see him again, and what the future may hold for the two of them. Lost in her thoughts, she hadn't noticed that all of the passengers are on the plane, but the doors are still open until the pilot came on and announced that they have to fix the brakes on the plane and that is the cause of the delay.

Oh hell, here we go, she thinks to herself. She repeats her prayer that she says before she gets ready to fly and asks the Lord to give her patience and strength to make it through this trip as well as to watch over Levy and Phillip.

Two hours later, they finally take off and are on their way to the United States. She manages to text Levy before they take off to let him know they were just now leaving. By the time they land and go through Customs and

Suddenly Single

Immigration in Miami, Jordyn has missed her connecting flight back to Dallas.

Before Kia goes out to the curbside to wait for the hotel shuttle bus to come and pick her up, she tells Jordyn to call her once she figures out what she is going to do about getting home. As Kia is walking out, she texts Alex to let him know that she has made it to town and where she will be staying. While she is standing out there waiting, she decides to get on Facebook and look up Levy Brathwaite. She finds him and just as he said there is a picture of Flash as his profile pic. She sends him a friend request, then she gives him a quick call to let him know she has made it. She is not sure of the cost but she does not care at this point.

"Hello?"

"Hey. I made it back to the US."

"I'm glad to hear that. I was worried. So you all left late?" he asks.

"Yes, they had to fix the brakes on the plane. So we ended up leaving two hours late."

"Well, I am glad you made it back safely. So, where are you now?

"I am in Miami. I have an overnight layover here before going home tomorrow."

"Ok. Ok. What time will you make it home tomorrow?"

"I am supposed to land sometime in the 9:00 hour in the morning. I leave here like at 7:30 and there is a one hour time difference."

"I see. Well you be careful going home. I don't want anything to happen to you."

"I will. Listen, I sent you a friend request on Facebook."

"Ok good. I will go in a few minutes and accept it. Then maybe we can chat on there later," he says enthusiastically.

"Sounds like a plan to me. Talk to you later," she tells him

"Ok, bye."

Kia is a little excited thinking about the possibilities of what could be with Levy. So far he is saying all of the right things. She is more excited though about seeing Alex. She has not seen him since before he moved, and it just doesn't feel right. This was her buddy in college, and she misses him.

Meanwhile, Kia waits what seems like an eternity for the hotel shuttle to arrive. Apparently, they only run on the hour, no matter what time you arrive. Finally, after forty-five minutes or so of waiting in 45 degree weather (a cold front came through that day) the hotel shuttle arrives and Kia gets on takes her seat.

At the next stop, a rather nice looking gentleman gets on the shuttle. Kia couldn't help but take notice. It was hard for her to discern his ethnicity, but it really didn't matter. This man was gorgeous, and he smelled good. *Mmmm there is nothing like a good smelling man,* she thinks to herself and hopes she didn't say that out loud.

Kia couldn't help but admire his 6 foot something frame. His muscles are draped over his body perfectly, and he is wrapped in the smoothest, most flawless, milk chocolate skin you have ever laid eyes on. His hair is jet black and straight and he speaks with some sort of accent. He is simply delicious. Kia could take him and eat him up, and they are staying at the same hotel too. He definitely would be a delightful ending before returning completely back to reality.

Kia snaps out of her trance when a 5 foot 9-ish, slender-built man gets on and sits right next to the decadent chocolate mound in front of her. The smaller guy is talking on the phone and he is talking a bit louder than Kia thought he ought to be for being in public. Kia should not know how he had to "read" the flight attendant on the plane for asking him to turn off his cell phone. Once he hangs up, he apologizes to Chocolate Drop for being loud and kisses him on the cheek.

"You've got to be fucking kidding me!!" Kia murmurs to herself. This time she knew she said it out loud, and she didn't care.

Disheartened and disappointed, Kia rides in disbelief to the hotel. She recalls a conversation she had with her good friend Raquel about being single: *"This is why women my age are screwed in the game if we are not already married. Men my age are either married, or divorced. If they are divorced, they don't want to get married again and if they do they want a 20-something or an early 30 something woman. They don't want a woman in her late 30's. If they are single and never have been married then most of them don't want to get married. Same goes for older men and well younger men just aren't emotionally mature or don't want to get married."*

"And the rest are either gay or on the down low," Raquel added. *"You can't forget about that."*

"Oh absolutely," Kia co-signs.

That is why Kia is hoping perhaps things will work out with her and Levy, then she won't have to worry about being single any more.

Once at the hotel, Kia collects her bag and checks in. She texts Alex to let him know her room number, and she orders some food because she is starving. She generally does not eat too much on days that she has to fly because she hates using the bathroom on the airplane, plus she is very regular and generally has to go after eating.

While waiting on her food, she takes a much needed shower. Shortly after she gets out of the shower, there is a call from the front desk that her food has arrived. She goes to pick it up and hurries back upstairs so she can devour it before Alex gets there. She sees Chocolate Drop and company in the lobby looking like they are getting ready to step out for the evening. *Damn he is fine,* she thinks to herself as she is shaking her head.

Just as she is finishing her food, there is call from the front desk. "Ms. Simonton, there is an Alex here to see you. Should I send him up?"

"Absolutely!!!"

Kia is excited because she misses not seeing her friend. They would always have a good time back in the day. No matter whom she would bring to hang with them, he and his boys always showed them much love. She glances at the clock to see it is 9:25PM and hopes they will not be up too late reminiscing about old times and such because she has to be on the 5:00AM shuttle, but if they are then so be it! This is her boy, and she doesn't know when she will see him again.

She opens the door when he knocks, and they exchange the biggest, longest hug you could imagine. They hug like it has been a lifetime since they have seen each other. In a way, it has. It feels like it anyway.

"Here I got these for you," he said handing her a beautiful flower arrangement.

"Awww. They are beautiful. This makes me feel special."

"You are special to me. It is not too many people that I consider to be special in my life, and you are definitely one of them."

"Awww boy stop. You trying to get all mushy and shit."

"So what's been going, Ms. Barbados world traveler?" he teases.

"Not too much. Just on my way back to reality from being on vacation. What's going with you?"

"Not too much. You know the wife is pregnant again."

Suddenly Single

"What?!!"

"Yep, this is number 4. It's a wrap after this."

"Naw, don't try to make it a wrap now, shit, you should've been wrapped it up 4 kids ago. I'm just saying. I love my godchildren though, and I'm gon' love this one too!!"

"I know you are. So, how was Barbados? Did you get your groove back?"

"Excuse me, I never lost it. Thank you very much," she laughs, "it was cool. I really enjoyed it. It was beautiful, and yes I did meet somebody. We will see what happens with that. He is just so far away though."

"Well, just be careful because I would hate to see you get hurt behind some BS."

"I hear you. Me too."

The two spend the next couple of hours reminiscing and catching up on old times. Kia hates to see him leave, but she knows he has to get home to his family.

"Well, it was definitely good seeing you. I miss you," Kia says as she is hugging him tightly.

"I miss you too! You know you are my girl. We had some good times together. Oh wait! We have to take some pictures. I told the wifey I would take some. She misses you too."

"Well, come on let's take some then. Tell her I miss her too and to kiss the kids for me."

The two snap a couple of pictures before they part ways. Kia almost has to choke back tears because she does not know when she will see her friend again. She does know that she wants to talk to Levy so she hurries back inside and checks her phone.

Chapter 10

Kia arrives back home in Houston and is greeted by her mother, sister, and dog, Sisi, when they pick her up from the airport. Being back home is a little bittersweet for her. While she is happy to see her family, she misses Levy and being in paradise. At least Christmas is in a few days, and she loves Christmas time.

She tells her family all about her trip. Now that she is back and is safe, she tells her mother about how she had to fly over there by herself and how Jordyn and Haleigh did not make it until the next day. She didn't want to tell her when it happened because she did not want her to worry. When they make it to her mother's house, she pulls out her camera and her phone to show them all of the pictures she took. They are amazed because they have never seen anything so beautiful.

When she and Sisi make it home, she calls Levy to let him know they made it.

"Hello?" he answers on the first ring.

"Hey. I just wanted to let you know that I made it back to Houston, and I made it home."

"Well, I am glad you made it safe, and I am glad I met you. I have not stopped thinking about you since you left. I really hope that was not the only time that I will get to see you."

"Awww, you are making me blush. I'm not sure how or when but I'm sure I will see you again."

"Well, that makes me a happy man!"

The two chat for a little while longer before getting off of the phone. They promise to chat on Facebook later because that does not cost them anything.

Over the next few weeks, Kia and Levy talk everyday via phone, text or Facebook; some days, it is all three. She has somehow fallen for this man, but she is not going to tell him how she feels just yet. Her past experiences have taught her to let the man express his feelings first.

"Hello?" Kia answers the phone seeing it was her friend Jasper. Jasper is one of Kia's best friends and confidant. He knows all of Kia's secrets and guards them dearly.

"Hey what's up? What's going on?"

"Not too much how are you? How are things with you and Levy?"

"I'm good, and things are going good between us. I really miss him. I think I have fallen for him which sucks because he is so far away. Did you know it is 2554 miles from here to Barbados? You know I had to look it up," Kia laughs.

"Girl, you are crazy, and no I did not know that. Only you Kia...only you." Jasper laughs at his friend. Kia could hear him shaking his head through the phone.

"You know I can be a little off sometimes," Kia laughs. "You know things have happened so quickly with Levy, I just pray that he is on the up and up and does not have some sort of hidden agenda."

"Just pray about it and ask God to show you."

"I have. I asked God that if he is not the one for me to remove him from my life but not to let anything bad happen to him. I just wish he would tell me he loves me. It just feels like that is next you know?"

"I feel you. Well hopefully he will say it soon, but you know men sometimes will drag it out."

"Hopefully that is not the case and he will just say it."

"Do you love him?"

Kia pauses for a second before answering the question. "You know, I do love him. I love him as much as I can being this far away. I had no intentions of meeting somebody much less falling for someone that lives so far away. This is not exactly what I want but at the same time it is so much better than what I have, which is nothing, by way of relationship anyway."

"I can understand. I just want you to be happy, and if this makes you happy, then so be it. I just don't want to see you get hurt because he is so far away, and anything could happen."

"I know. He has been so sweet to me and has said all the right things which is more than these fools over here."

"I hear you, and I completely understand. Just remain prayerful."

"Absolutely!"

Kia continues her normal routine each day of waking up to a "good morning" message from Levy. Early one January morning, Kia takes a short break from work to talk to Levy.

"Good morning," Kia says to Levy.

"Good morning. How are you this morning?"

"I'm doing fine, just missing you," Kia says sounding a little sad.

"I miss you too. How is work going for you?"

"It's going. Not too bad today, so far anyway."

"Well that's good. I'm glad to hear that. I don't want anything to make you upset, especially since I am not there to comfort you and rub your feet and kiss you."

"Awww that's sweet. I wish you were here to do those things."

"I do to. Well listen, I have to get back to work, but I love you and will talk to you later."

Kia's heart explodes! She can't believe what she just heard. Did he just say "I love you"? "Ok Levy. Well you have a good rest of the day, and I will talk to you later." Kia plays it cool and does not say it back right away because she does not want to seem desperate or something, but she is elated because she does indeed love this man, and these are the words she has been waiting to hear.

"Ok. I will speak with you soon. Bye."

Kia floats through the rest of the day. She is on cloud nine because he has finally told her the words she has been longing to hear, but she also hopes that he is serious and not just playing with her emotions. She has been through a lot in relationships over the years, and she does not have time for games. Her heart is not a toy to be played with and tossed aside like trash when it is no longer fun.

The next day, Levy calls Kia at work like usual, "Good afternoon. How are you doing today?"

Suddenly Single

"Hey. Good afternoon. I'm doing well, how are you?"

"I'm doing better now that I hear your voice."

"Awww, that is sweet. You know just what to say to make me feel special. Speaking of, yesterday, did you tell me you love me? Did I hear you correctly?"

"Yes, you did hear me correctly. I did say that I love you because I do love you."

"Do you mean it?"

"Kia, I don't say things I don't mean."

"Mmmm ok. Well Levy, I love you too!!!" Kia exclaims. Her heart is overcome with joy when she says this.

"I know you do," he tells her.

"What? How do you know?" She is a little taken back. She scratches her head. This is not what she was expecting him to say.

"I can tell by how you act and what you say."

"Well ok then. I see."

"Well I see me loving you more and more each day."

"Aww me too!"

"Well look, I have to go. I will talk to you later. I love you," he tells her. It feels good to hear him say that again.

"I love you too!!" she tells him. "I will talk to you later."

"Ok. Bye bye."

Kia is beaming from ear to ear. One of her co-workers just so happens to see her as she is walking out of the back supply room where she goes to talk privately since she is in a cubicle at work.

"Girl what is going on with you? You are just smiling and shit. What happened?"

"Chiiilld, Levy told me he loves me!!" She can hardly contain herself.

"Good Lord. You would've thought he told you, you won the lottery or something the way you're cheesing."

Kia laughs because she can feel her cheeks in a smile so she knows it must be true. "I'm just happy you know?"

"I can see. Well I'm glad you are happy. Just be careful."

"I am. Talk to you later. Hey, where are we going for lunch?"

"Now you already know it's your turn to pick," she says as she is walking off.

"That's not helpful," Kia reminds her as she heads back to her desk. She feels like a weight has been lifted. Finally, someone who loves her and doesn't want to just have sex with her. There is no better feeling than falling in love.

To help her channel her emotions since Levy is so far away and they cannot always talk, Kia starts keeping a journal to express herself during times that she wants to talk to him but can't. The next time she sees Levy, she will give him the journal so he can read her thoughts and notes to him. Maybe he can find some comfort in the words she has written.

She puts an introduction in the journal that reads:

My Dearest Levy,

There are times when I wish I could talk to you but for whatever reason I can't. These are my thoughts during those times. I hope you enjoy them.

Love,

Memi

He gave her a nickname of Memi.

January 16, 2013
Dear Levy,

We made it through the first 30 days of knowing each other!! Yesterday was the one month anniversary of the day we met. I am not the type of person to track each month, but I wanted you to know that I have been counting the days. I miss you. A lot has happened in our first 30 days!! You expressed that you love me, and I feel the same way. ☺ I wish that I could talk to you more often and that we could see each other every day, but I guess those things will come in time. I just want you to know that you have really touched me, and I hope it is for a lifetime. I can't wait to see you again. I love you! <3

Love,
Memi

January 17, 2013
Levy I miss you!! I want to see you and hug you and kiss you. I fell in love with you a little more today. Earlier, we had a conversation and you asked me why I did not ask you why you did not call me back last night. I was a little taken back because no man has ever asked me that before. I love the fact that you acknowledge when you say you are going to do something, and you don't do it. To me, that is what a real man is supposed to do. It makes my heart smile. ☺ You also told me today that you have blue balls. I'm sorry that I

cannot help you. I wish I could. ☹ I tell you what though; when we are together for the rest of our lives you won't ever have to worry about that!!!! I have to go to bed now, babe. I love you. Good night. MMMUUAH!! XOXOX

January 18, 2013
Levy, I wish I could talk to you for hours at a time. I mean since we can't go on dates for months at a time...☹ I can't wait to go on a date with you. Even better I can't wait for the kiss at the end of the date....Sleep tight. I love you.

Kia feels all mushy inside all of the time. She can honestly say she has never felt this way before. Her last relationship was not bad by any stretch of the imagination, but she finally admitted to herself that it was one-sided. She was in love with her ex-boyfriend, and he loved her but was not in love with her. There's a difference. Something about this relationship with Levy is different. Even though, he is so far away, he makes her so happy.

January 19, 2013
Levy what have you done to me? I think about you all the time. You are the first person I think about when I wake up and the last person I think about before I go to sleep....

January 20, 2013
I think you are mad with me. I don't know. When I spoke with you BRIEFLY earlier you said I deserted you all day, which is not true. We had a family event today and I text you and sent you a pic on Facebook, not to mention I text you last night, but you didn't text me back. But anyway, in the midst of all that was going on today, I had the WORST allergy attack!!! I kept sneezing and my eyes were itching and watering, then I was fair out of it. Not a good feeling at all. I called you but you were on the road and you said you would call me back but you didn't. I will find out why tomorrow. Until then, I hope you sleep well babe. Love you!!

January 21, 2013
Oh Levy. I think you were trying to torture me today. I called you several times but you didn't pick up. I text you but no response. I was able to chat with you on Facebook though, which was good. I

didn't feel well today, but chatting with you helped me to feel better. I hope we can be together soon. I miss you terribly…….

Chapter 11

Kia is woken up by her phone ringing. She is a little concerned because her phone does not normally ring this early but she will get a message from Levy sometime at this hour.

"Hello?"

"Good morning sleepy head."

"Hey babe, what's going on? What time is it?"

"It's 8:00 here."

"Ok so it's 6:00 here right now. So what's going on babe?"

"Nothing, just on my way to work and I wanted to hear your voice. You were on my mind. I love you Memi."

"Well, babe that is sweet. I love you too."

"I know you do. Let me ask you something, if we are to be together for the rest of our lives where would we live?"

"I don't know Levy. I would love to live there, but I would hate to leave my family and friends."

"I feel like we could have a better start here. I am going to grow a crop of onions that could make a lot of money."

"How much money are you talking about?"

"If it is a good crop it can be at least $15,000 BDS per crop."

"Ok well that would be good, but we need more than one crop per year and what if that crop fails then what?"

"I would still work so we could have other money coming in and you could stay at home or go to the beach or whatever you would like to do."

"I hear you but I feel like we would be off to a better start in the US. Once you get your work permit, you can work for one of these oil and gas companies and make some good money. It will probably be manual labor at first but you just need to get in before moving up. Then maybe in five years or so we can move back to the island or maybe move to The Grenadine Islands."

"I was in the process of starting a taxi business back home on my island. I had the money, but the guy I was working with stole it."

"Oh that's horrible. Why would anybody do something like that?"

"I don't know but I don't want to talk about that right now because I will get mad."

"I can understand babe. I don't know. I just think we would have a better start here. We can always move there once we save some money. Besides with the children and all, we will have a better support system here."

"Child you mean…Just one child. I hear you, but I just feel like we could do more here."

"Levy, I want two kids. What's wrong with having two kids?"

"Nothing is wrong with it. Kids are just expensive and we can do more for one child than we could for two."

"You don't know that, but ok. But since we are talking about kids, how am I going to get pregnant with you know…." Kia's voice fades.

"Listen, I know you have what you have, but I love you, and I'm not going to wear condoms with you forever, ok? End of story; we don't ever have to talk about it again."

Kia is completely shocked by what he has just told her. She can't believe that he would risk himself like that to be with her. "Ok babe. I love you!!"

"I love you too!!! Now, let me ask you something."

"What is it love?"

"Will you marry me?"

Kia is caught completely off guard as she was not expecting a marriage proposal like this. Her head is instantly flooded with all kinds of questions but her heart instantly overflows with overwhelming joy. "Yes, Levy, I will marry you."

"Ok good. I'm so excited. I love you so much."

"I love you too!!"

By this time, Kia has gotten out of bed and has started her morning hygiene routine. She completes the routine out of order due to being on the phone with Levy but that is okay because this is her man and she loves him. The two talk for about another 20 minutes before Kia absolutely has to go. She does not want to get off the phone, but she has to.

Talking with Levy has put her in a good mood this morning especially since he asked her to marry him. She is excited but then all of a sudden fear starts to creep in but Kia tries to keep it out. She will not let anything ruin this day!

The next couple of days were like a dream for Kia. She started thinking about all the different options for she and Levy. Fear did eventually set in, but talking to him always calms her down.

"Levy, remember a couple of days ago when you asked me to marry you?"

"Yes."

"Were you serious, or were you asking me to just to see what I would say?"

"No, I was asking you for real. If I was there, I would have been down on one knee with a ring in hand. I was serious babe. I love you and I want to spend my life with you."

"Ok. I was just checking. So technically, you are my fiancé then."

"Yes, that would be correct. I am your fiancé and you are mine!"

Kia couldn't help but smile. This was like a fairytale. "Well, should we put something on Facebook?"

"I don't really care but if that is what you want to do then you can. I don't know how to do that sort of thing on Facebook, so you will have to do it for me."

"Well, babe, to change your relationship status, I would have to be logged on as you."

"Ok, so log on as me."

"I need your e-mail address and password."

Levy gives her this information, and Kia is in disbelief. She cannot believe he willingly gave her the information. In this day and age of social media, this is a big deal. She knows that this is just one social media outlet, and he could have several but still it is a big deal none-the-less. Almost immediately, he starts to warn her about what she may see in his inbox should she choose to look at the messages. Of course, this is the first place she goes once logged in as him. You can't give women that type of information and then expect them not to check it out. She doesn't find anything worth questioning.

She changes their relationship statuses to "in a relationship". She isn't going to put engaged just yet because she needs to make sure it is going to work out.

In the meantime, Levy and Kia continue to have their daily talks and messages. Kia loves getting texts from him that simply say: I love you. This helps her to make it through the day and somehow eases the angst of missing him. She also continues to write in her journal in the hopes of one day sharing it with him.

January 24, 2013
Good morning babe!! I'm sorry I have not been able to write you in the last couple of days but I wasn't feeling well the first day and yesterday I just plain forgot. I did talk to you yesterday for a long while in the morning. We started to talk about our future together and I was excited. That was the first time ever in my life that anyone ever seriously spoke of having a future with me. I'm scared Levy. Scared about what the future holds for us. I pray and ask God to make a way for us to be together if it is His will. I know we as humans want things on our time but we have to realize it is God's time. You know Levy for me to move there or you to move here we both would be giving up a lot, but I am willing to try if you are. I miss you babe and I want us to be together. I know for that to happen we will encounter some bumps in the road just given our locations, but anything worth having is worth fighting for!!! I love you!!!

January 27, 2013
Hey Babe!! I'm sorry I haven't written you in a few days but I've been busy. I have talked to you every day though including today. I get excited when I think about us building a future together. We have nowhere to go but up. I look forward to the day we will get

married which we have set for March 2014. It may be sooner or it may be later, but it will be. I know we have to continue to get to know each other, but the more I know, the more I love. Well love, it is late and I must go to sleep and dream about you. Talk to you soon!! Love you!!

January 30, 2013
Oh Levy!!! I feel like my heart is about to bust. I love you sooooo much. I miss you and I want to see you. <u>I LOVE YOU!!!</u>

February 6, 2013
Hey babe! I miss you. I talked to you a little earlier today and you were working just like I was. I was telling you about the phone bill for January and about the paperwork we need to file to get you a visa. Then you told me I was yapping. WHAT THE HELL?!?! You have not even begun to see "yapping". But anyway I am excited thinking about marrying you and our wedding. For as long as I have dreamed of this day and for as many times as I have thought about it, I am at a loss now that it is for real and not just a fantasy in my mind. I have ideas but now it's time to make them come to life. I can be picky but I will do my best to pull this together. I have some time. Anyway, take care. I love you. Talk to you soon!!

Kia talks to Levy day in and day out. Her love for him grows by the day. She starts looking at wedding magazines trying to get some ideas. There are so many ways she can go with this, but she really is somewhat at a loss and seeks some input from her future husband.

"Levy, what do you want at the wedding?"

"Kia, listen that is your day. Whatever you want is what I want. The day is yours, and the night is mine. Besides I'm the one who gets the prize because at the end of the day, you will be mine."

"Awww, babe that is sweet. You always know what to say to make me feel special."

"Well, you are special!!! I love you."

"I love you too!!"

Kia is so thankful she met Levy. He has truly made her happy. This is a kind of happy she has never felt before.

February 14, 2013
HAPPY VALENTINES DAY BABY!!! I hope you had a good day today. I talked to you a little earlier. I wish I could've talked to you a little longer, but I guess your schedule didn't allow it. Next Valentine's Day, we will either be married or getting ready to get married depending on the immigration forms. Anyway babe, I must go to bed now. I love you!!

February 24, 2013
Hey Babe!! It seems as if this is the only way I will be able to speak with you today. I have been calling you all day, but I think the system is down over there. Anyway, today has been a difficult day for me because I have not talked to you. I have grown used to talking to you every day, and my day is not right if I don't talk to you, so one day of not talking to you throws me off a little. I don't know how many more days of not talking to you I can take. NONE!!! I love you and I miss you and I need you. I wish you were here with me, or I was there with you. Babe, fold yourself up in a suitcase and ship yourself here!!! I wish I had the money to just come and scoop you up right now. Today was extra hard for me because the last time we spoke, you were crying. And it hurt me because you were hurting and there was nothing I could do to physically comfort you. And what makes it even worse is just that a few days ago we were talking about men crying, and you say you rarely cry so it has to be something really big if you shed a tear. I wanted to hold you, kiss you, and tell you everything was going to be alright, but I couldn't do any of that. Well what keeps me going is knowing that this time next year we will be married or getting ready to get married. I just love you and I want us to be together. I LOVE YOU BABE!!! God willing I will talk to you tomorrow. XOXOXO

March 1, 2013
I love you. #thatisall

Suddenly Single

Kia has had enough. She can't take being away from Levy and decides to go and see him for his birthday in May. She prices airline tickets and they are reasonable, but if she has to also pay for lodging, it will cost her quite a bit. She will see if Levy can take care of the lodging.

"Hey babe, how are you?" she asks.

"I'm doing good today. How are you?"

"I'm good. Listen, I decided that I want to come see you for your birthday. I looked at tickets, and they are pretty reasonable. I will be ready to buy it in the next few days, but I need somewhere to stay. Do you think I could stay with you?"

"Oh babe, I'm so excited to see you!! I will have to ask the owners of the house if you can stay. But I tell you what, I did some work for a lady who owns a guest house. Let me see if I can work it out where we can stay there. Are we going to split the cost because you know I don't have a lot of money?"

"Well, I was thinking you could pay for it since I'm buying my ticket, but if it would help for us to split it, then that is fine. It just can't cost too much. And why would you need to ask the owners of the house if I can stay with you, don't you pay rent there?"

"Just to be sure it's ok and to be respectful. Let me work on the guesthouse and let you know what I come up with."

"Ok, babe. I'm not going to buy my ticket until I have somewhere to stay and I want to get my ticket in the next few days, so please let me know."

"I will honey. You don't have to worry about it."

"Ok...I'll take your word for it."

Over the next couple of weeks Kia and Levy go back and forth on the guesthouse, and Kia has set a deadline for herself. If Levy does not come up with something by her deadline, then she will not go.

"Levy, where are you on talking with the guy about the guesthouse since the first one did not work out?"

"I have not been able to reach him. I will continue to try and get a hold of him."

"Ok because the deadline for me to get my ticket is approaching, and I'm not going to purchase a ticket not having anywhere to stay."

"I can understand babe. Can I tell you something?" he asks sounding nervous.

Kia gets anxious because she does not know what is about to come out of his mouth. "Of course you can babe, what is it?"

"I feel bad with you coming to see me because I am getting all of the benefit."

"What do you mean?"

"Well, *you* have to *come here* to see me, and then it's *my* birthday. I just feel like you are getting nothing out of it, and I would hate for you to spend your money like that to benefit me. I am a man, and I wish I could do more for you."

"Levy, ummm I'm getting the benefit too. I will be on vacation, and the best part is that I will get to see you!!! So please believe you are not the only one benefitting."

"Ok babe. If you say so. I just feel bad."

Suddenly Single

"Babe, there is no need to feel bad. OK? I love you."

"I love you too."

Kia's deadline came and went and since Levy did not get the guesthouse situation together she did not buy her ticket. That is too far to travel not having accommodations secured.

"Kia, I feel bad that I couldn't get this worked out for us."

"It's ok, Levy. I just wanted to be there for your birthday. I tell you what," Kia says looking at her calendar, "How about I come at the beginning of September? This is right after my birthday, but we can still celebrate!!" Kia is excited because this will actually work out better for her. It gives both of them more time to get their finances together.

"That sounds fine to me but I'm still getting the benefit."

"Oh stop, I'm getting just as much benefit as you!!"

They look at the dates and decide she will leave Houston September 1, 2013 with a layover in Miami and reach Barbados on September 2, 2013, and she will come back home September 11, 2013 because that was the cheapest day to fly. It did not even dawn on Kia that she would be flying on September 11. That is the day life as people knew it in America changed forever.

"I tell you what babe, let me just look for my own lodging. I don't want to burden you with this, and I'll be damned if I let another deadline pass. I still love you, but I'm just saying."

"I hear you babe, but I will still look too."

"Okay."

Over the next few, days Kia starts a feverish search for somewhere to stay in Barbados that won't cost her an arm and a leg for the length of time she is staying. She finds a place that seems descent and is in a good area. Kia remembers passing through this area when she was there the last time. She inquires with the owner about it, decides to make the reservation, and pays the deposit. Since she has secured her lodging, she books her plane ticket.

"Babe, guess what?" she tells Levy when he picks up the phone.

"It's official, I am coming to Barbados!!!!" Kia screams. "I bought my ticket today, and I will be there in 63 days! I can hardly wait!!!"

"Kia!!!! This is great, I can hardly wait to see you," he says sounding doubly as excited as she did. "Where are you staying?"

"I found a place by the Quayside shopping center."

"Ooh, ok. That's a good area." His voice seemed to drop just a little bit as if this was a problem, but it was not enough for Kia to be concerned.

Kia is so excited that later that night she posts a message on Levy's Facebook page that simply said: *63 days...I can't wait to see you again*, and when they were chatting that night, he liked the post.

Kia starts counting down the days until she gets to see her man again. She can hardly sleep at night she is so excited. She goes about her normal day to day routine, but she just floats through it. She starts looking at wedding dresses and bridesmaid dresses and even picks out some different styles. Of course, she will not actually try on any or pay any money towards this wedding until she gets her official proposal when she goes. She wonders if Levy will have a ring for her or what because she knows his money is limited. At this point, she doesn't care. He can string some sea shells together and that would be okay with her.

Suddenly Single

When she is about two weeks out from coming, Levy calls her one afternoon like normal.

"Babe, two more weeks, and you will be here!! I can't wait to see you."

"I know I can't wait to see you either. I'm so excited. We are so close yet so far."

"Can you do me a favor?" he asks her knowing she would do anything for him.

"Sure babe. What is it?"

"My cousin is always showing off to me about his girlfriend. Can you send me a text saying that you got some time off work, and you are coming to see me in Barbados in two weeks? I just want to show off to him."

"Sure babe, but are you not friends with him on Facebook because I have put plenty of posts on there about me coming there?"

"I just want to show him. Please can you do it for me?"

"No problem love."

"Thank you!!"

The next two weeks seem to drag on for Kia. She begins to pack her things and get stuff ready for her trip. She and Levy often speak about the things they are going to do to each other when they meet again in a few days. He wants to ravish her body and she wants to feel every inch of his.

She can hardly stand it, and just when she can't take waiting another day, the day arrives for her to see her man again.

Chapter 12

As the flight is making its final descent into Barbados, Kia could see that the weather is ugly outside. It looks nasty and like it has been raining all day. She is extra careful when going down the stairs off the plane because she has on flip flops that will slide on a slippery surface. The breeze is even a little cool because there is an overcast, or it could be because she has on the strapless dress she had on the day she met Levy. She wore it by request.

Kia makes a beeline for the bathroom once inside the airport. She can hardly contain herself. She is so ready to see this man that has made her come to know the meaning of happiness. While using the facilities, she pulls out her phone to call Levy but the way the international calls are set up on her phone, she cannot call him because she is not in the U.S. so she has to text him.

> Hey, I am here. I can't call you so you will have to call me or text me. I am in the bathroom now because I can't use my phone in the Customs line or the other parts of the airport. The line to Customs is long but I should be finished in about 20 minutes.

Kia is hoping Levy hurries and responds because she wants to go ahead and get in the Customs line because another flight has just arrived. And he does respond right away.

> Hey babe. Am glad you made it safely. I can't wait to see you. Meet me out front when you get finished. I love you.

Kia hurries and picks up her carry-on items and heads for Customs with her blue form in hand. She feels like she is in a whirlwind. She is so close yet so far from seeing the man she loves and the man she intends to spend the rest of her life with. She is only about 3 rows back in the roped off line, and it doesn't seem like it should take too long but then she realizes there are only 2 agents working on the visitors side. *Really?* she thinks to herself.

In line in front of her are 2 children that look to be about 4 and 6 years old that are traveling with their mother. From what Kia has overheard, their father is a pilot and was the pilot on their flight from Miami so he goes through a different line. They are from Canada but travel to Barbados quite often. Both of the children are acting out and causing quite a scene. Kia loves children, but she is not in the mood today. She is trying to get to her man. The little girl who is the youngest keeps looking at Kia and Kia is giving her the "if you don't shut yo' ass up and turn yo' ass around look". She really wants to handle her how she would handle her 3 godchildren if they were acting up, but these are not her kids, and this is a different country. She would hate to be out of town with an issue. She instead focuses on seeing Levy.

She has been in line for what seems like an eternity. She manages to sneak and text Levy to let him know she is still in line because 35 minutes have passed and there are still about 20 people ahead of her. At least some of them are in groups, so hopefully it will go a little faster.

Alas, after 52 minutes of standing in line Kia has cleared Customs, and she retrieves her suitcase, which she didn't see at first and got scared. She heads out the doors of the airport to look for her future husband. She doesn't see him right away so she texts him and asks him where should she meet him. He responds:

```
Hey babe.  I am coming.  When you walk out of the airport
walk straight ahead and I will come right there.
```

Before she could reply, she sees him rolling up in the passenger side of the car looking better than what she remembered. This is it; this is the moment she has been waiting for the last 9 months. When the car stops, he gets out, grabs her bags, and puts them in the trunk. Then he comes back and gives her a hug and tells her to get in the front seat. This is not as a big of a welcome as she had hoped for, but it didn't matter. She is here…with her man.

"Hey babe. I can't believe you are here," he tells her while rubbing her shoulders from the backseat. "Meet my brother, Caleb. This is Kia; Kia, this is Caleb."

"Nice to meet you, Caleb. I can finally put a face with a name," she tells him.

"Yes, yes...nice to meet you too. Levy talks about you all the time."

"Does he? Well, it's all good I hope," she laughs.

"Of course it is, so where are we going?"

"We are going to the Merriville Apartments by the Quayside Shopping Center. Babe, can you call the guy to get directions?"

"Ok, I know where that is." Caleb tells her as they drive along.

"Sure babe, I can call him. What's the number?" Levy asks.

Kia gives him the number, and the guy gives him the directions on where it is and tells him he will meet them there with the key. Meanwhile, Levy is sitting right behind Kia and he is rubbing her bare shoulders. She turns around and leans back to give him a kiss, and their lips meet for the first time in months. That tingly sensation that she used to get when he was rubbing her feet is returning. She is trying to hold it together in front of Caleb. She asks if they can stop at KFC because she is hungry, and she knows that she and Levy will probably not leave the apartment anymore that day even though it is only 4 something in the evening. That is what she hopes anyway.

They stop at KFC in Oistins and pick up some food and head off to the apartment. Where it is located is not that far from the airport, but it seems like it is taking forever because the road is only 2 lanes. Caleb has a nice stereo system in his car, so Kia asks can she plug up her phone so they can listen to some of the songs she has downloaded.

"Of course you can plug it up. There is a spot where you can put in your SD card as well if you want to do that," he tells her.

"Whaaat? I didn't know they made them like that. I knew they had stereos where you can plug up your USB cord to it, but I have never seen one where you can put your memory card in there. I see you. That's fancy. You fancy, huh?" Kia laughs.

Caleb laughs and shows her where to plug in the cord. She turns on one of her current favorites, *Bitch Don't kill My Vibe* by Kendrick Lamar. "Please don't judge me. I am very eclectic when it comes to music. I can go from hood to something in Portuguese or French to some smooth jazz. I just don't like country."

"No worries, babe. I love you the way you are. Besides, I like country music, old school country. Like Kenny Rogers and Willie Nelson," Levy reassures her.

"Aww, I love you too hun."

Caleb is laughing at the two of them being all lovey dovey. He tells Kia he has never seen his brother this happy before.

"Well, I hope I have something do with that," she smiles.

"You have everything to do with that babe," Levy tells her as he leans up and kisses her on the shoulder.

"Oooh weee. So look ummm, how far are we from the place?" she asks to distract herself from the moisture that is building in the place where moisture builds.

"It's just up the road," Caleb tells her.

In all of the excitement, Kia forgets to look to her left to see the water. She turns as they are leaving Oistins and she is able to catch a glimpse of the water. Even though it is ugly outside, she can still see the beauty in the water. The waves are a little high but not too high to get in.

"So, I see it was raining here today."

"Yes, it has been raining here for the last few days," Levy replies.

"Well, I am bringing the sunshine with me from Texas so it will be fine the next few days. Mark my words."

"Okay. You have that power?" Levy laughs.

"I asked God for sun during my trip and I have him on my side," Kia says sternly,

"Well, you can't argue with that." Caleb says.

Once arriving at the apartment, Levy and Kia walk over hand in hand to greet the man to get the keys, and Levy gets the information regarding check out, the phone, etc. In that moment, she felt like this is what it is supposed to be like being in a relationship with somebody. The man taking the lead and she not having to worry about anything, at least not in that moment.

He unlocks the door, and they go in together. Kia looks around and is slightly disappointed in the accommodations, but it doesn't really matter at this point anyway. She sits at the table and is eating her food while Levy brings in her luggage. After he brings in everything he comes over by her and sits on the bed and is gazing at her like he is in disbelief.

"What is it?" Kia asks.

Suddenly Single

"I don't believe you are here. I have waited for this for so long, and it is finally here. You are here in Barbados with me," he tells her.

"Yes I am here. With you, and I couldn't be happier."

She gets up and walks over to him and throws her arms around him and gives him a big passionate kiss, chicken breath and all.

"Finish eating your food. I don't want you to be hungry."

"Oh, I am just about done. I would rather nibble on you." Kia says as she kisses him on the lips and cheek and neck and lips again. Kia is about to explode.

"Are you done eating?"

"Yes, I am done," she tells him breathlessly. Her heart rate has increased and she can barely catch her breath she is so turned on right now.

Levy grabs her by the hand and leads her to the bed, where he begins to peel off her dress ever so slowly kissing what seems like every inch of her exposed skin along the way. Kia can hardly take it. Finally, her dress is off and she is there in her matching strapless bra and panty set. Levy steps back to admire the view.

"Damn, you look good," he tells her, "and you smell good and I'm guessing you taste good too," he says in between kisses.

"It's only one way to find out," Kia says with a devilish grin on her face.

Levy chuckles as he removes her undergarments and tells her to lie on the bed where he proceeds to taste the sweet folds of her skin. Kia explodes.

Kia wakes up lying on Levy's chest and glances at the clock that reads 9:22. She looks up and finds him awake and looking at her as she moves.

"How long have I been sleep?" she asks.

"About an hour and a half," he answers as he kisses her on the forehead. "I told you I could last longer than 12 minutes."

Kia busts out laughing. "You don't forget nothing do you?!?!"

"No, I don't," he says seriously then starts laughing himself.

"Well, at least I didn't tap out, like my friends thought I would. It did hurt a little bit though."

"Tap out?"

"Yes, like the song. You know like give up, stop, quit, tap out like I'm done, I'm done, I can't take anymore."

"Oh okay. I see. Well, no you definitely didn't tap out."

Kia laughs. She put an "H" on her chest (like Superman) and "H"andled that. She is feeling good right now.

"Babe, are you hungry?" she asks Levy.

"A little bit. Are you?"

"A little. But not for a big meal, maybe just something to snack on."

"Ok, well maybe we can go to the store. It is one at the bottom of the hill," he informs her.

"Ok well, I have to take a shower first."

"Ok. I will join you."

Kia turns the water on in the shower and is unpacking her bathroom items while she is waiting for the water to heat up. She forgot the hot water heaters in Barbados are solar powered, and if the sun has not been out the water will not be hot. She and Levy get into a lukewarm, at best, shower and begin to clean themselves up after indulging in each other's essence a little while earlier.

Once out of the shower, Kia throws on a pair of shorts and a t-shirt. There is no need to be dolled up going to the bottom of the hill.

"You are such a woman," Levy tells her.

"Why do you say that?"

"Look how long it took you to get dressed. We are just going to the bottom of the hill."

"I know Levy, but damn I like to air dry," she laughs.

"That's bad for you, you know."

"Why is it bad?"

"Because of the bacteria the water leaves on your skin. Plus you can catch a cold," he tells her.

"Levy, that is crazy, but ok. I'm still going to do it you know."

"I know. Are you ready?"

"Yes, I am. Let's go. You got the key?"

"Yes, I do."

He locks the door and the two of them are off down the hill, to the store. They are walking hand in hand and Kia notices that she is a little sore from their session earlier in the evening. She smirks to herself.

"You see that window right there with the light on?" he tells Kia.

"Yes."

"I was looking into us staying there."

"Oh, ok. So what happened?"

"It wasn't available."

"Oh. I see."

They arrive at the store and Kia picks up some water, cookies, and guava pineapple juice.

"Don't get that brand of water," Levy tells her.

"Why?"

"Because it comes from Trinidad and we don't support things from Trinidad."

Shaking her head Kia puts that water back and picks up another brand. They make their way to the register and Levy also grabs a box of condoms. Kia gets a little excited. Kia pays for their things then they head back up the hill to the room.

Chapter 13

"Good morning sleepy head," Levy tells Kia as he leans over and kisses her on the lips.

"Good morning babe. You doing okay this morning? What time is it?"

I'm doing good, as long as I can wake up next to you. It's 10:00."

"Aww, that's sweet babe. That's why I love you. So what's the plan for today?" Kia asks as she sits up in the bed.

"Well, I need to do some work at Pearl Gardens. You can go with me, or you can go to the beach."

"I came down here to see you, so I will go with you, but I will also hit the beach today. Remember what I told you: I need to go to the beach every day that I am here."

"Fair enough. Well, let's get ready so we can catch a van over to Pearl Gardens."

The two of them get in the shower and freshen up after their midnight tasting and photo session. They brush their teeth and complete their hygiene routine. Kia couldn't be happier. She is with the man she loves, and this is a small peek into what being married to him will be like. She is ecstatic.

Levy is dressed by the time she finishes in the bathroom. She decides to put on a maxi dress and some flip flops. She takes her swimsuit and a towel with her because she is not sure exactly when she will make it to the beach, she just knows she will go at some point today. Once dressed the pair head down the hill to the main road to catch a van.

"Are you hungry?" Levy asks Kia.

"Not really, but I could eat. Are you hungry?"

"A little. We can stop at the store in Oistins and get something to eat. Do you have some cash because I only have enough for us to get a van?"

"Yea, I have some. I'm cool with getting something at the store."

They continue walking towards the bus stop where Levy is able to flag down a van for them to take to Oistins. Kia is loving it because she does not have to worry about anything. Once in the van, they sit next to each other and he puts his arm around her. Thankfully it is not too many people on here so they can sneak kisses along the way.

"I love you," he tells her while gazing in her eyes.

"I love you too."

Before they know it, they arrive at their stop in Oistins. They get off across from the grocery store, which is directly across from Oistins Bay. It is a beautiful day and Kia can't help but get lost for a second in the richness of the turquoise water. The water in this area is a different shade of blue, and it is absolutely gorgeous. Kia is snapped out of it by the passing of a city bus.

"Babe listen, there are some girls in this store that have eyes for me. I am telling you because they may look at you crazy."

"Are you fucking them?" Kia asks calmly, never turning to look at him.

"No!" Levy exclaims with all seriousness.

"Ok. Let me just go ahead and handcuff you then," Kia says as she grabs Levy's hand and holds on tight. She is laughing as she says it, but she is very serious. She doesn't play when it comes to her man. As they approach the door of the store, she looks at him and gives him a kiss and not on the cheek.

They walk over to the counter that sells the hot food and pick out what they are going to eat. Kia is hyper vigilant when interacting with the girls that are working this area because she is trying to see which ones may have eyes for her man. None of them seem to be phased by him or her. Kia is glad because she does not want to have to read one of them. Kia pays for the vittles, and Levy grabs the bags. They head across the street so they can sit on a rock and dine on their food.

"Babe, you see that lady over there in the black pants?" Levy asks.

"Yes, what about her?"

"She reminds me of you."

"How so? She does not look anything like me," Kia says as she is a little put off.

"You don't think so? I think she does. Her butt reminds me of yours as well."

"Really Levy?" Kia says giving Levy the side eye.

"Relax babe, I'm just kidding," he says rubbing her shoulder with his one free hand. "The way she looks reminds me of you. I think she looks like you. You are more beautiful, of course."

"I know I am," Kia smirks.

The two of them walk down to the cross walk to cross the street, and they settle on a rock close to the boat yard in Oistins. The view from here is stunning. The water is calm today and looks just right for taking a dip. Kia wants to get in right now, but she can't. As she is sitting there taking in the scene, enjoying conversing with Levy, and eating her fried fish, a rooster comes out of nowhere. Kia throws him a small piece of her bread she is eating, and he gobbles it up faster than the blink of an eye. The roosters seem to be everywhere around the island and they crow all day long. Kia is thinking they only crowed in the morning, but this is not the case over here.

"Babe, are you enjoying your food?" Levy asks.

"Yes I am. That fish was on point," Kia responds. "Do you want my salad?"

"Sure if you are not going to eat it. You need to eat it, it's good for you."

"I know. I eat salad, I just don't want any today," she says giving him her salad.

"Thank you," he tells her as he leans over and kisses her on the cheek.

When they are finished eating, Kia shares her scraps with the rooster before Levy discards the containers. Levy calls his brother and tells him to come and pick them up to carry them to Pearl Gardens. While they are waiting on Caleb, they decide to snap some photos. They pose individually and then snap some together. When they finish up, they walk through the boat yard to wait on their ride.

A few minutes later Caleb beeps the horn, and they get in the car. They head off to Pearl Gardens and arrive in about 5 minutes. It was closer than what Kia thought. Pearl Gardens is a set of 6 townhomes, and Levy is installing the pool. The pool is in the ground, and the shower has been built. The concrete around the pool has to be poured, but the supports in the concrete have to be welded together first. Today, Levy is cleaning out the pool so the electrician can finish installing the lights so it can be filled with water overnight.

Suddenly Single

Levy has the key to one of the units. He pulls out a chair for Kia and puts it in the shaded area on the porch. He makes sure she is taken care of before he starts working. Caleb has his radio blasting so Kia is jamming while she is sitting there watching them work. This is not Caleb's job but he helps Levy from time to time when he has time.

"Ummm babe?" Kia yells.

"Yes, love?"

"I have to go to the bathroom." Kia is hoping the water is working in this unit so she can use the bathroom. She is very regular so she figured this was going to happen.

"Ok hun, there is toilet paper in the upstairs bathroom."

"Ok. Thanks," Kia yells.

Kia goes in and goes upstairs to handle her business. This is a nice, cozy 2 bedroom townhouse, and the bathroom is equally as cozy. The toilet is between 2 walls and it is kind of tight, but she can fit. Once back downstairs and outside, Kia takes her seat back in the chair and she moves it to shade because the shade has shifted.

Kia loves being on vacation on the island however; the heat is starting to get to her. She has been sitting out here for about an hour and has already put her hair up in a ponytail. Her dress is raised as far as she can raise it and still be decent in front of her man and future brother-in-law. She is trying not to complain, but she is definitely struggling with the heat. Maybe she should've opted for the beach instead. At least she could've gotten in the water.

"Babe do you want some water?" Levy asks.

"Yes, do you have some?"

"Not here but Caleb can take you to the store."

"Oh he doesn't have to make a special trip for me. That's okay. I'm good."

"It's just right down the street. It's really no problem," he insists.

Kia agrees because she really could use some water or something to relieve some of the heat. She has started to sweat, and she has just been sitting in the chair. It almost feels like the sun is singeing her skin. She and Caleb get in the car and head to the store. Kia does not know how far it is but she was shocked when they drove for about 45 seconds. The store is in the front of a house that is literally down the street. It is only a few houses down from the entrance to Pearl Gardens. Kia would have never known this was a little neighborhood store. She gets a couple of bottles of water and some cookies to snack on, and then they head back.

Kia retakes her seat in the shade and she sees Caleb and Levy talking. Levy comes over and tells her they are leaving in a few minutes to go over to his mother's house so she can meet his family. Kia is glad to be meeting her future in-laws. She has something for little baby Jewel and she can't wait to give it to her. So far Caleb was cool, and she hopes the rest of the family is cool as well.

Levy's mother lives in a neighborhood a little further in-land but you can still see the coastline if you are on a hill. When they arrive at the house, Levy enters first and then Kia. He introduces her to his mother Naomi, his sister Alesha, and his sister Anya.

"It is very nice to meet you," Kia tells each of them as she greets them. "This must be Little Baby," she says as she is waving at his niece.

"Yes, this is Jewel," Alesha says.

"She is too cute," Kia says.

Suddenly Single

Kia takes a seat on the couch and tries not to wrinkle her face at the heat. It feels like it is hotter in the house than it is outside. Obviously they do not have an air conditioner, but they do have a fan that is on and circulating.

"So Kia it is so nice to meet you. Levy talks about you all the time," Naomi says.

"Does he? Well, I hope it is all good."

"It is, of course. This is the first time he has ever brought someone here to meet us so I am just so excited."

"Awww, I'm excited too."

"So what part of the US are you from?" Anya asks. She is the youngest of the sisters at 16 years old.

"I live in Houston, Texas."

"Which do you like better: cars, buses, or trains like a subway?"

"Well, I have a car, and I have only ridden the bus in Houston one time and we don't have subways. We do have a train though but it only goes to certain parts of the city. So I would definitely say car is my preference."

"What do you think about Obama being President?" Anya continues.

"I think it is great. I wish the Republicans would not challenge him on everything he does. I mean they just ride him for no reason. If he says go up, they say go down. If he says the sky is blue, they say it's red just to challenge him, you know? They just mess with him on everything. But he is a true example of what is for you is for you and nothing can get in the way. That was shown especially with his re-election."

"What is your stance on corporal punishment?"

Kia chuckles to herself because this Anya is letting her have it with these questions. She was not ready for this. "I think it is okay to spank children as long as you do not spank for every little thing, and it is not excessive and as long as it does not leave any marks or bruises."

"That's what I think to. We got spankings growing up," Anya says while staring at Kia. "Look at your dress. It is so pretty. Ooh, and I like your fingernail polish."

"Aww, thank you," Kia responds trying to keep up.

"So when did you know you loved my brother?"

"Anya, that's enough questions, leave Kia alone," Levy orders.

"What? I'm just trying to get to know her. We girls like this kind of stuff."

"It's ok Levy. I don't mind," Kia reassures.

"See," Anya tells her brother. "How did y'all meet?"

Kia tells them the story of how they met in the Shell station and how she feels like they were destined to meet because nothing went according to plan that day and if it would have went according to plan then their paths would not have crossed. Almost in unison they all say "Awwww". Kia couldn't help but smile.

"Well look I have something here for Jewel," Kia says as she pulls 5 outfits out of her bag. She had them in there just in case she would meet them today. Truthfully, she was just going to carry them until she met them because she did not know when that was going to be.

"Oh my gosh! These are so cute!" Alesha exclaims, "thank you so much for these. You didn't have to do that for my daughter. I mean you have never even met her. I really appreciate it."

"Oh, you are welcome," Kia says. It really was no problem. "I enjoy shopping for baby clothes."

"Oh, thank you God," Naomi says. "We asked you for shoes for the baby and you provided some."

One of the outfits Kia picked out had shoes that came with it. Kia's favorite was the pink and brown Osh Kosh romper.

"I just want to tell you thank you for helping my niece that was really sweet of you. You have never even met her and you did this for her," Anya tells Kia.

"Oh, you are very welcome. It really is no problem," Kia tells her.

Jewel walks over to Kia and starts playing with her and smiling at her. All of the women are in surprise because they say she is normally not too friendly with strangers. Kia loves children and has a way with them. She is like a child magnet.

Over the next hour and a half, Kia laughs and talks with Levy's family. Naomi tells of how she named Levy and then of how Levy came to be his nickname. She does not seem as bad as Levy makes her out to be, but anybody can put on for company. Kia learns that she is only 10 years younger than Naomi which makes her feel some kind of way but she knows that Naomi started having children young and Levy was her first child.

The family starts telling Levy about their plans for Christmas, and he tells them that he hopes to be in the U.S. by then. Kia is excited to hear this but knows it probably won't be likely because the paperwork can take up to six months to be processed. She hopes this will be a reality sooner rather than later.

They look at old baby pictures, and Kia even shares some of her pictures that are on Facebook. Come to find out Anya is really into Sci-Fi and ended up on the cover of an online magazine with her friends. Kia sees something in Anya. She will be the one to make it off the island if that is what she chooses.

"Babe, are you ready to go to the beach?" Levy asks Kia.

"Yes, I am but I need to put on my swimsuit," Kia tells him. While she has enjoyed her time with his family, she is about to fall over from being in the heat. She is not used to not having AC. That is something that obviously she has taken for granted living in America. In Barbados in a community of 50 homes, you may find one that has air conditioning. Kia was dumbfounded when she learned that.

"You can change in my room," Anya says and she shows her to the back of the house where the heat seemed to get worse.

"Thank you. I will be out in a minute."

Kia closes the door and puts on her swimsuit under her sundress and returns to join the others in the living room. She can't help but wonder how anybody can sleep in there with all of the heat.

"It doesn't even look like you have on a swimsuit," Anya says to Kia.

"I assure you I have it on," Kia laughs.

"Wow, I'm not trying to look at you, but I see why my brother said 'wow' when he looked at you," Alesha says trying not to stare at Kia's backside in that dress.

Kia laughs. "Thank you. Yes, it is big, and yes, it is real."

Kia gives hugs to each of the ladies, including baby Jewel, before leaving out. They tell her that it was a pleasure to meet her and that they hope she will come over again before leaving the island. Kia tells them that she is really glad to have met them and that she indeed will try to make it back over to their home before she leaves. This of course will depend on Levy.

Kia and Levy get in the car with Caleb and his girlfriend, and they head off to Miami Beach.

"Babe, let's put our things over here. This is a good spot, but we will have to still keep an eye on them," Levy instructs.

"Ok. Just make sure you keep a watchful eye on them," Kia tells him.

"That's your job. I gave it to you," Levy laughs as they walk down the beach to the water.

Kia can't help but think X-rated thoughts that involve that rock where they put their things, the beach and the water. She has always wanted to do bad things on the beach with her boo. This may not be the place though because there are children out here.

"Oooh, this feels so good," Kia exhales.

"Yes, it does feel good," Levy agrees.

"Babe, I know you said you can't really swim, but we need to go out a little further. I mean you at least need to be able to pick me up," Kia laughs.

"I can swim enough but we can't go too far past waist deep."

"Ok, that sounds cool."

Kia is looking at the sky and the clouds are rolling in. She hopes the rain holds off because she is enjoying frolicking in the water with her man. This is surreal for her because she has always wanted to go to the beach with her love and "play" in the water with him.

Kia and Levy splash around in the water stealing kisses in between laughing and splashing each other. At one point, they are locked in a passionate embrace and Kia can feel something brushing up against her inner thigh.

"We better stop before the kids think we are doing it," Levy tells her.

"Let them think what they want," Kia says almost breathless. Her heart has started to beat fast because she is getting turned on. "Levy, I love you. This is what I have always wanted to do."

"What is that?"

"Go to the beach with my man, play in the water with him, make out in the water with him, and just have a good time…just me and him."

"Well, I am glad I could make that happen for you, anything to make you happy."

"You make me happy," Kia tells him as she steals one more kiss from him before swimming off from him. "Betcha can't catch me."

"Ha ha…You got jokes. Umm Babe, when was the last time you looked at our things?"

"A little while ago. Why?"

"Because a known criminal just came on the beach and he walked by our stuff. I'm going to go check."

"Ok. I will come with you."

As they were leaving out of the water, the sky opened up. They had to run to get their clothes before they got wet or they would be forced to walk around in their wet swimsuits. Luckily, all of their things were still intact. Kia is saddened by the fact that her time at the beach with her boo has been cut short by a passing shower. Levy does not want to get back in the water because he has to do some more work at Pearl Gardens before dark and it gets dark at 6:30 every evening.

"Babe we can take a shower here and get the salt and sand off"" he tells her.

"Ok."

"When you finish go in there to the dressing room and change your clothes. I will hold the bags."

"But can't you come with me in there?"

"No. I will be okay. Just go in there."

"But I want you to come in there with me."

"Kia, the sign says it's for ladies only."

"Oh," Kia blushes because she didn't see the sign. She gets her towel and dress and goes into the dressing room and locates the cleanest stall so she can change her clothes. She hates being wet and not in a place where she can air dry.

When she came out Levy is waiting for her at the door looking sexy as all get out because he is still a little wet and the water is rolling off his bare chest bead by bead. Kia almost needs to go back in and dry off some more.

"Babe, did you hear that man ask me if you were my boyfriend on the way in?"

"No, I didn't hear him. What did you say?"

"I told him you were my husband."

"Ahh, I like that. Yes, I can't wait to be your husband."

Levy and Kia walk off down the road towards Pearl Gardens and Levy stops at a street vendor selling coconuts.

"Would you like a coconut or some coconut water?" he asks Kia.

"No. I don't eat coconut, but thank you.

Levy tells the guy he will take a coconut with jelly. Kia can't fathom the idea because in her mind she is thinking grape jelly, like what she puts on her toast, but apparently that is not the case. The "jelly" is a part of the coconut. Levy eats it all right there in a matter of a couple of minutes. Once he is done they start off back down the road again.

"Umm babe, how far is Pearl Gardens?"

"It is about half a mile," Levy answers. "Okay maybe one mile. Is that okay?"

"It doesn't matter as long as I am with you and you carry this bag." Kia laughs but she is serious. She is not prepared to walk. She has on flip flops.

"Babe, did you see that man with the coconuts tell the other man to look at your butt?"

"No, I did not. What did you do when you saw them?"

"I grabbed your butt."

"Oh, is that why you grabbed it? I thought you just liked what you saw and wanted to touch it," she laughs.

"Well that too, but I want them to know this is MINE."

"Yes, I am babe. Yes, I am."

Suddenly Single

The two walk along the winding road dodging cars that come flying around each curve. They even stop and take a few picturesque photos. Levy picks a couple of flowers and puts them in Kia's hair and they take a few photos together.

They are walking for what seems like forever before they get to the street to turn where Pearl Gardens is located. When they do make that turn Levy stops on the side of the road and pulls out his log to relieve himself on a tree.

"Levy! You are just going to pull it out right here?!?!" Kia exclaims but she is a little excited to see her love piece.

"What's wrong with that?"

"It's in public and people can see."

"Kia, nobody is around us."

"I guess. It's just not fair. Men can just whip it out anywhere and go. Women, well me anyway, need a toilet and toilet paper and such."

"You know you can squat if you need to go."

"I will not. I am too big to squat. Fuck that. I need a toilet," Kia laughs.

Levy shakes off, and the two take off down the road. Before they know it, they are walking up into Pearl Gardens. It is almost dark but there is still enough light for Levy to do what he needs to do. Kia takes her seat in the chair on the porch after Levy pulls it out for her. She can't help but watch him work. She is totally in love with this man. He has made her very happy. She smiles, and he catches her smiling.

"Why are you smiling? What's going on?" he asks her.

"I was just looking at you. Levy you make me happy. There is no place on earth I would rather be at this moment than here with you. I am glad I came to see you. Now once you officially propose to me, it will be perfect."

"Kia, I love you too, and I am glad you came to see me. You make me a very happy man," he tells her as he walks over and gives her a kiss.

Kia grabs at his love log because it has gotten a little darker, but it didn't matter because he has the key to the house she is sitting in front of. Nobody is here anyway and she wants to feel her man.

"Not now. I have to finish my work so we can go. I will cook, for you tonight so we need to stop by the store."

"Okay, but 5 minutes won't hurt," Kia insists.

"No," Levy says and kisses her on the nose and walks off to finish cleaning around the pool.

Kia is a little bothered, but it is okay because they have all night. Levy continues to work around the pool and Kia watches him wondering will it be like this when they get married. She can't help but think about him working around their house while she watches the baby and then them doing it once the baby is sleep. The thought excites her, and she can't help but smile again.

Once Levy is finished for the day, Kia makes one more failed attempt to get her future husband to give her some loving before they go. She is a tad bit frustrated because he always says he has a high sex drive, but so far, they have only been intimate the night before. Besides she was expecting 10 days of back breaking, mind blowing, marathon love making like she has never done before, but it has not been quite what she has expected on that point so far.

They are going to take a van back to the room where they are staying so they have to walk up to the main road. As they are walking, Levy is carrying the bags, and they are talking about what he is going to cook them for dinner. He says he is going to cook some fish and potatoes so they will need to stop at the store in Oistins. Kia is loving this because it feels complete to her.

Almost as soon as they get to the main road, a van passes, and they get on. They did not have to wait at all. Once seated in the van, Levy puts his arm around Kia, and she lays her head on his shoulder. They don't say too much during the ride, but to Kia, not too much needs to be said. She is in the arms of her man. That is all that matters to her.

They get off the van in Oistins close to where Caleb picked them up earlier this afternoon. They stop by one of the stands that are still open. Levy talks to the guy and purchases the fish while Kia stands closer to the street because the seafood smell is overpowering. Once he is finished, they walk up the street towards the store.

"What kind of fish did you get?" Kia asks.

"Tuna Steak, do you like that?" he asks her.

"No. I have never had it though."

"Aye Aye Aye, this girl here does not eat anything but chicken," Levy mumbles to himself.

"What did you say?" Kia says sarcastically.

"I said, you only eat chicken. Woman, why you only eat chicken?"

"I eat more than chicken. I eat beef and fish, just not tuna. But I will try it since you have already bought it. And just so you know, the food I eat has to moo, cluck, swim or oink. And if it swims, it has to swim like this," Kia says as she is imitating the motion of a fish, "not like this," and she imitates the motion of a squid or octopus propelling through the water.

Levy looks at her and laughs. "I love you."

"I love you too!"

Once in the store, Kia is on the lookout for any heifers that might want her boo because they are in the same store as earlier today.

Once Kia and Levy arrive back at the room, Levy begins to prepare the meal but is not able to cook it because there is not any gas left for the stove. He calls the guy that got them checked in, and he states he will bring some right over. Kia is annoyed at the situation, and Agatha is starting to get stirred up. She needs to keep her calm and out of sight. While they are waiting for the guy, Levy sets the table for the two of them, complete with a pitcher of water and everything.

"Aww, look at you babe trying to spoil me. I feel special," Kia tells him.

"You are special, and I look forward to spoiling you every day when we are married."

"I do to!!" Kia says as she leans in and gives him a kiss. As she is kissing him, her hands begin to wander along his back and front and down one side and up the other. She starts kissing his neck, and she is getting more and more turned on thinking they can get in a quickie before the man comes with the propane, but Levy stops her.

"Not right now, just wait," he tells her as he stops her and returns to the kitchen. *What the fuck you mean just wait?!?!* almost came out of her mouth but it didn't. She is glad it didn't because that would have been more Agatha talking than her. Kia retreats to the bed and begins to flip channels on the TV.

The guy finally arrives after what feels like an eternity. By now, it is almost 9:30PM. He and Levy get things together, and he is quickly on his way. Kia loves having a man around. She does not have to worry about the little things like this. This is how it is supposed to be.

Levy finishes preparing the meal and he tells her to go sit at the table where he proceeds to pour her drink and then he brings her a plate of pan grilled tuna steak, skillet sweet potato fries with onions and green peppers and green beans.

"Here you are my love. This is the meal I was supposed to fix for you the last time you were here," he tells her.

"Why thank you. It looks delicious and smells wonderful."

Levy takes his seat at the table, and he grabs her hands and proceeds to bless the food before they eat. Kia is beaming because she loves this man with all her heart. She feels like she is the luckiest woman in the world.

"Babe, this is good," she announces as she practically inhales the first few bites. She is not sure if it is really good or if she is just hungry. She figures it is a little of both.

"Thank you. I try sometimes," he laughs.

"Well you should try all the time, because this is good. I mean it. I don't try new food often and I actually like this so that speaks volumes. Kudos to you, babe."

"Thank you. That means a lot to me. This is something that swims so you should be okay," he laughs.

"Ha, ha...you got jokes," Kia quips.

"It's only because I love you," he tells her.

The two finish their meal, and Levy clears the table while Kia prepares the shower for them. Once out of the shower, Kia puts on one of the many pairs of sexy panties she has brought with her and climbs into bed where Levy is there watching TV. She snuggles up to him and lays her head on his chest. She begins to kiss his neck and chest and stomach while her hands go wandering along his midline.

"Babe, what's wrong?" Kia asks sensing something is wrong because he is still flaccid.

"Nothing is wrong. I'm just tired."

""I'm tired too, but I'm only going to be here a few more days and I want to make the most of our time together."

"Kia, I can tell you have never lived with a man."

"How can you tell that?" Kia says almost instantly getting defensive.

"I just can."

"Well what does that mean? Is that good or bad because you are making it sound bad?"

"Listen, I don't want to start an argument. I was just saying," he tells her.

"Nobody is arguing. I'm just trying to get an understanding," Kia tells him. Her whole tone has changed now. She is trying to figure out what is going on. She dismisses his rejections to him being tired. Her gut is starting to tingle, and she doesn't like it.

Chapter 14

The next morning, Levy gets out of bed at what feels like the crack of dawn. Kia wakes up when he gets back in the bed from bathroom. She still has her mask on, but she takes it off so she can cuddle up to her man without the mask and tube being in the way.

"Good morning," he tells her as he is lying there.

"Good morning babe. How are you this morning?"

"I'm good. How are you?"

"I'm doing okay. How did you sleep?" she asks him genuinely concerned because after their little discussion she put on her mask and went to sleep.

"I slept okay. How did you sleep?"

"I slept okay. I would've slept better if you would've put me to sleep," she smirks as she kisses his chest.

He chuckles. "I can tell you have never lived with a man."

"Aww here we go with this. Levy what does that mean? How can you tell?"

"Listen, obviously you were horny last night, but you just went to sleep."

"You kept rejecting me. What was I supposed to do?? Take it?" Kia says a tad bit annoyed because she does not want to be having this conversation right now. She would rather be feeling him inside her. "I'm only going to try for so long, and if you keep telling me no, then what else am I supposed to do?"

"I watched you sleep for a little while and I could not believe that you went to sleep. When I am horny, I can't sleep."

"Well, Levy, that's you. I stay horny so I have learned to deal with it."

"Hmmmm. Ok. Anyhow, I'm not trying to start an argument. I need to get up and go run an errand right quick," he says as he gets up and proceeds to put on his clothes. "I should be back about 9:00. I will call you or text you if I can't make it back. What are you going to do today?"

When he said that, Kia knew he wasn't coming back. "I don't know. Go down to the beach I guess if I can't spend it with you."

"Ok. Well take your phone because I will call you." He walks over and gives her a kiss on the lips before leaving out the door.

Kia is a little perplexed by the conversation, but she brushes it off and turns on the TV. She wants to go to the beach now, but honestly, it's too early. It is only 7:00 in the morning. She lays there and watches *Good Morning America*. She doesn't normally watch it when she is home, but there is nothing else on. Somewhere in the midst of the weather and leading stories of the day, Kia dozed off only to be awakened by her phone ringing. It was Levy.

"Hello?" she answers in her sleepy voice.

"Hey babe listen, I'm not going to make it back to spend the day with you. I have some work I need to finish up. I will see you tonight though."

"Well...ok", Kia sighs. "I can come with you. I mean, I came here to see you and spend time with you."

"It's not really some place where you would like it. You would be bored, and I don't want you to be bored watching me work. Listen, you will see me tonight. I promise."

"Well what time are you coming Levy? I need to know so I can make sure I am here."

"I should be there around 7:00. I will call you and let you know for sure. Ok? I love you."

"I love you too. Bye."

"Bye."

Kia is disappointed because she wants to spend the day with Levy, but she will have to take in the beach by herself. She looks over at the clock, and it is 9:10. She decides to get on up and head down to the beach. She is hungry, but she doesn't recall seeing anywhere where she can get breakfast. She really would love some Happy Days for breakfast but she would have to catch a bus or van down there and she did not want to do that by herself. She will have to be content with whatever she could get at the store at the bottom of the hill.

She changes into her new swimsuit she bought just for this trip and she heads for the water. She stops at the store where she picks up some snacks and a big bottle of water. This is not what she had in mind, but it will have to do. As she is crossing the street to the beach, Kia is feeling some kind of way because she is by herself in this country. She was expecting to spend every day with Levy even if it meant going with him to work. She knew that she probably would have to spend some time by herself, she just did not expect it would be so soon. She hopes it will be worth it in the end because he is supposed to officially propose to her while she is here.

Kia pays for an umbrella and lounge chair on the beach, and the chair guy puts her in a prime spot on the beach, right next to the flags in front of the lifeguard stand. It seems she is the only one out here at the moment. There are other umbrellas set up, but nobody is under them just yet. Kia takes off her cover-up and gets her phone out of her bag so she can listen to music and hopefully Levy will call her and come join her.

After she gets situated and puts on her sunscreen and headphones, she scrolls through her list of songs and decides on *Wey U* by Chante Moore. It is nice and mellow and is perfect for her mood and the environment she is in. She can't help but think about her co-workers for a split second. She wonders what they are doing, probably somewhere complaining about the boss. Kia gets tickled because she is enjoying a gorgeous view of the ocean, watching the waves crash into the beach while they are at work in front of a computer.

Wey U stops playing, and Kia looks at her phone to see what happened and she sees that she received a text message. Anxious and hoping it is from Levy, she hurries and opens it. She is disappointed to see that it is a notification from her cell phone carrier letting her know her data charges have exceeded $50. She decides to give them a call so she can properly turn off the data and stop all roaming charges. She absolutely does not want to incur another high phone bill. She apologizes to the lady who is helping her because the waves are loud, and she can barely hear. They lady tells her no problem and to enjoy her vacation. Kia gets the settings fixed on the phone, hangs up with the lady, and starts *Wey U* over again.

As time passes, more and more people arrive at the beach. You can tell these are people that are on vacation. Kia can hear them talking, and some of their accents are un-mistakenly British and the others are not discernable. There are a lot of couples here on the beach and Kia can't help but be a little sad because she is out here without her man. She decides to send him a quick text and let him know where she is on the beach in case he can make it out here.

```
Hey babe I am at the beach across the street from where
I am staying.  I am right by the flags in front of the
lifeguard stand if you can make it out here.  I love
you.
```

Suddenly Single

She puts up her phone and decides it is time to get in the water. She has been out here people watching long enough. That first step in the water is a little chilly but not enough to stop her from trekking farther out. With each step the water is warmer and warmer and she couldn't help but smile. This is it. This is what she needed. It is something about being in the water that calms her soul.

She lounges around in the water enjoying the warmth of it and how the waves crash into her. She is loving this. She only wishes that her man was here to enjoy this with her. She enjoyed their time at the beach together yesterday and she wants to experience that joy again.

Kia stays in the water another 30 minutes or so before deciding to take a break. She can see that she has gotten a shade or two darker from being out in the sun, and that's okay because she wants to work on her tan while she is here. As she gets settled back in her lounge chair, a guy approaches her and asks her if she is okay and does she need anything. He explains that he sells Rum Punch, Pina Colada's, whatever she wants to drink, out of the little stand by the parking lot. Kia did notice the 4 stands over there and wondered what they were. She tells him that she will get something in a little while. Right now, she just wants to relax and dry off.

A few minutes later another guy comes and asks her does she want anything. This one told her that they also have food. She has him run down the menu to her and she decides to order a flying fish sandwich and some fries. Fifteen minutes later he brings her a tray with her food. He also offers her something to drink, but she declines because she has water in her bag, plus she promised the other guy that she would get something from him.

She looks at the fish on her sandwich before diving in. She has never heard of flying fish and is not sure of what it would taste like but at this point it did not matter because she is hungry. She takes the first bite and is pleased with the taste and the flavor. The water calms her soul, and the food calms her stomach. As she is eating, she watches the couples walk along the beach hand in hand, and some very publically displaying affection. This makes her sad because her honey is here on the island but not here with her. So close, yet so far. She almost gets a little emotional, but she shakes it off because she wants to enjoy being here on this beautiful island and not be overcome with sad emotion.

Kia orders a rum punch from the first guy when she sees him again. She needs to wash down that flying fish and fries. She is very pleasantly surprised that her meal was delicious. She did not quite know what to expect for beach food. When her drink arrives, she pays the guy and takes a sip. It is stronger than what she expected and she almost spit it out but instead she swallows it and endures the burning sensation as it is going down. She instantly knew that she has to sip slowly otherwise she will be out there on the beach, tore up, by herself, especially since the sun is beaming.

She pulls out her music and lands on *There It Go* by Juelz Santana. This is perfect because it is upbeat and she needs something to keep her awake because between a full stomach, that rum punch, and the afternoon slump, staying awake doesn't look promising. Kia turns the volume up on her headphones and slips into the zone.

When she comes around she looks at her phone for the time and it is almost 2:00. She decides to go for another quick dip before heading back to the apartment but before she does that she sends Levy another text:

```
Hey babe.  I am getting ready to leave the beach in a
few minutes.  Do you want me to order you something and
bring it with me? I wish you were here.  I love you.
```

Kia goes for her dip while she is waiting for a response from Levy. She stays in the water just long enough to soothe her soul but not long enough to get a shade darker. When she returns to her umbrella, she checks her phone for a text from Levy, but there is nothing. She decides to order him something anyway because she figures he may be hungry when he gets in from work. She flags down the guy and orders him the same thing she ate earlier. While she is waiting for the food she packs her up things and dries herself off.

Suddenly Single

When she makes it back to the apartment, she puts the food in the refrigerator while she is letting the water warm up in the shower. Once she is finished washing the sand off of her body, she checks her phone for a response from Levy but still nothing. A little put off, Kia proceeds to flip channels and she settles for whatever is playing on the Discovery Fit and Health Channel. She dismisses Levy's non-response as him being busy, and she thinks no more about it.

Before she knows it, she is awakened by the sound of her phone ringing. "Hello?" she answers.

"Hey babe. Listen I will be there around 7:00 ok?" Levy tells her.

"Ok well I bought some food for you from the beach in case you are hungry, but I was thinking we could go get something to eat."

"Ok, we will talk about it when I get there."

"Ok, I will see you then. I love you," she tells him.

"I love you too."

They hang up and Kia is relieved. She looks at the time and it is 6:30. "Where did the time go?" she thinks to herself as she had not realized she dozed off. She freshens up and puts on something she thinks is sexy and she waits for him to arrive. Just like clockwork at about 7:00, there is a knock on the door. Kia opens the door without even asking "who is it?"

"Kia, you didn't even ask 'who is it?' It could've been anybody," Levy almost snaps as he walks in.

"Well, I knew it was you. Who else would it be? But anyway, I am and fine, and you?" Deep down, she knew he was right. She was just so excited to see him she just flung the door open.

"My head hurts," he tells her as he strips down to his underwear and gets in the bed.

"Well babe, maybe you need to drink some water. Do you want some medicine?"

"No, I just need to lay here for a few minutes."

"Did you eat today? I don't know if you got my text but I bought you some food. It's in the fridge."

"I did get your text and thank you, but I just need to lay here. Can you wake me up in an hour?"

"Of course I can babe," Kia tells him as she climbs in bed next to him and kisses him on his lips that always seem to be begging for her to kiss them, or maybe that was her subconscious mind always wanting to kiss him.

She resumes flipping channels and settles once again on Discovery Fit and Health channel.

•———————————————————•

"Babe?" Kia says as she is gently kissing his lips while he is sleeping. "Wake up."

"What time is it?" he asks without opening his eyes.

"9:30."

"Why did you let me sleep so long?"

"You were sleeping so good, that I did not want to disturb you. Are you hungry?"

"My head still hurts. I know you are probably hungry so you can go on and get something to eat."

"But Levy I wanted us to go somewhere," Kia says disappointed.

"I know babe. I'm sorry. My head just really hurts."

"Well take some medicine then," Kia says as she is choking back tears. "I have some ibuprofen if you want some."

"Kia, why are you crying? You are scaring me. The last girl that cried like this was crazy."

"Well I can assure you that I am not that girl, and I am not crazy!" Kia is overwhelmed with the emotion of missing him the entire day, then he is not feeling well, and now she is disappointed because she wanted to have dinner with him, and it looks like that is not going to happen. "I just want you to be okay. I know that your head has been hurting for the last week or so." Kia always tends to think the worst and she is trying not to think brain tumor, but she can't help it.

"I am fine. Whenever I have my hair cut this low my head always hurts. I guess from the heat. I probably could stand to drink some water too."

"Ok, well as long as you are okay. I just love you and I want you to be okay. I guess I will go down here and get me something to eat right quick."

"Ok. I will see you when you get back."

"Ok."

Kia grabs her bag and the keys and heads off down the hill to see what she can get to eat. She does not want Chefette because that is like fast food, and she does not want any fried chicken. She walks through the shopping strip by the store because it says food court on the sign. She decides to check it out and see what they have. Kia spots an internet cafe' and she doubles back to read the sign, and it says they serve breakfast. She gets excited because she has wanted some breakfast food. She walks further along and decides on the New York Pizzeria. She orders a one slice combo and takes a seat outside to wait for her order.

Next door to the pizzeria is an ice cream shop, and it stays busy. People have been going in and out of there non-stop since she has been sitting there. She wonders if this is where Levy wanted to bring her when they first met. The thought quickly vanishes as she hears her order number being called.

She takes her food and decides to go back to the apartment to eat. The mosquitoes are hungry tonight and her ankles seem to be their buffet, besides her boo is in there. Hopefully he will be awake when she gets back.

She makes it back in no time. This apartment really is in a convenient location. When she opened the door, Levy was still sleep, in the same spot. Kia decides to sit at the table and eat her food because she does not want to disturb him.

She takes out her pizza and is quite surprised at how good it tastes. Jordyn said the pizza in Barbados tastes different because of the cheese, but she did not notice anything different about the taste.

When she is finished eating, she sits there and watches TV for a while. Levy is still sleeping, and she does not want to disturb his sleep. Eventually, she puts the trash in the trash can, turns off the lights, takes off her clothes and gets into bed. She snuggles up close to Levy and looks at him for a second before stealing a kiss.

"I'm sorry babe for stealing kisses," she says in a susurrant manner trying to wake him but not startle him.

"Why do you say you are stealing kisses? I told you, you could have them," he tells her equally as susurrant.

"I know. I just like saying that," she says as she snuggles closer to him, so close that he turns over on his back and finally seems to wake up.

"Did you enjoy your food?" he asks.

"Yes. It was good."

"Can I ask you something?"

"Of course you can, babe. What is it?" she asks a little nervous, could this be it? Could this be the moment she has waited for?

"How many times have you had sex since we met? I am man enough to say if I had sex."

Kia had to catch herself from saying *What the fuck?* Instead she asks him, "Have you?" trying to turn the attention off her.

"Yes," he says almost too nonchalantly. "Have you?"

Kia assumed he was over here fucking somebody, but she never imagined that he would so readily admit to it.

"Once, right after I got back." It just rolled off her tongue without much thought. Kia knew this is not the truth, but it is out and she had to stick with it. "Why do you ask that?" she asked totally perplexed.

"Because listen, for most women that have not had sex in a while, it is hard for them to take dick, but you did not seem to have any problems."

"Oh it hurt alright especially when you would go hard from behind, but I didn't tap out. I'm not a punk. I hung in there. Where is this coming from Levy?" she asked out loud but she is thinking to herself, *Is he trying to say my stuff is not as tight as he thinks it should be?*

"It's just hard for me to believe that you only had sex one time."

"So you are calling me a liar?"

"No I'm not calling you a liar. It's just hard for me to believe. That is all. Like I told you earlier when I am horny, I can't sleep, and you just went to sleep."

"Levy, let me tell you something, first, I have a 10-inch toy at home that I use, so no I'm not going to be as tight as perhaps you think I should be besides you don't have a point of reference anyway because we have never had sex prior to Monday; and second, I told you that I stay horny and have learned to suppress it so it is nothing for me to go to sleep."

"I see. I don't know. Something in my spirit is troubling me about this."

"What is it Levy? What is troubling you?"

"Have you ever been with a woman or had anal sex?"

"Levy!!" Kia exclaims. "Hell naw. I ain't never been with a woman. I LIKE DICK! And NO I have not ever had anal sex. I told you I was saving that for my husband, and by the size of you, we won't be doing it. Levy, where is this coming from?"

"The way you use your tongue is truly like no other women and is the best I have ever had, and it makes me think you eat pussy, and your ass is so big, I know you have to had anal sex before."

"Levy really?!? This is crazy!! What is really going on?"

"I just feel troubled in my spirit. I need to think about this."

"Think about what Levy, us?"

"Yes."

"Why? What is there to think about? Levy, where is this coming from?" Kia asks again feeling she has not yet gotten a response.

"I can tell you have never lived with a man."

"Levy, you keep saying that. What does that mean? How can you tell? Listen. That is a good thing. You know that right?"

"I know that is good, but it can also be bad."

"How so?" Kia asks exasperated because her perfect relationship seems to be dissolving right before her eyes and there is seemingly nothing she can do to fix it.

"Listen, I just need to think about this," he says as he gets up out of the bed and starts to put on his clothes.

"Where are you going?" Kia asks surprised that he is getting dressed.

"I just need to clear my mind."

"Levy don't go. Everything that you have said is fixable. If you need to clear your mind, I can understand that, but don't leave. Sleep on the futon or this is a king bed, just roll over and think about what you have to think about but whatever you do, don't walk out that door. Is this how it is going to be when we get married?"

"I need some time," he says as he walks towards the door.

"Levy, I am begging you, don't leave. Let's talk about this."

He puts his hands on her shoulders and looks her in the eyes. "I need to clear my mind."

"Levy, where are you going?"

"Home."

Did he just say home? "Levy, I am asking you again, please do not go."

"I have to clear my mind."

"Are you breaking up with me?"

"I'm not saying that. I just need some time to think."

Kia is relieved to hear that, but she is now troubled herself and is slowly succumbing to the reality that he is not going to stay. She just hopes that he is not walking out on her forever.

"How are you going to get there? Walk?" Kia asks out of concern for her man. She does not know what time the busses or vans stop running or even how far he has to go, but she does know it is late. Somewhere between the pizza and this discussion, the time has flown by, and it is now 1:00 in the morning.

"Yes, I am going to walk. It will help me clear my mind."

"Ok," Kia says feeling defeated. "Be careful. Please call me and let me know you made it. I love you."

"I will. I love you too. Lock the door," he says as he kisses her on the forehead before leaving out of the door.

Kia locks the door behind him and is a sea of emotion. *What the hell just happened?* she thinks to herself. Never in a million years did she see this coming. She retreats to the bed, physically, emotionally, and mentally drained...she just can't take it. She puts on her mask and attempts to go to sleep but to no avail. She lets about 45 minutes pass before she calls Levy, no answer, so she decides to text him:

```
Hey did you make it home safely?  Let me know please.
I love you.
```

At 3:30 AM, Kia is awakened by her familiar text notification. *Excuse me boss, you have a text message:*

    I made it home.

Chapter 15

Kia awoke the next morning still exhausted. She is emotionally drained, still pondering the events of the night before. She looks at the time and sees that it is 7:00AM. She reaches for her phone to call Levy but hesitates just a little before dialing the number. He doesn't answer. To tell the truth Kia is not really surprised that he didn't answer. She figures he is still trying to clear his mind or whatever he is doing. She decides not to text him and figures she will wait and see if he calls her back.

She grabs the remote and starts to flip channels on the TV. She is looking for anything to take her mind off of the uneasiness she is feeling in her chest. She settles on *Good Morning America*. That is all she can find that is even anywhere close to something she would watch. As she lay there looking at the TV, it seems to be watching her more than she is watching it. Her mind is racing with what ifs sparked by what happened just a few hours ago. She plays it over and over again in her mind wondering if she should have said something different or done something different. *Should I have been honest with him about having sex while we were apart?* she thinks to herself. *Should I go back and tell him the truth? No because if I tell him the truth then he will use that against me. Besides he was having uneasiness before I told him I only had sex once.* Kia is good at rationalizing things in her mind whether or not she is right or wrong it makes sense to her.

She decides to take a shower and decide what she is going to do with herself for the rest of the day. She stays in the shower longer than normal seemingly trying to wash away that feeling she is having, but it is the kind you can't wash away with soap. She knows the only thing that will wash this away is talking with Levy. When she gets out of the shower, she decides to send him a text regardless of the fact that he hadn't called her. She wants to talk to him and is of the mindset that if you want to talk to somebody, call them or text them.

Suddenly Single

```
Hey babe. How are you this morning? Am I going to see
you today?
```

Kia anxiously waits for a response and before she knows it her phone is ringing. It is him.

"Hey. How are you?" he asks when she answers the phone.

"I'm okay Levy, how are you?"

"I'm okay. So you want to know if you will see me today?"

"Yes, will I see you today?"

"Yes, you will see me. I have some work to do but I will come this evening."

"Ok. Do you have an idea of what time so that I can make sure I am here?" Kia knew she would be there no matter what time.

"I will come around 7:00," he tells her.

"Ok. I will see you then."

"Ok. Enjoy yourself today," he tells her before they end the phone call.

Kia puts on something to lounge around in. She really does not feel like going to the beach today, but she made herself a promise that she was touching the water everyday while she is here. She decides to lie around a while and watch TV before heading to breakfast and the beach.

After about 2 hours, Kia couldn't take it anymore. Her mind is racing and all she can think about is Levy. She needs to get out. She puts on her swimsuit and cover up and heads to find some nourishment for her body. What she really needs is nourishment for her soul because she is still troubled.

This is not how this is supposed to be, she tells herself as she strolls down the hill by herself. Before she knows it, she is at the bottom, and she decides to try Picasso's, the internet café, she saw the night before. She has been craving some breakfast food, and this was the only spot within walking distance that she knows about.

After she places her order, she pulls out *50 Shades Freed,* the third book in the 50 Shades of Grey trilogy, and catches up to the characters, Anastasia and Christian. They keep her going although she has not spent much time with them on this trip. Before she knows it, her plate with pancakes, bacon, and a side of fries has arrived, and she can hardly put her book down before digging in. She is pleased because this is what she has been craving….besides Levy. She takes a sip of the fruit punch she ordered and is pleasantly surprised because it is absolutely delicious. *Some coconut rum would set this off nicely.* It tastes better than it looks. She sips slowly because in Barbados there is no such thing as a free refill.

She finishes up breakfast and pays for her meal. She sits a little while to let her food digest and resumes catching up with Anastasia and Christian. She finishes that chapter and decides it is time to go across the street to the beach. She is glad that she chose this location because it is less than a five minute walk to the beach, and it is close to everything else she needs: food, ATM, and a convenience store.

She stops in the store to get a bottle of water before sitting out at the beach. She has developed a fine heat rash from being out in the sun. As much as Kia loves being out in the sun at the beach, she is sensitive to being outside. At least her allergies have not bothered her. She hopes drinking more water will help with this rash because it is not sexy. She gets the water then starts her two minute trek across the street. Before she knows it she is paying the chair guy for her chair and umbrella. He gives her the same spot each time she has come out here. It is right in front of the lifeguard tower next to the flags. It is the prime spot on this beach. She settles in and puts on her sunblock. She feels like she is just going through the motions because she is pre-occupied with thoughts of Levy. She decides to pull out her phone and choose a song that will serve as an audio distraction to the reality that her fantasy is crumbling. She starts off with *You (78's House Mix)* by Negghead. This is perfect because it goes with the atmosphere and is upbeat enough to get her lifted but not so much that she becomes overstimulated.

She decides to pull out her book and continue on with Anastasia and Christian before going out in the water. It is only one other family out here, and she does not want to get in the water by herself even though the lifeguards are at work.

Kia tries for what seems like hours to get back into the book. She has reread the same page at least four times. She is distracted by thoughts of the night before and the uneasiness in her chest. Deep down, she knows the only thing that will make it go away is speaking with Levy. She decides to get in the water to try and take her mind off of things. She gets in and soaks up the warm, wet goodness that seems to soothe her soul, at least for the time being. She goes out at least waist deep and she lays back and floats on her back and lets her mind drift to the other side of the island.

She can't help but wonder what Levy is doing as she lays out there floating. She can't help it, but she loves this man. She wants her relationship to work out because it is the first time in her life that she has felt this happy. She floats and floats aimlessly checking her position every few minutes to make sure she has not drifted too far. The sea is relatively calm so she has not drifted far at all. After checking her position for about the 20th time, Kia decides to stand upright in the water because her front side is longing to be submerged in the Caribbean Sea.

Kia has lost track of time and it doesn't really matter at this point. She knows it is nowhere near 7:00. She takes her seat back under the umbrella and proceeds to dry naturally in the 85 degrees air. She attempts to listen to music but it is too much for her at this point. She just sits there taking in the view of the waves lightly crashing into the beach. Every now and then she will see a crab come out from its home in the sand and scurry in front of her chaise. If she wants to move, she has to be careful because the crabs are the same color as the sand.

For now she just relaxes on the chaise lounge, under the umbrella and tries to stop her mind from racing. She flags down the guy she ordered the food from the day before and orders a rum punch. There is nothing like sitting on a beautiful beach, looking at the waves, and sipping on rum punch. She just hates that she is out here by herself. It is not supposed to be this way. She is supposed to be with Levy.

Two rum punches later, Kia decides to head back to the apartment. She is loving being out here, but she is not really enjoying it like she wants to because she is consumed with Levy and trying to get to the bottom of what has happened.

After she arrives back and takes a shower, she does what she has always done: flip channels on the TV. She, of course, decides on Discovery Fit and Health channel because it is the only channel that has anything interesting on. She is laying there half asleep when there is a knock on the door. It startles Kia and her heart almost leaped out of her chest because she is not expecting anybody. "Who is it?" she asks approaching the door.

"Housekeeping," a young sounding female voice responds.

Kia opens the door at first with the chain on it to peep out because there is not a peep hole and she sees a young woman standing there with a bag and a mop and bucket. She closes the door, takes the chain off, and opens the door to let her in.

"Hello. I am here to clean," the girl tells her.

"Ok, do I need to leave?" Kia asks.

"No, you don't need to leave. I can work around you."

"Ok. Thank you." Kia is relieved because she didn't know that she would have housekeeping services, and she isn't going to leave anyway. "I didn't know there was housekeeping services," Kia tells the young lady.

"Yes, I do some housekeeping for Orville from time to time. This is not my regular job."

"Oh ok. What is your regular job, if you don't mind me asking? What is your name?"

"Oh no problem. My name is Misha. I work at a day care for my regular job," she tells Kia as she starts her cleaning routine.

"Oh ok. That's cool. I love children. I don't know if I could work in a day care though. My name is Kia, by the way."

"Ok, nice to meet you Kia. It's not that bad. What do you do? Where are you from?"

"I'm from Houston. I work for Family Services."

"Ok, like Child Protective Services?"

"That's exactly it," Kia tells her.

"Oh ok. We have that here. They don't do anything though. Some of the things I see sometimes make it rough."

"Like what?" Kia asks because her curiosity is piqued.

"There was this toddler where I work, and he came in with his ankles and feet burned. We asked the dad what happened. He said the boy was in the tub, he stepped away for a minute. The boy turned on the hot water, and by the time he got back, the boy was already burned."

"Was a report made?"

"Yes, and they came out and talked to us and the family, but they didn't do nuttin'. I mean come on the boy is a toddler. Number 1, how could he have turned on the water by himself? Number 2, children are not going to just stand in hot water without crying or trying to get out, and number 3, where was the father and how long was he gone for the child to have gotten burns that bad? You know it just makes me sick," she says as she sucks her teeth.

"That sounds like a submersion burn to me, and CPS would've taken some sort of action in that case."

"They didn't do nuttin' here. They left the boy in the home."

"Do y'all watch out for him and check for marks and bruises?" Kia asks as she shakes her head at the situation.

"Yes we do, and so far nuttin' else has happened. So what brings you to Barbados? Is this your first time here?"

"No, this is my second time here. I am here to see my boyfriend."

"Oh ok, so you are on holiday. How long are you here for?"

"I leave next Wednesday. I got here this past Monday."

"That's a long time. Are you having fun?" she asks Kia.

"I am having fun. I have truly enjoyed going to the beach. I wish I could spend more time with him, but he has to work. He is at work right now. He is supposed to come when he gets off, but I don't know because we kind of had a little bit of a falling out last night."

"What happened, if you don't mind me asking?"

"I don't mind. He says that he can tell I have never lived with a man and I asked him how can he tell that what gives that away, and he has not given me a clear response. Then he says he is troubled in his spirit because I told him that I was horny, and I just went to sleep. The killer part is that he rejected all of my advances."

"Whaaaat?!? After you came all the way down here to see him?"

"Yes girl."

"Where is he from?"

"He is from The Grenadine Islands, but he lives here and has been here for a while."

"Girl you better watch it. Grenadine men including Vincy men, Lucy men, and men from Trinidad are no good. Bajan men are ok, but some of them are no good too. They lie and manipulate to get what they want. Let me ask you a question. If he lives here, why aren't you staying with him?"

"Well, he says that he rents a room in a house and he would have to ask the owner if I could stay. That sounded like bullshit to me, but I told him don't worry about it. I wanted to come so I came on."

"That's what he told you?"

"Yep."

"That makes no sense. If he pays rent you should be able to stay with him."

"That's what I said, but I didn't question it too much."

"Girl, dem men are something else. They come here and meet these women and use dem for whatever they want. Most of these tourists, especially the older white women just want them a piece of black dick. They fall for the men with the pretty black skin and the pretty white teeth."

Kia thinks damn has she met Levy because she has just basically described him. "Here's a picture of him. Do you know him?"

Misha takes a look at the picture on Kia's camera, looks at Kia with amazement on her face, and looks back at the camera before saying, "Girl, that is a bitch you are battling. He has a woman. I don't know him, but watch what me tell you. A man look good like that has a woman. When did you say you fell out? Last night? He probably had to get back home to her."

"You think so?"

"Watch what me tell you. He looks too good. I really hope that is not the case because you have come all this way to see him, but deep down, something is telling me that is what it is. I really hope not though."

"I hope not either because I did come all this way to see him and spend time with him. I mean damn, he could have told me before he let me spend the money on this trip. That's okay though because I needed a vacation anyway so if nothing else at least I got that much."

"Girl, my gut is telling me that is what it is. I knew it was a reason I came here today. You needed to hear this. Those Grenadine men are something else. If I were you, I would try and get a baby out of him."

"We talked about having kids, but I don't want them like that though." This conversation with Misha is enlightening but, it is making Kia a little more anxious to speak with Levy. "I hope it all works out. We will see when he gets here tonight."

The two ladies continue talking as Misha finishes cleaning the room. Once she is done, she sits at the table because her head has started to hurt. Kia offers her some ibuprofen and the food she bought for Levy the day before that he did not eat.

"Thank you for this food. I haven't eaten today and that may be why my head is hurting."

"You are most welcome. It is not a problem at all."

"So are you going down by Oistins tomorrow night? You know Oistins right?"

"Yea, I know Oistins on Friday nights. No, I don't plan on going," Kia tells her not sure of what was going to happen with she and Levy.

"You should come. Look here is my phone number. Call me if you want to go, and I will come pick you up. You really should come. We will have a good time."

"I will think about it. It depends on what happens with him. I appreciate it though."

"Girl, it's no problem. I hope it works out for the best for you because that man there is fine!!"

"Thank you."

After Misha leaves Kia lounges around the apartment to wait for Levy. She takes a nap, but it does not last too long because she does not hook up to her CPAP machine. She looks at the time and realizes it lasted a little bit longer than she thought, or did Misha leave a little bit later than she realized? She did get carried away in conversation with her. Kia almost feels a little sorry for her because she has a son by an older Bajan man that moved to London, but he comes back home on holiday to visit her and the son. That's why she works two jobs, to be able to provide for him. While Kia does not have any kids she can only imagine that it is tough being a single mother.

Kia appreciates their conversation because she knew Levy is sleeping with someone here, but she did not have any solid evidence until he readily admitted it. Hearing Misha talk about how the men here will tell their local woman that their woman from the states is coming on holiday and to chill while she is here hit close to home for Kia.

As Kia mills about the apartment, she stands outside the back door and takes in her view. From where she is standing, she can see the ocean. She lets her mind drift out there on the waves to keep it off of Levy and the big elephant they had to discuss. She is startled when a man walks past her and speaks. She is not expecting to see anyone back here especially since it is on the side of the property which is out the back door for the residents and guests. Kia has seen this man before since she has been here, and he seems to be fairly friendly. Well, at least he speaks whenever she sees him.

Kia can tell it is getting close to 6:30 because it is getting dark outside, and right on cue, the familiar cry of the frogs start. Kia goes in and sees what is playing on television while she waits for Levy. This time she settles on HGTV.

Excuse me boss you have a text message: `Hey, I am not finished working and I have a lot more to do so I'm not going to make it tonight.`

Kia reads this and wants to scream. But she calmly replies: `Ok Levy. Are you coming tomorrow because we need to talk?`

Excuse me boss you have a text message: `I will be there tomorrow when I finish work. Probably around 9:00 in the evening.`

`Ok Levy. See you then.`

At this point, Kia is frustrated because she is at a loss for what is going on with Levy. She constantly replays what he has told her, and she cannot for the life of her figure out what is going on. She decides to walk down to Jus' Grillin' to get some dinner and hopefully take her mind off of things. Besides she could use some fresh air and some cookies from the store.

Suddenly Single

Chapter 16

Kia awakes to a new day. She is hoping that Levy keeps his word and comes to see her that evening. *This muthafucka better come see me shit. I came all this way to see his ass and this is not even how it was supposed to be. He should have his ass here!* Kia thinks to herself. She tries not to get all worked up, but she couldn't help it this morning.

She flips channels on the TV as she has done every morning, and as usual, there is not really anything on that she watches. She looks at the clock and sees that it is already 9:30. This is good because it will help the day to go by a little faster. At least she hopes so anyway. She lies in bed for a while before taking a shower and getting ready to get breakfast and go to the beach.

As she makes her familiar trek to the internet café, she can't help but wonder what the conversation will be like between she and Levy this evening when he comes over. "What the hell is going on?" she says not realizing she said it out loud. She was hoping she did not look like a crazy person talking to herself. Then again, that may be okay since she was by herself.

She makes it to Picasso's and gets the same breakfast she ordered yesterday. She hates to be so repetitive, but she finds something she likes and sticks to it. She eats her food slowly because she is not really hungry and knows she needs to eat if she is going to be at the beach most of the day. That was her plan anyway.

After breakfast, she heads across the street to the beach. When she arrives she notices there are people sitting in "her spot". Just as she gives the chair guy the money, he yells to the people, "Hey!! Get up!! Let the lady have the chair." Without hesitation the man quickly gets up so Kia can have the one that she has had each time she has been out here.

Suddenly Single

"Thank you," Kia tells the chair guy.

"No problem sweetheart," he replies.

Kia makes her way over to the chaise lounge under the umbrella she has become accustomed to over the last few days and begins her ritual of unpacking her bag, putting on sunscreen, and turning on an audio distraction to her thoughts. Today she decides on *Elle (Criola Remix)* by DJ Gregory. It will serve as background music and help to take her mind off of the situation with Levy.

Kia is tempted to call Levy but fights the urge and settles into the lounge chair and takes in the scenery. She cannot believe she is in a place so beautiful. She chuckles to herself as she thinks about what her co-workers are doing. *Hell they are probably glad I am not there!!* She thinks to herself. Little do they know, she is glad she is not there either.

"The beach seems to be a little more crowded today," she mumbles to herself. *Maybe some people have arrived from different countries on vacation, or maybe it could be because it's Friday.* Whatever the reason for more people, Kia didn't care. All that matters to her at this moment is getting in the water, that seems to be calling her name louder and louder with each crash of the waves, and talking to Levy to figure out what the hell is going on. She hates to be consumed with thoughts of him but this is the man she loves and she couldn't help it.

After about 30 minutes or so, Kia decides to answer the call of the waves and makes her way out into the big hot tub that is called the Caribbean Sea. As she is out there, she notices a man looking at her and making eye contact. Kia really does not feel like being friendly with her world seemingly falling apart, but she manages to crack a smile. She wasn't in the water long before he makes his way over to her.

"The water is warm this morning," he tells her with that familiar Bajan accent.

"Yes it is," Kia replies. "It feels good."

"It does. It's been a long time since I have been out here in the water."

"Why is that?" Kia asks. "Where are you from?"

"I'm from here. I don't' have time to go to the beach. I work a lot and pass by here every day, but I just have not had time for a swim," he tells her.

"Man, I just don't understand that. If the water where I live looked like this, I would try and be in it every weekend. I guess it can get old though."

"Where are you from?" he asks her.

"Texas."

"Aww ok. The States. Is this your first time here?"

"No, it's my second."

"How do you like it?" he asks inquisitively.

"I love it. I think it is beautiful. The people are friendly, the food is good and this water is good for my soul!"

He can't help but smile as she says that. "So what brings you here?"

"I am here visiting my boyfriend. He is at work," Kia tells the guy not really knowing where Levy was.

"Ahh...I see. So when are you leaving?"

"I'm leaving Wednesday. I have been here since Monday." Kia figured she would just go ahead and tell him because she figured that would be coming next.

"Ok. I see. So you will be here a while. Are you having a good time?"

"I am having a great time, but I need a cigarette now!"

"You smoke?" he asks sounding surprised.

"Not really; sometimes socially."

"Why do you need one now? You are on vacation."

"True. I just have some things on my mind. That's all."

"Well if you get a pack let me know. I will smoke one with you."

"Will do. What is your name?"

"Michael. Nice to meet you and you are?"

"Kia, nice to meet you as well." Kia is grateful for this conversation. It was a great distraction to her impending talk with Levy. "So what brings you to the beach today?"

"Well, I drive a cab and I don't go on duty until 1:00 so I decided to make time for a dip in the water."

"Oh ok. I see. I may need to get your info because I may need a ride to the airport next week."

"Yes definitely, I will give it to you when we get out of the water. I drive the cab most afternoons. I work another job in the mornings, so you will have to just call me. What time will you need to be at the airport?"

"I don't know off the top of my head I believe my plane leaves at like 3 something in the afternoon, so I would probably need to be there around 1:00 or so."

"Ok well we can work something out."

"Cool. That sounds like a plan."

The two of them stay in the water a few minutes conversing about a variety of things before getting out and exchanging numbers. Well Kia takes his number and locks it in her phone. Kia is surprised she is managing to hold a conversation being that she is consumed with thoughts of Levy. She has gotten caught up in the "what if's" again: *What if he wants to break up with me? What if he is married? What if he has a secret family? What if he really doesn't love me?*

Kia just shudders at the thought of what if he doesn't love me. She snaps out of her mental rant and tells Michael good bye and that she will definitely call him if she needs a ride to the airport and if she buys that pack of cigarettes.

Kia relaxes and tries to enjoy the rest of her day at the beach. She lies out under the umbrella but is still enjoying the beams of sunlight that is warming her already tanned skin, and right on time here comes a young man asking her if she would like something to drink. She figures why not and orders a rum punch. This is a different guy than the one that has helped her before. This one is much younger. When he returns with the drink, she pays him and they strike up a conversation.

"Why is a pretty lady like you out here by yourself?" he asks her as he takes a seat at the foot of her lounge chair.

"Well my boyfriend is at work right now, otherwise he would be here."

"Oh ok I see. So your man lives here then?"

"Yes he does."

"Where do you live? Where are you from?"

"I live in Houston, at least right now anyway. I would love to move here to this tropical paradise."

"So why don't you?"

"Well," she seemed to perk up just a little bit, "we actually talked about getting married and possibly moving here in about 5 years or so. But I don't know if that is going to happen."

"Why do you say that?"

"He has been acting funny the last couple of days, and we are supposed to talk tonight, so depending on the outcome of the conversation..." Kia's voice drifts off as she tries not to think the worst but the anxiety has taken over.

"It will be ok, mon. Don't worry about it. "

"I sure hope so!" She tells him.

"Yea mon, it will. I will talk to you later ok. I have to go check on these other people."

"No problem. Thanks for the drink," Kia tells him trying to muster up a smile, but deep inside, she is feeling very uneasy.

She wants to turn on some music but decides against it because she is too anxious right now and listening to music might overstimulate her, and she does not want that. She decides to take in the breathtaking view in front of her instead and listen the crash if each wave. She puts on her sunglasses and decides to take some pictures with her phone. She takes a couple of herself and but mostly takes shots of the scenery. She even takes a couple of the crabs that have made their home at the edge of her umbrella.

Kia manages to stay put for another couple of hours. She checks her phone and she is able to get a Wi-Fi signal so she gets on Facebook. She sees where a couple of her friends posted on her wall for her to post pictures. She posts a couple of the ones she just took and let them know this is all she has and she will post more later. She doesn't stay on long because she does not want to risk running up the phone bill even if Wi-Fi is supposed to save on her data usage.

As she is packing up her things and putting on her cover up her phone rings, her heart skips a beat or two because it is Levy. She was not expecting him to call, but she is glad he does.

"Hello?"

"Kia?"

"Yes Levy. What's up?" She said barely able to speak because she is glad he called. It took all she had not to pick up the phone today and call and/or text him.

"Hey I just wanted to let you know that I will be there tonight around 7:00 or 7:30. It looks like I will finish up a little early. Will you be there?"

"Of course Levy, where else would I be?"

"I just wanted to make sure. I will see you then."

"Ok Levy. I love you," she tells him needing to hear 'I love you too' to help ease her mind.

"Ok. I will see you tonight."

That is not the response she was hoping for and that adds to the anxiousness that has already taken over her body, but she is glad that he called.

Suddenly Single

"Ok Levy. See you tonight."

Kia hurries across the street back to the apartment so she can take a shower and try and calm herself before seeing Levy. She really needs a cigarette to help calm her down but resists the urge.

Kia glances at the clock and sees that it is five after seven. She sits at the edge of the bed flipping channels until she finds something that she can stare at. She is there, but her mind is elsewhere racing with thoughts of the unknown.

She sits for what feels like an eternity before there is finally a knock at the door.

"Who is it?" she asks already knowing it was him.

"Levy."

She unlocks both locks and opens the door to let him in. She is relieved to see him with his smooth black skin and his pearly white teeth. She can tell he has been at work because he has some paint on his arms. "How are you?" she asks as she lets him in.

"I'm fine and you?"

"Levy, I'm not good and you should know that. We have a problem here, and I am trying to understand what is going on."

"Yes, we do have a problem. Come, sit here," as he points to a chair at the table.

Kia obliges and sits at the table even though she would rather sit on the bed. Sitting at the table feels so formal.

"What is it Levy? What is going on?"

"Kia listen, I have been thinking over the last two days and something is troubling me."

"What is it, Levy?"

"Listen, you said you have only had sex one time after you left the last time, right?" he begins.

"Right," Kia agrees knowing this was not true but it was her story, and she is sticking to it.

"When I get horny I can't just go to sleep."

"Ok, but Levy I can. Besides I told you already that I have toys that I use. I'm not understanding what the problem is? Are you trying to say that I was not as tight as you might have expected? You don't have a frame of reference so how would you know anyway?"

"Listen, I just feel like you had sex more than once."

"So now you are calling me a liar? Levy, this is bullshit. What is the real problem?"

Levy looks at her and shakes his head. "I can tell you have never lived with a man either."

"How can you tell Levy and what does that mean? You keep saying that, but what does that mean?" Kia yells growing more frustrated by the second.

"You tried with buying me dinner, but I can just tell. I don't know."

"Levy, you do know that is kind of a good thing right; the fact that I have never lived with a man?"

"Yes, but I don't know. I can just tell."

"Tell what Levy?" Kia says just about at her wit's end with this fuckery coming out of his mouth.

"The other thing is with that tongue of yours I think you eat pussy. You say you don't, but I think you do. I have never felt anyone use their tongue the way you do."

Kia rolls her eyes at him because she cannot believe what he is saying. "Levy, this is bullshit!! Tell me what the problem is."

"Listen, I just don't think we should stay together. I don't crave you the way I thought I would or how I should. I don't feel any chemistry between us."

At that moment, Kia's world comes crashing down around her. The man she loves just breaks her heart into a million tiny pieces. She tries everything to keep from breaking down in front of him but once the first tear drops the flood gates are opened.

"Are you fucking kidding me? Levy, this is bullshit!!!" she yells through the tears. "What is really going on because surely it can't be this? What is really going on? Tell me. What's the real reason you don't want to be with me because everything you have said is bullshit. AND NO I DON'T EAT PUSSY BUT SO WHAT IF I DID!! Don't bullshit me anymore. What the fuck is the problem?"

Levy sighs and looks down at his hands before looking at her in her eyes, "There is someone else."

"Now we are talking. Tell me. I'm listening."

Levy takes a deep breath. "I live with a woman."

"Uh huh."

"I only live with her because I don't have anywhere else to go. I have been living with her for about a year."

"A year?" Kia says in disbelief.

"Yes. She is crazy, and if she finds out we are still together, she will kick me out then I will be homeless."

"Levy, this is not making sense to me. I mean it makes sense as to why I couldn't stay with you but that's about it. This is not adding up. So she knows about me? Are y'all together?"

"Yes, she knows about you, and no, we are not together, but she wants to be with me. It was her idea for me to tell you about her. She said as a woman she would want to know."

"So let me get this straight, you live with a woman that will kick you out if she thinks we are still together? BUT she knows about me and encouraged you to tell me about her? Is this correct?"

"Yes."

"Do you want her?"

"No, I don't want her. I'm only there because I don't have anywhere else to live," he says solemnly.

"Do you love me?" Kia asks.

"I do love you."

"Then why the fuck would you let me come all this way to break up with me? Why didn't you tell me a long time ago? I could've saved all this money and did something else with it. This is bullshit Levy. This is bullshit," Kia says as she stands up and begins to pace the floor back and forth.

"I didn't know how to tell you."

"How about you say 'hey I live with a woman, and if she finds out we are together she is going to kick me out, and I will be homeless.' How about that?! You could've said that!"

"Yes, but I didn't want to hurt you. You were so excited to come, and I was excited to see you as well."

"Didn't want to hurt me?" Kia says in disbelief. "You got the au-damn-dacity to say you didn't want to hurt me but here you are breaking up with me halfway through my trip. Then you have the unmitigated gall to try and blame it on me rather than coming clean. FUCK YOU LEVY!" Everything in Kia wanted to tell Levy to get the fuck out, but she didn't because then she would virtually be alone for the rest of her stay. "Do you love her?" Kia asks giving him a deep side eye.

Levy pauses for way too long for the answer to be no. "She asked me the same thing about you."

"And what did you say?"

"I didn't say anything, and she said that must mean that I do love you."

"You didn't say anything?! What the fuck?! Answer my question though: Do. You. Love. Her?" Kia pauses after each word to make sure he understands the words that are coming out of her mouth."

"No. I don't. I love you, and I want to be with you."

"Levy, this is bullshit," Kia says as she walks over and picks up the papers she brought to complete on this trip, "Look at this. This is why I came here."

"What is this?"

"Look at it. These are the papers you need to come over so we can be together. This is what we need to get married."

Levy looks at the papers flipping through them slowly. "Can you hold these for six months?"

"For what? Why would I do that?" Kia says in disbelief that he would even ask her such a thing.

"I need some time to get myself together."

"No shit! How long have you been in this situation? And what about your family? Can't you stay with them?"

"I can't stay with my family. We don't really get along. Any money I get, my mother takes from me because she is sick and needs medication. I just need some time to get myself together. I need at least until the beginning of the year."

Kia stops and looks at this man deep in his eyes searching for some sign of his love for her. She takes a deep breath before saying, "Let's just fix it. Let's just go down to the magistrate and get married. Fuck it. I love you and want to be with you and you say you love me too. Let's just fix it."

Levy looks at Kia with shame in his eyes. "I can't do that. It's not that simple."

Kia's heart sunk. She did not think it could drop any lower, but it did. "Why not Levy?" she asks as she drops her head and starts rubbing her forehead.

"What I am about to tell you no one knows except my mother, me and now you."

Suddenly Single

Kia is not sure that she wants to hear this because she needs plausible deniability should it ever come up, but the heartbroken girlfriend in her needs to hear what he is about to say. "What is it Levy?"

He sighs deeply, "I have an issue back in my country, in my village. People have said the authorities are looking for me. It was in the paper and everything."

Kia's stomach churns a little because she does not know what else could possibly come out of his mouth. She hopes and prays that he is not about to say he killed somebody. She very calmly asks, "What did you do?"

"It's nothing bad. I didn't kill anybody or anything," he could sense her uneasiness. "My friend had something that was in my name and I was paying the bill before I came to Barbados but when I left, he stopped paying the bill, and since it is in my name, they are looking for me."

"So you are paying somebody else's bill, and they are looking for you?"

"Something like that. Yes."

Kia arrives at her wit's end. She can't take anymore. It all starts coming together for her. "So is this what you needed to take care of back home? Is this the news you got a little while ago that had you upset?"

"Yes."

"How much do you need?" Kia asked out of curiosity.

"Listen, I don't want your money."

"Oh, you weren't getting it. I just want to know how much you need."

"I don't know how much. I haven't tried to find out yet."

"Well, Levy don't you think you need to find out?"

"Yes. I do."

Suddenly it all comes together and hits her like a ton of bricks. "So this is why you can't go home. This is why you didn't want me to give your name at the airport. You are over here illegally!"

"Yes. If I leave, I can't come back."

"This is why you can't really look for a job then either?"

"Yes."

Kia is overwhelmed at what has just happened. She cannot believe what she is hearing. This man she loves has just crushed her world and here she is suddenly single. She does not know what to do or what to say. She is out of words.

"So, what are you going to do?" he asks her.

"About what Levy? You have just shattered everything I came here to do," Kia says defeated.

"Are you going to go home early or are you going to stay?"

"Oh, I'm staying here. I'm not cutting my vacation short because you decided to ruin it."

"So where do we go from here?" he asks her.

"I guess you go home to your woman, and I go to bed or something."

"Kia that's not what I'm talking about," Levy says pitifully to her. "What do we do about us?"

Suddenly Single

Kia looks at Levy with incredulity. "There is nothing to do about us. We are over. That's what you wanted right? That's it. We are done." Kia cannot believe she is saying these words because those are the last words she expected to say on this trip.

"I guess so then," Levy says as he gets up from the chair. "Do me a favor?"

Did he just ask me for a favor after all he has just done?!?! Kia thinks to herself. "What is it Levy?"

"Please do not go anywhere tonight. I want you to be safe."

"Why should you care? You are leaving me anyway."

"Please, Kia. I know you are upset and I just want you to be safe."

Kia's eyes well up with tears that never really stopped flowing since they started. "Whatever, Levy."

They both make their way to the door. Kia looks at Levy through the tears in her eyes not knowing if she will ever see him again. Part of her wants him to get the fuck out, but the rest of her longs for him to stay. She almost wishes he would've kept the lie going. At least she would still be happy and could enjoy her vacation instead of standing here somewhat terrified not knowing what is going to happen in the five days she has left on this island.

Levy puts his arms around Kia and hugs her tight. Kia doesn't put her arms around him at first because she is too hurt and too upset, but then she embraces him like this is the last time she will see him. After all, love doesn't die in a day.

He looks at her and kisses her on the forehead before turning and walking out of the door and what she secretly hopes is not out of her life forever.

Chapter 17

Kia closes the door behind Levy and sits on the bed feeling like the wind had been knocked out of her. The stream of tears that had been flowing turned into a river. She is trying to process what has just happened, but she can't get past the fact that the man she loves, the man she had hoped to build a future with, just walked out the door.

Eventually, sadness and disbelief give way to an ounce of fear. She is 2554 miles away from home, she is by herself, and she has five days left on this island. She quickly dismisses the fearful thoughts and reminds herself that she is grown and the same God that is in America is the same God over here, and He will protect her here as He does at home. "He did not give me a spirit of fear but of power, love and of a sound mind," she tells herself.

Kia needs to talk to somebody but she does not know who to call first. She doesn't necessarily want to talk to anyone at home, at least not yet, because she needs time to calm herself and process what happened. She knows they will ask questions that she does not have the answers to. She decides to call Phillip whom she has not spoken to since she has been here. He does not know exactly when she came but he did know that she was coming.

"Yes, good night," he answers on the first ring.

"Phillip, how are you? This is Kia," she says trying not to sound as if she has been crying.

"I'm doing well. How are you? Are you here?" he asks enthusiastically.

"Yes, I made it in."

"Where are you staying? I want to come and see you when I get off work."

"Ok, that will be cool. I am staying at the Merriville Apartments by the Quayside Shopping Center. What time do you get off? Are you still at Divi?" she asks.

"Ok, I know where that it is. I am still at Divi but not right now. They were cutting hours so I had to take on a second job. I get off at 10:00. I can come there when I get off."

"Ok, cool. I'm in number 23."

"Ok, perfect. I will see you when I get off."

"See you then," she tells him before hanging up the phone. She is grateful to have Phillip come over and help her take her mind off of things. She feels bad for just now calling him especially when things are going bad but after all she did not come here to see him, per se. She came to see Levy.

Kia pulls herself together because she does not want her face and eyes to be puffy when Phillip gets there. She does not want him to necessarily know that she has literally just broken up with the love of her life. She goes to the bathroom and washes her face. While she is doing that, she takes a good look at herself in the mirror. Her eyes are red and burning from the tears. They are puffy underneath from crying, and they are filled with sadness. As she looks at herself, she starts to cry all over again because she can see the pain and sadness in her own eyes.

She finally gets it together and sits on the bed letting the TV watch her as she waits for Phillip to arrive. She has a little time to spare so she decides to call Mack. He is the one unexpected person that can comfort her in times of need. Talking to him is like pouring peroxide on a cut. He tells you what you need to hear but does it in a manner that doesn't sting or burn like alcohol on a cut. She hopes he is still up, but he should be because Houston is now an hour behind Barbados.

"What's going on?" he says as he answers on the first ring.

"We broke up." Kia says trying not to tear up because she does not want him to hear her cry.

"What?! What happened?" he says with a hint of anger and unbelief.

"Ummm," Kia starts fighting hard to choke back the tears, "He broke up with me. He basically told me that he lives with a woman and she wants him, and if she finds out we are still together, she will put him out and he will be homeless. Or something like that anyway and some other stuff, but that is the main reason."

"I had a feeling something was going to happen. I just felt like he wasn't going to show up to the airport to get you or that you wouldn't see that dude, and you would be stuck out down there."

"Oh no, it wasn't that at all. He was there to get me. But now here he comes with this bullshit."

"How many more days do you have left? Are you going to stay or are you coming back early?"

"I have 5 days left, and I'm staying because this is a vacation for me you know."

"I know. I just hate that happened man. That's not cool at all. If I ever see that nigga, I'm going to bitch slap him like the bitch he is for doing that to you. I don't care if it's 10 years from now. You don't do my homie like that."

"Well thank you I appreciate that. I doubt you will ever see him though."

"But if ever do, you already know it's a done deal. So are you ok though?"

"I'm ok. Just in shock you know," Kia says sniffling trying to stop the tears.

"I know. I know it can be tough. Just hang in there. You will be home soon."

"I know. I'm loving the beach and the water though. This just sucks. Anyway, how are the kids?"

"They're fine. They are getting ready for bed."

"Kiss them for me."

"Will do. Will do."

"Well, I will let you go because I don't want no high ass phone bill," she chuckles.

"I can dig it."

"I love you. Thank you for listening."

"I love you too. You my girl," he tells her.

This is comforting to Kia. "Thank you. Talk to you later."

"Bye."

"Bye." She hangs up. She is feeling a little bit better. Talking to her buddy always does her some good. She paces around the room trying to pass the time and calm her mind. She evens steps out of the back door just to take in the sounds of the night. As she is standing out there, the guy that she had seen before walks up towards the pool from around the corner. This startles her because she did not see or hear him coming up. He speaks as he passes and keeps on along his way.

Kia decides to go back inside because she does not want to be startled anymore tonight. She can't take anymore. She lies in the bed and stares at the TV. She is not really watching it because she cannot focus right now.

Suddenly Single

She needs to vent some more because that is how she processes things. She decides to call Aunt Betty because she always gives her sound advice and can make her laugh. Aunt Betty is not really her aunt by blood but rather an aunt figure in her life. They met while working together before Aunt Betty retired a few years ago.

"Hello?" Aunt Betty says as she answers on the second ring.

"Hey Aunt Betty," Kia says trying to sound upbeat.

"Hey. What's going on? Are you okay?"

Kia sighs deeply. "He broke up with me."

"Bastard. What happened?"

"I'm ok. I'm not hurt physically or anything like that. He broke up with me. He says that he lives with a woman and she will put him out if she thinks we are still together or some bullshit like that."

"Fuck him. Let him go, bastard."

"I know. I just was not expecting this. I'm so pissed right now."

"Well, I know you are upset. Just try and enjoy the rest of your vacation, and when you get back, don't you go anywhere else with a 'B'. The bedroom and the bathroom, that's it. Muthafucka. I can't stand him."

Kia can't help but be tickled. Aunt Betty makes her laugh every time she cusses because she doesn't really cuss a whole lot. "I know you can't, shit."

"What are you going to do for the rest of the night?" Aunt Betty asks out of concern.

"Phillip is coming over. I called him, and he agreed to come. I'm not going to tell him we just broke up because I don't want him to feel like I only called because we broke up."

"Well, fuck him too if he hurts you."

"I know. That's unfair to him though. He has been nothing but nice to me since we met. He really is a good guy."

"Well, shit you should've went after him hell. He'd a been better one than this other bastard. Oooh, that just makes me upset. I can't stand a no good ass muthafucka, with his onion raising, gay ass."

Kia couldn't help but laugh. "I know. Phillip is cool. He is just so short. I know that's shallow but damn. I do have to be attracted to you at least a little bit. Speaking of, there he is now knocking on the door. I will talk to you later.

"Ok, you be careful now. You hear?"

"I will. I promise. Bye."

"Bye."

"Who is it?" Kia asks just out of safety. She already figures its Phillip because nobody else should be coming here.

"Phillip."

"Heeeyyyy," Kia says as she opens the door. She gives him a big hug and lets him in. It was refreshing to see him after all these months and after all she just went through. "Come on in. How have you been?"

"I've been well," he says smiling from ear to ear. "I'm really happy to see you. How have you been?"

"I've been okay," Kia says trying not to think about what happened a couple of hours ago.

"Just okay? Are you and the guy from here still together?"

"No. we broke up. I came anyway because my ticket was already booked and I needed a vacation."

"Okay, okay. I see," he couldn't help but smile. "Yea, I just got off work. I drive an ice cream truck. I met a guy who owned the truck. He needed a driver so I tried it out for a week, and he liked me so he asked me to start driving it for him in the evenings."

"Well, that's good. It's nothing wrong with making a little extra money. Hell, I need to find me a side hustle to make some money. Shoot. Does your friend still work at Divi?" Kia asks.

"Yes, she does. She is still the manager. She dropped me off here tonight."

Kia instantly wonders how he is going to get home and what time the busses stop running since he doesn't have a ride. "Oh ok. I see. Well that's good."

"Are you hungry? Have you eaten?" he asks her.

"No, I have not eaten. I'm not really hungry, but I need to eat a little something. What do you have in mind?"

"We can go down to Chefette right here if you want to."

"That will be fine. I have never been to Chefette before."

Kia gathers her purse and the two of them head off to Chefette. Kia isn't really hungry, but she needs to get out of this apartment. She didn't care what Levy said about going out. She is grown and she is going out anyway. At least she has Phillip there with her for the time being.

When they get to Chefette, Kia orders a two piece fried chicken meal with French fries and a drink. Phillip knows the lady that is helping them so he introduces her to Kia.

"Nice to meet you," Kia says trying to keep a smile on her face.

"Nice to meet you as well. Is this your first time in Barbados?"

"No, it's my second."

"How long have you been here?" she asks seemingly out of curiosity.

Before she knew it, Kia tells the lady she has been here since Monday.

"Monday?!" Phillip says shocked. "Today is Friday. You see how she does me," he tells the girl.

"I know today is Friday, but I needed time to clear my head. I told you me and the guy broke up and I just needed to get myself together," Kia tells him trying to sound convincing because she knows this is not exactly the truth.

"Yea Yea," Phillip says as he takes out the money and pays for her food.

"Thank you Phillip. You didn't have to pay for my food," Kia says almost apologetically.

"I'm a man. I'm supposed to pay for your food, and you are most welcome."

With food in hand, the two head back to the apartment to eat. When they arrive, Kia unlocks the door, and they go in and sit at the table. He sits on the futon couch that is in the room. Kia tears into her food, which is pretty tasty. It's not Popeye's, but it will do.

Suddenly Single

"So, why did you all break up, if you don't mind me asking?"

"Well," Kia starts and has to fight back tears as she becomes overwhelmed with emotion, "he has somebody else, and he lives with her. He claims that she wants to be with him, and if he stays with me then she will put him out and he will be homeless."

"Aww man. That is messed up. You don't do people like that. I hate that happened. Are you ok?"

"I'm doing okay. It just sucks being here knowing we were supposed to be together," she says as a tear rolls down her cheek.

Phillip walks over to her and rubs her shoulders and tells her not to cry. "Listen, let me stay here with you tonight. I want to make sure you are okay."

"Oh Phillip, that is not necessary. I am okay," she tells him. She really wants to just be by herself so she could process the events of the evening and cry herself to sleep, if necessary, but she didn't have the heart to tell Phillip, especially after how nice he has been to her. She suspects he wants to stay until morning because he does not have a car, and it is getting late.

"Nonsense, you are here crying. I would hate to leave you knowing you are not in the best of spirits."

Not having the energy to go round and round with him, she tells him he can stay. "Ok Phillip you can stay, but you have to stay on your side of the bed. I am not in the mood for you trying anything."

"What kind of man would I be if I tried something with you in this emotional state?" he asks her sounding a little insulted.

"Ok. I was just letting you know." Kia finishes up her food and goes to wash her hands and changes into her night clothes. While she is doing this, Phillip strips down to his underclothes before they get in the bed. Kia puts up a pillow barrier between them. She knows this may be a bit extreme, but she really is not in the mood for him to try anything even though he said he wouldn't. She isn't chancing it.

"You know this is like a dream come true for me," he tells her.

"Why so?" she asks confused, but she had an idea why and wants to hear what he has to say.

"Because I get to sleep next to you," he tells her.

She expected he would say this. Nonetheless she is flattered. "Thank you, Phillip."

Chapter 18

Kia awakes the next morning and tries not to disturb Phillip as she gets out of bed and goes to the bathroom but to no avail. When she returns to the bedroom, Phillip is awake and looking at her.

"Good morning," he says to her.

"Good morning. How did you sleep?"

"I slept fine because I was next to you," he tells her.

Kia is flattered but is not in the mood for flirting. "Aww, you are too kind. I hope the CPAP wasn't disturbing to you."

"No, it wasn't. It was okay."

"Well, that's good to know. So what do you have planned for the day?" Kia asks so she can try and gauge how soon he will be leaving. She needs some time to herself, but she doesn't want to be rude and ask him to leave. He has been nothing but kind to her and she doesn't want to be a bitch to him just because of what happened to her.

"I have to go to work this afternoon, but right now I need to go home, clean up, change clothes, and get ready for work. What are you going to do?" he says as he gets up and starts getting dressed.

"I am going to the beach. I mean, I came here to get away and clear my mind, and nothing does that better than going to the beach."

"Well, that sounds like fun. Listen, I am off on Tuesday so maybe I can rent a car and take you around."

"That sounds nice," Kia says. "I would like that. It would be nice to see some other parts of the island especially since I will be leaving on Wednesday."

"Ok, cool. I look forward to that. What time do you leave on Wednesday?"

"I don't know exactly. I think at 3 something. Why?"

"I can have one of the taxi drivers at Divi come and pick you up and take you to the airport if need be."

Kia's heart just melts because Phillip really is a good man. "Ok cool. I will let you know that morning if I need a ride. Is that okay?"

"That sounds perfect. Give me a hug."

Kia walks over and gives him a hug. "Thank you Phillip for everything. I really appreciate it. And thank you for not trying anything."

"You are most welcome my dear. I will text you later today and check on you and we will be in touch about Tuesday," he tells her.

"That sounds like a plan to me," she says as she opens the door to let him out.

"Cool. Goodbye now."

"Bye." She waves and closes the door behind him. It is already close to 9:00 in the morning so she decides to go ahead and get dressed for breakfast and the beach.

Once dressed, she makes the familiar hike to the breakfast spot, this time stopping at the corner store on the way to pick up some water. She is relieved that the truth has finally come out, but she is saddened by what the truth is. Now she has to spend the rest of her time here without Levy and this is not how she envisioned it.

She takes her seat under an umbrella closer to the building and orders her same breakfast as the days prior. She really is not that hungry but she needs to eat if she is going to stay at the beach all day. She tries her best not to get caught up in the thoughts running through her mind. She replays her conversation with Levy the night before and she tries to rationalize it in her head but it just is not sitting well with her. *How could he do this to me?*

Even though their relationship had some unique circumstances, it was still very real to her, and she was hurt by the ending of it all. She did everything she could to be the best girlfriend she knew how being 2554 miles away from her man. She tries to take her mind off it by staring across the street at the beautiful water but to no avail. The thoughts keep invading her, leaving no segregation from the reality of it all.

She nibbles on her breakfast until it is gone. She pays the lady what is owed and heads across the street. She stops at the ATM to get some cash to pay the chair guy. Once at her destination she pays the guy for the chair and umbrella and she gets settled. She lets her food digest and, as usual, she pulls out her phone for some music but decides against it for right now at least. Instead, she takes in the view and all its majesty.

She gets in the water because it is beckoning her with each ripple. When she gets to the water's edge, she stands there and lets it run up on her feet while she looks out onto the horizon. As far as the eye could see, there is nothing but water. She walks out slowly adjusting to the temperature with each step. Once out far enough, she lays out on her back and just begins to float, letting go of her weight, trying to somehow let go of the emotional weight of the broken heart she is carrying. She closes her eyes so she can feel the warmth of the sun on her face. She floats and floats checking her position periodically to make sure she has not floated out too far when she feels water on her face. This is strange to her because her face had not been under water. Then she realizes it is a tear. She is so lost in the waves that she did not realize water had begun to escape from her eyes.

She pulls herself down so she can stand up and get herself together. She comes in from the water and is sitting on the side of the lounge chair when her phone starts ringing. This startles her because she is not expecting any calls. She grabs her phone and it reads: Incoming call from Levy.

"Hello?" Kia answers after the second ring.

"Hey good morning," he says.

"Hey Levy, what's up?" she asks rather dryly but deep down she is glad he called.

"Listen, I was wondering if you want to spend the day with me," he says.

Kia sighs deeply before responding. "I probably shouldn't, but I will. I came here to see you and spend time with you, so I will." Going against her better judgment, Kia agrees to spend the day with Levy.

"Where are you now?"

"I'm at the beach. I just got here really."

"Well, I am close by where you are staying so can you go there now?"

"I can but I have to change clothes, so I need a few minutes."

"That's fine," Levy says "but hurry because I am almost to you."

"Ok Levy. I will see you in a little while."

"Ok."

Kia hurries and gathers her things. She makes it back across the street and up the hill in record time. *Wait, why am I rushing?* she thinks to herself. *This muthafucka broke up with me. Let me slow my ass down.*

Suddenly Single

She makes it back to the room and jumps in the shower to wash off the sand and freshen up just a bit. She puts on some shorts and a tank top and right as she does that, there is a knock at the door.

"Who is it?" she asks knowing who it is.

"It's Levy."

Kia opens the door, and he stands outside not coming in. She can see that the car is parked in the middle of the driveway. "Are you ready?" he asks.

"Yes, I'm coming. Let me get my bag." Kia grabs her bag, locks the door, and follows him to the car.

"I need to get to Pearl Gardens by 12:30. I'm doing some brazing work today, and I need to meet the guy there."

"Ok. That's cool," she says as they start off in the car. She is happy to be getting out and about and away from this part of the island.

"How have you been?" he asks as if he did not shred her heart into a million strands the night before.

"How do you think I've been?" she says rather sarcastically and looks at him as if he has lost his mind. "I'm alive, so I'm good. Just out of curiosity, what made you call me today?"

"I was just worried about you."

"Worried about me? You weren't too worried when you walked out that door."

"Listen, I'm not trying to start an argument. I was worried about you, and I wanted to see you. For what it's worth, I'm glad you said yes. I do still love you, you know."

"I guess Levy. So did you tell her we broke up?"

"Yes, I did."

"I see. What did she say?"

"She didn't say anything."

"MMMM. Ok."

"Do we have to talk about this?" he asks sounding slightly irritated.

"Not right now we don't," she says as she inhales the ocean breeze. "Listen, before I go home, I want you to take me to get some seasoning or some spices. That food you cooked was really good, and the bar-b-que sauce they use at Jus' Grillin' is off the chain I want to figure out what is in it."

"We can do that. Don't let me forget."

"Oh trust me, I won't. So, are you going to be over here all day?"

"I will probably be there at least until dark, unless I get finished earlier than that. Caleb is supposed to come and help me so hopefully it won't take that long. Are you hungry now, do you want to eat?"

"No, I'm good for now, but I will be hungry later."

"Ok cool. We can get something later when you are ready to eat."

The two ride along having moments of silence in between bits of conversation. Kia is trying hard to understand why Levy has done what he has done, but she doesn't feel like it turning into some big argument. She just doesn't have it in her.

They stop at the little house store that is on the same street as Pearl Gardens. While Levy is getting the items, Kia, being the detective she is, looks at a piece of mail that is in the door of the car. It is addressed to a Ms. Chevelle Wilcox, and it is an invoice for Cool Spot Ice Cream Shop. Kia looks at it for a second trying to memorize the address in Speightstown before putting it back in the door.

"Well, I'll be damned," she thinks to herself, "this is *her* car and she owns the ice cream shop where he works." It had not clicked with Kia until this moment that Levy does not own a car. She just assumed this was a family member's car. Not *her* car. When Levy returns, she did not say anything to him about what she just discovered, but she can't help but be a little perturbed at the fact that he would pick her up in *her* car.

When the two of them pull into Pearl Gardens, Caleb is already there with another gentleman Kia has not met. The man Levy is waiting on has not yet arrived.

"Did you tell Caleb we broke up?" Kia asks before getting out of the car?

"I haven't told anybody anything because I'm not giving up on us," he tells her.

"Humph. Ok," she says before opening the door.

"Hey Kia. How are you today?" Caleb asks.

"I'm ok, Caleb. How are you?" Kia says desperately trying to act as if everything is kosher.

"I'm ok. Are you enjoying your vacation?"

"I am. It has been a nice getaway."

"Kia I want you to meet my cousin Ian," Levy says as he walks over towards where they all were standing.

"Ian, nice to meet you," Kia says as she shakes his hand.

"Nice to meet you as well. I have heard a lot about you," he tells her.

"I hope it was all good," she says as she tries to muster up a smile.

"Of course it was. It has been a long time since I have seen my cousin this happy."

"Really now? So did he tell you I was coming here to visit him?"

"Ok, ok, enough of the questions," Levy interrupts. "Let me get you a chair so you can sit and be in the shade."

"Ok. That is fine," Kia tells him.

Ian and Caleb walk over to the rebar and start assessing what needs to be done as far as the brazing. While they are doing that, the man who Levy is waiting for drives up and Levy greets him at his truck to get the Chlorine tablets for the pool. Once he finishes with him, he pulls the chair over to the shade so Kia can be comfortable and not too hot. He looks at her, and she walks over to where he has put her seat. As she takes her seat, she calls him close to her so Caleb and Ian cannot hear what she is telling him.

"Levy, since you did not tell Caleb we broke up we probably should kiss or something every now and then to make it believable," Kia whispers to him.

"You are probably right," he says as he leans in to kiss her and gives her a peck on the lips.

He walks over to the other two and Kia gets up to follow. She is not ready to sit just yet. Levy, Caleb, and Ian start discussing who will start brazing the rebar because they all want a piece of it. Levy, being the oldest and this being his job, says he will kick it off. Kia watches the three men carefully solder each joint of the rebar together. Levy explains this has to be completed before the concrete can be poured. This strengthens the concrete once it is down.

Suddenly Single

Kia asks can she sit on the edge of the pool while they are working so she can stick her feet in the water. Levy tells her it is okay but to be careful because the chlorine level is really high. She agrees and takes her seat. She watched them work for a little while before getting out to get her phone. She notices some of the polish has come off of her toes and this reminds her that she is going to give Anya her fingernail polish since she admired it so. She will give it to Levy this evening.

She walks over to get her phone but decides to sit in the chair for a while because her butt is hurting sitting on the edge of the pool. She picks up her phone and decides to take a couple of selfies and some pics of Levy and the crew. She wants to post them to Facebook however, there is no Wi-Fi network out here and she is not going to run up her data charges. Instead she opts for flipping through the few pics she has taken so far on this trip. This is a bad idea because she sees the first few pics that she and Levy took and she instantly becomes overwhelmed with emotion and the tears start flowing. It is like somebody turned on the faucet. She discreetly wipes her tears because she does not want anyone to see her crying. Levy catches a glimpse of her wiping her face and he makes his way over to her leaving the brazing to Ian and Caleb.

"What's wrong?" he asks kneeling down to see her face that she has dropped and hidden behind her hands.

"Nothing," Kia sniffs. "I was looking at some of our photos."

"Don't cry" he says as he wipes her tears, "you are going to mess up your pretty face."

"I can't help it. I'm going to go into the house and go to the bathroom and put some water on my face." Levy kisses her cheeks then gives her a peck on the lips. And with that she goes in the house to rinse her face and use the bathroom and Levy rejoins his brother and cousin.

She takes her time in the bathroom because she wants to be sure she could put on her game face and maintain it while they are there. When she comes out of the house, she sees they have made their way halfway around the pool and Kia walks over to watch them work.

"Kia, please be careful and watch where you walk, especially with flip flops on. This is so hot it will take your skin off if you touch it," Levy instructs her.

"Take my skin off?! Damn ok. I'm being careful," she tells him. "I'm going to just sit on the edge of the pool again."

"Ok. Just be careful," he tells her.

"I will."

Kia sits there and listens to waves in the distance and ponders what her life will be like without Levy. She supposes it will be like life was before him the only difference is that she now knows what real happiness (well to her anyway) feels like and what it feels like to truly have your heart broken. She tries not to get too caught up in those thoughts because she does not want to start crying again. She is also trying to keep the hurt off of her face which is where she wears her emotions. She stares at her feet in the water only looking up every now and then to see them virtually arguing over who is going to do the brazing next.

Levy comes over to Kia when he finished most of the work that was left. He leans down and gives her a kiss in an effort to keep the facade going that they are still a happy couple. They even pose for a couple of pics after Kia gets finished soaking her feet in the pool. He starts to clean up after they finish with their mini photo session, while he is doing that Kia musters up some strength and looks at all of the pictures from her trip so far, and she can see the sadness in her eyes now. She looks different from when she first got there. She tries not to focus on that right now and rather focuses on getting through the rest of the time here in front of Caleb and Ian.

She walks over to the chair Levy brought out for her, and she takes a seat. She fiddles with her phone and decides to get on Facebook for a minute risking running up the phone bill even though the data is supposed to be fixed where this won't happen. It is the same ole, same ole with her Facebook friends. She doesn't stay on too long, but she does make a post so her friends and family will know that she is safe and alive.

Levy and Caleb finish cleaning up while Ian talks on his cell phone. Kia gathers her things and gets the rest of the bottled waters out of the refrigerator in the house before getting in the car. It is getting dark so she knows it is close to 6:30. She has not eaten since breakfast and wasn't really hungry. She didn't have much of an appetite. She tells Caleb and Ian goodbye before retreating to the car.

Since she is in the car alone again, she looks around on the surface for anything else she can see in an effort to help her gain some sort of comprehension about what is going on. She did not see anything until Levy opens the door and pulls out a pink digital camera from the middle console. He snapped a few pics of the work he completed today. Only if Kia could get her hands on that camera she would be able to see what she is up against, but she knows that would be damn near impossible.

When he finishes taking pictures, he gets in the car and Caleb says something to him as they drive off.

"Did you understand what Caleb told me?" Levy asks.

"No, I didn't. What did he say?"

"He asked me what I did to you because you seem different."

Kia thinks, *Damn, is it that obvious?* "So what did you tell him?"

"I didn't tell him anything."

"Mmmmm. Why not?" Kia asks.

"It's none of his business. Besides I told you I'm not giving up on us."

"Is that your camera?"

"No. It's not," he says.

"It's hers," Kia asks but not really asking, more telling. "So I think I will snap a pic of myself with it," Kia says seriously but knows she is just kidding. She would not do that because she is too old to play those types of games.

"Babe, you know you can't do that," Levy says as he turns and looks at her with all seriousness in his face.

"I know," she sighs. "I know."

"Are you hungry?"

"A little. Are you?"

"Yes, I am. What do you want to eat?"

"I don't know. How about KFC, I guess?" Kia didn't know what else to suggest because she is not from here.

"Ok, cool."

The two drive along in an awkward silence for a bit. Kia is enjoying feeling the breeze on her face after being hot all day long.

"So let me ask you a question," Kia starts, "do you love her? I know you have said you don't but I don't know."

"Kia, I don't love her. I love you, but I don't want to be homeless."

"What about the house at Pearl Gardens? You have the key and it has electricity. Can't you stay there for a little while?"

"I can't squat there. I don't own it. What if the owner comes?"

"I thought you told me the owner lives in Canada?"

"He does but what if he comes? I can't just be in there, that's illegal."

"But you have a key? And it's not quite finished, and it's a bed in there." Kia tries any solution to help Levy so he can somehow get himself together and they can be together.

"I wish I could, but I can't."

Kia drops it. She doesn't feel like getting worked up. They arrive at KFC and decide to go through the drive through. It is bittersweet because this is the same one they stopped at when she first got here. She orders her food and to her surprise Levy pays for it. They get their food in their separate bags and head towards the room.

When they arrive, Levy drives Kia to the door. He leaves the car running and he gets out and opens the car door for Kia. He walks her to the door to make sure she gets in safe.

"Thank you for today," she tells him. "I was glad to spend it with you."

"No, thank you for spending it with me. I enjoyed our time together even though I was doing some work."

"You're welcome. Hold on." She runs in and gets the fingernail polish for Anya. "Give this to your sister. She really admired it, and I want her to have it."

"She will like that. Thank you." He reaches out to hug her, and she gives him a hug. He kisses her on the forehead and turns and heads for the car. "Lock the door. I will call you tomorrow."

"Ok. Goodnight."

With that Kia shuts and locks the door, eats her food and takes a much needed shower before retreating to the bed to let the TV watch her.

Chapter 19

Kia rises to a new day. She is not expecting to see Levy today so she tries to find something different to do for the day. She would like to venture out on this island but she is cautious about adventuring too far out by herself. She flips through the tourist book that is on the nightstand. She wants to see if she can set something up for the Jammin' Catamaran in the next couple of days since she really enjoyed it the last time. There is a phone in the dresser drawer the owner said could be used for local calls. She will just need to add some minutes to it. Much to her delight, it has a few minutes left so she doesn't have to add any at that moment.

She called Jammin', and they are not sailing this week. She is disappointed. She thinks about calling Cool Runnings, but she decides against it because she is not familiar with them. She flips a little more in the book, and she sees an ad for a massage. She thinks this would be great. She calls and makes an appointment for later that evening as the spa is at the hotel right across the main street from where she is staying. In the meantime, she will do what she has been doing since she has been here which is get breakfast and go to the beach. She is sure she will make a whole day of it today until it is time for her massage.

She gets dressed and gathers her things. She is in better spirits today, probably because she spent time with Levy yesterday. She locks the door and heads down the hill not caring what the day has in store because it will all be rubbed away this evening with her massage. She gets to the breakfast spot and orders her usual. She decides she will turn on some music now rather than wait until she gets to the beach. She decides on *Hunger* by Rhye to start with. It is upbeat and matched her mood right now.

When she is done with breakfast, she stops by the store before walking across the street to the beach. She wants some cigarettes. She has been through enough and needs something to calm her down if she gets a little riled up. She buys a pack of Newports and a lighter and puts them in her bag. When she gets to the beach, she can see that her spot is taken and she is a little disappointed. She is used to sitting in the same place. The chair guy calls out to the people sitting in her spot and tells them to move. Much to her surprise, they all get up and walk off.

She struts over to her umbrella feeling special and proceeds to get settled in. Once everything is in place, including her back against the lounge chair, she resumes the music with *Sweetness Alive (featuring SLL)* by Goldroom. Just as the song reaches the chorus she is startled by a man that approaches her. He is saying something, but she can't hear because of the music. She slips off her headphones and asked him to repeat what he was saying.

"Hi, good morning. I was just saying that I wanted to see who this was I had to give up my chair for."

"Oh, ok. Well, now you see," Kia says trying not to sound to sarcastic, but she was really enjoying her music.

"What's your name?" he asks.

"Kia. What's yours?"

"Javel, nice to meet you Kia. I am one of the lifeguards here, and since this is the second time I had to give up my chair for you, I wanted to come and meet you."

Kia couldn't help but smile. "I'm sorry he made you give up the chair, but this is where I have sat since I arrived a few days ago."

"Where are you from, if you don't mind me asking?"

"I'm from Houston."

Suddenly Single

"The States. Ok, so what brings you to Barbados?"

"Do you really want to know?"

"Yes. Do you mind if I sit in this other chair?"

"Please, have a seat. Well," Kia sighs, "I came to see my now ex-fiancé. He broke up with me a couple of days ago and I still have a few days left on my trip."

"Oh, you are breaking my heart," he says as he is clutches his chest as if his heart is really breaking.

"Yea, right," Kia says trying to keep the mood light.

"Seriously, he's a coward. You don't do that to somebody."

"Well, thank you," Kia says to him.

"One man's trash is another man's treasure you know. And that's all I'm going to say about that."

"That's true. So how do you like being a lifeguard?"

"I love it. I wouldn't trade it for anything."

"That's cool."

"Can you swim?" he asks out of curiosity.

"Like a fish," Kia snaps. "Well, maybe not like a fish, but I do swim pretty well."

"Ok, I see," he laughs.

"Can I ask you something?"

"Sure, what's up?"

"What is that out there?" Kia points to the buoy looking thing offshore.

"That is a man-made reef."

"Oh, ok. That's pretty neat."

"I can take you out there if you want. We take people out for $10 USD," he informs her.

"Ok, cool. So by take out there you mean swim out there?"

"Yes ma'am. Do you think you could make it?"

"Of course I can, well how deep is it?"

"It's about 15 feet at the deepest point. I can tow you out there so you won't have to swim much if you don't think you can make it."

"I may have to take you up on that a little later this afternoon. That sounds like fun."

"That will work. I will have to check on you then for sure."

"Let me ask you something: Do you know where I can jet ski?"

"I sure do. I have a jet ski. It is not out here right now because the guy that runs it for me brings it out a little later."

"Ok, cool...cool. How much does it cost?"

"It's $40 USD for 30 minutes and you can go down the coast with one of us or $20 for 15 minutes by yourself but you have to stay right around in here."

"Ok, cool. I definitely have to do that. That is something that I love to do whenever I go on vacation."

"Cool. Well let me know when you are ready, or I will give you time to get settled and I will check back in with you."

"That sounds like a plan," Kia says, "I guess I will see you later."

She resumes listening to *Sweetness Alive*; this time starting it over from the beginning. Before the song is over (and it is only a little over four minutes), another younger looking gentleman approaches her.

"Good morning. How are you this morning?" he asks with a big grin on his face.

"I'm good. Trying to relax and enjoy the beach," she says with a tad bit of sarcasm hoping he would catch the hint but he didn't.

"That's good. I couldn't help but notice how beautiful you are, AND you are sitting here all by yourself."

"Thank you," Kia tells him as she manages to crack a smile. He reminding her that she is by herself started to take her down a little. So she pulls a cigarette and lights up. She is secretly hoping this would make him leave.

"So, why is a pretty lady like you out here all alone?"

"Well, if you must know, I came to see my now ex-fiancé. He broke up with me 2 days ago," Kia tells him as she takes a puff of her cigarette.

"Awww, that sucks. Who would do something like that? That's bad."

"Well, gee thanks," Kia tells him not quite expecting that response.

"I can understand how you must feel though because something like that happened to me..." He proceeds to tell Kia about what happened to him and she is zoning in and out. She did hear him say that he got over that girl by basically getting under another one. He doesn't word it like that, but that is what he means. She hopes he is not thinking he would like to help her in this way because Kia's mind is not on sex and definitely not with him.

"So, where are you from?" Kia asks in an effort to direct his mind in a different direction.

"My mom is from here and my father is from London. I actually live in London."

"Do you now? So what brings you here? Visiting your mom?"

"Well, that and working."

"Oh, ok. So what do you do?"

"I work on different plumbing accounts that my company has."

"Ok, I see. So how long are you here for?"

"This time around I'm here for 6 months. It may get pushed to 7 months."

"Oh, okay. So your company pays for you to come home basically and pays a per diem then?"

"Yes, that is correct. So what is your name? I'm Amani."

"Nice to meet you Amani, I'm Kia."

"Ok Kia. Good to formally meet you. Have you been in the water yet this morning?"

"No, I have not. I will go in a little bit," she says as she puts out her cigarette.

"Well, I think I'm going to go in now. Do you mind if I leave my things under your umbrella?"

"No, that's fine. I will go ahead join you in the water. It looks too inviting."

The two go out into the water and soak up each wave while engaging in conversation. They talk about a multitude of things from what type food they eat to Amani wanting to massage Kia and suck her toes. Kia does not want him close to her in that capacity. Activities like that lead to sex and Kia just is not having it. Amani even asks can he take her out to the boardwalk that evening and she agrees. She tells him to pick her up around 8:00 PM that evening. That will give her time to get in from her massage and get dressed.

Kia comes in from the water leaving Amani out there. They have been out there so long Kia's fingertips are wrinkled. She sits on the side of the lounge chair to dry off some in the sun before laying in it the correct way. She decides to smoke another cigarette so she lights one up.

"Good afternoon, pretty lady."

"Hey, how are you?" Kia says. It was the young guy from before that was selling drinks on the beach.

"I'm doing okay. How are you? I see you are smoking today, I didn't think you smoked. You don't look like the type."

"I don't know what the smoking type looks like but thank you. I don't really smoke. Only in certain situations like when I'm really stressed out or on some social occasions."

"I see. I see. So are you stressed out now? What happened with your boyfriend?"

"We broke up," Kia says trying to keep a straight face and not think too deeply at that moment but she is impressed that he remembered.

"Awww, well that sucks," he says as he takes a seat next to her and rubs her on the shoulder. "Some people just don't know when they have a good thing. You'll be okay mon. It's plenty of other Bajan men that would love to pick up where he left off."

"That's sweet. Thank you," Kia smiles, "but I'm good for now. I need time to process this you, know?"

"Absolutely my dear. So are you going to have a rum punch today?"

"I will have one, but I am going to go snorkeling out on the reef in a little while so I will have one when I get back."

"Oh ok, cool. Who is taking you out to the reef?" he asks.

"I'm going out there with Javel."

"Javel, yea he's cool. He's a really good swimmer, one of the best out here."

"Ok cool. I'm glad to hear that."

"Ok love, I will check on you when you get back in."

"Cool," Kia tells him before he continues on down the beach.

Kia sits there and finishes her cigarette and relaxes looking out onto the horizon. She is pleased with how the day is going so far. She cannot wait for her professional massage this evening. She decides to put on some music, this time not with her headphones on, just playing openly. She chooses *Blow the Whistle* by Too $hort. She decides it's time to tap into her hood side.

"Hey, are you ready to go out snorkeling?" Javel asks as he approaches Kia's umbrella.

"Yep. I'm ready when you are," Kia says. She couldn't help but smile because she is finally getting to do something different besides her same routine, and she loves to snorkel.

"Ok, cool. Let me get the gear. I will be right back."

"Ok. Do you want me to pay you now or when we get back?"

"Now is fine if you want. Whichever."

"I will go ahead and pay you now for the snorkeling and the jet skiing. Don't bring me back dead from snorkeling and don't make me have to hunt you down to go jet skiing. I do have to be back from both by 4:00 because I have a massage at 5:00," Kia says jokingly but she is very serious.

"It's no problem. You will be back in time. I promise. I tell you what, if it will make you more comfortable why don't you pay me when we get back from both."

"Well ok then. I can do that. Thank you."

"No problem. Let me get the gear. Be right back." He goes to the lifeguard stand behind her and returns a short while later with the fins and mask they would need and a float called a torpedo. When he returns they walk down the beach some so that they can swim straight out to the reef. Kia is sure to bury her phone and money deep in her bag and cover it with her cover up dress and shoes and other things before they leave out. "Here put the mask on but you don't have to put it in your mouth yet and turn around and put the fins on," he instructs.

"Turn around?" Kia asks a little perplexed.

"Yes, turn around so you can walk backwards out into the water. Otherwise it will be impossible for you to walk."

Kia thinks for a second, and he is right. The way the fin is made it would be impossible to walk with it on. She leans down and attempts to put on the first one but she almost falls over in the process. She is sure this is quite a sight for anyone that may be watching.

"Hold on. Let me help you," Javel tells her as he walks over so she can lean on him.

"Thank you. I was struggling," Kia laughed.

"I could see."

Kia manages to get both fins on and she puts on her mask on top of her head but not completely on just yet.

"Are you ready?"

"I am," Kia says beaming but feeling just a little bit self-conscience about how she must look but at the same time not really giving a damn.

"Alright, we are going to swim out about halfway and put the mask completely on. You will be able to still stand at that point in the water. Ok?"

"Ok. I'm ready."

The two walk backwards into the water until they are in deep enough water where they could turn around and swim. Kia does not want to risk getting separated from Javel so she holds on to the torpedo and kicked as he towed her out to the half way mark where they put on their masks.

"You good?" he asks her.

"I'm good."

"Ok, we are going to go all the way to the reef then we will stop for a minute and rest. Ok?"

Kia gives him a thumbs up because she has already put on her mask with the snorkel in her mouth. The two continue on in the same manner they did before. He is towing her but she is kicking and she even lets go a couple of times. Each time she does this, he turns around to make sure she is right there with him. By the time they make it to the starting point at the reef Kia catches a cramp in her foot. Javel quickly grabs her foot and takes off the fin and starts to rub her foot. It feels good, but it is kind of awkward because they are in the ocean and their feet are not touching the ground. They are leaning on the rocks but have to be careful because the rocks are very sharp and jagged.

"How does that feel? Does it feel better?" he asks her as he continues to rub.

"It does. Thank you."

"Ok, good. I'm going to put your fin back on and we will start down the reef."

"Sounds good. I'm ready. How far down does it go?"

"It's 100 meters out here, 200 meters down each side of the reef and 100 meters back in so all in all it's about 600 meters total."

"Ok, cool. Let's go!"

Both of them mask up and head off down the reef. This time hand in hand. This gave Javel a break from having to tow Kia and gave Kia a chance to really swim. About halfway down the reef, they see a man out there fishing with a spear. He looks startled to see them swimming up. Javel looks at Kia and shakes his head no as if to say that is a not allowed. Kia understood what he is saying, but she is too caught up in the colorful schools of fish she is seeing. There are all kinds of fish out there. She is loving it. As they approach the end of the reef on that side, they stop on a flat rock to take a break and catch their breath.

"You swim pretty good," Javel tells Kia. "Most people don't make it this far. They get about halfway and want to turn back."

"Thank you!! I finish what I start," Kia sasses. It's no way I was going to start this and not finish it." As she says that, she looks back towards the shore which seems farther away than it did when she first started out and questions herself in that moment. She gets tickled because she thought of Aunt Betty who always tells her she does not have any fear. If she could see her now she would really talk about her and call her fearless.

"Well, that's good to know. Are you enjoying yourself so far?"

"I am. This is fun!"

"How is your foot? Not cramping anymore?"

"No, it's good. I just had to get used to the fins."

"Yea, it takes a minute especially if you're not used to it. Well, are you ready to go down the other side?"

"Yes, I am," Kia says as she replaces her mask and snorkel.

The two head off down the other side of the reef hand in hand again. Not far down this side of it Kia sees a sea turtle. It is just one, and since it is not too big, so she knows it is not too old. There seemed to be more fish on the other side of the reef but there are still some colorful ones on this side. The two take their time swimming taking in all that they can see. They stop once more at the first pylon, where they first stopped, before swimming back to the shore.

Suddenly Single

"I saw a turtle!" Kia exclaims.

"Where?" Javel asks sounding as if he does not believe her.

"Right after we first started out on this side. He was right there. He was about this big," Kia shows him with her hands how round he was.

"You should've tapped me. I didn't see him. You are lucky you know. You rarely see a turtle out here but every now and then you can catch one feeding out here."

"I'm sorry. I thought you saw him because he was like right there."

"No, I didn't see him, but it's okay," he smiles as he looks at her. "Are you ready to head to shore?"

"Yea, I guess," Kia drags. "I'm enjoying being out here."

"We can stay out a little longer if you want."

"No, we better go on back in because we still have to jet ski before I go for my massage and I don't know what time it is."

"Ok then. We can go when you are ready."

"I'm ready."

This time Kia swims completely on her own, but she is right beside Javel not letting him out of her view. The torpedo is within her reach so she can grab it if she needs to. She makes it within standing distance of the shore and she stops to take off her fin and mask as does Javel. She gives it to him, and he carries it the rest of the way in for her.

"I will check on the jet ski and let you know when it will be ready."

"Ok, that sounds like a plan."

"I enjoyed myself out there with you. You really swim very good."

"Awww, thank you," Kia blushes. "I enjoyed myself as well."

As Kia is walking back to her umbrella, she sees Amani playing paddle ball with another guy on the beach. The first thing Kia does is check for her things in her bag. Thankfully, everything is intact just as she left it. "Ooh, thank you Lord!"

Kia takes her seat under the umbrella and lets the rays of sun that are peeking through dry her off and warm her skin. She checks her phone and there are no missed calls or text messages.

"Hey, so you made it back in?" Amani says as he comes over.

"Yes, I did. I had a really good time."

"That's good. It's nothing like having a good time to take your mind off of things."

"True....so true," Kia says as she exhales.

"Excuse me, I don't mean to interrupt," Javel says talking to Kia, "I talked to the guy running the jet ski and he says there is somebody on it now that should be back in about 15 minutes and then it will be ready alright?"

"Ok, cool," Kia says, "You are coming with me right?" she asks him.

"Of course I am, if that is what you want," Javel smirks.

"It's what I want."

"Ok, then. I will come and get you when it's ready."

"Perfect. See you in a few minutes then," Kia tells him before he walks off.

"So, you are going jet skiing too?" Amani asks.

"Yes, I am."

"You are having quite the day then. I see you," he laughs.

"Yes, I am. Yes, I am. I need this fun to help get my mind off of things," Kia says as she pauses for a moment of reflection.

"Well, that's good. I can help you too, you know."

"How so?" Kia asks. This ought to be good because all he has tried to offer Kia is sex or some type of way to touch her. She agreed to going out to the boardwalk, but it comes with the understanding that she is not doing anything sexual in nature with him.

"I can come over to your place and rub you down and rub your feet and kiss on your curves."

"That sounds nice but that is not what I need. Let's just go to the boardwalk and chill."

"Of course we are going to go there. I was trying to give you a little extra to help keep your mind on something positive."

"Well, thank you. But that's not what I need right now. Okay."

"I understand."

The two sit and chat for a little while before Javel comes over and gets Kia to go jet skiing. They walk off down to the end of the beach where the jet ski is parked. They put on their life jackets and climb on. Kia drives with Javel sitting behind her. He is sitting close but not too close that she is uncomfortable. They head South down the coast. It takes Kia all of about 1 minute to get warmed up driving this thing. She hits it almost full throttle and is taking each wave like a champ. As they pass popular beaches in Barbados Javel is pointing them out to her. They fly by St. Lawrence Gap, next passing Dover Beach which is down by Divi and there is literally nobody out there. Kia is quite shocked that the beach looks deserted. Next they pass by Maxwell beach before heading up towards Oistins. When they get in Oistins Bay, she and Javel switch just for a little while because he takes her up by the pier to see if they can see some sea turtles. They inch along barely revving the engine. They stayed in that spot about 5 minutes hoping to catch a glimpse of one but no luck.

Javel drives out back into the open water, and he and Kia switch back to Kia driving. Once again, she guns it. Even though she has never driven a motorcycle, she imagines it feels something like this. It is absolutely exhilarating! The further down the coast they go Kia notices the waves get bigger and bigger so she slows down a little bit. Javel tells her to gun it and take the waves head on. Each time she does that they go airborne for a second hitting each wave as they come down. It becomes a rhythmic motion, and Kia tries not to go into a trance. Javel scoots up just a little closer to Kia and tells her the turnaround is coming up. She slows down in anticipation of the turn but he tells her they have a little further up to go.

He asks her if she is having fun, and she yells yes over the roar of the engine. They drive a little farther up and he tells her to make a right turn and then to look how far out they are from the coast. Kia makes the turn and then looks over at the coast, and he is right. They are out far as hell. In this moment, fear tries to creep up, but she shakes it off. She reminds herself that she is out here with a trained lifeguard, and the coast is in sight which means if something awful happens she can swim to shore come hell or high water, literally.

"Daaaaayum!!" Kia exclaims. "How far out are we?"

"We are about 1/2 a mile out."

Kia heads in towards the coast some but Javel tells her to drive straight, heading back North. When they get somewhere between Dover and St.

Suddenly Single

Lawrence, Javel tells Kia to stop. Kia instantly became nervous, but he tells her that he needs to get in the water and rinse off for just a little bit because the salt from the water coupled with the wind from going so fast is stinging his face. Kia stops the jet ski and he gets off into the water.

"Oh, this feels so good. Do you want to come in and join me?" he asks.

"No, I'm good. I'm afraid that if I get in I won't be able to get back up here," she laughs.

"Oh, you will be fine. I can help you up."

"I'm good. I will just wait for you."

"Don't leave me now," he jokes.

"Of course not, I wouldn't do that," Kia smiles.

Javel stays in the water only for a minute before rejoining Kia on the jet ski. They head off in the direction of Accra beach and before Kia realized it, Javel was telling her they are back and to go ahead and turn up towards the beach but to go slow and barely push the throttle.

Once they arrive back, Kia's butt was tingling from all the vibration. She takes off her life jacket and heads down the beach ahead of Javel. She sees Amani out in the water as she approaches the umbrella. Once again the first thing she checks is her bag to make sure everything is intact, and it is. She takes her seat and decides to light up a cigarette. She sees Javel is still down the beach talking to one of the other lifeguards.

Amani spots her and comes in from the water. "Smoking is not good for you, you know," he tells her as he is walking up.

"I know," she says as she takes a puff. "I don't really smoke."

"So, what do you call this then?"

"Trying to enjoy my vacation that got turned upside down," Kia snaps but tries to laugh it off. "So, what's up?"

"Did you enjoy jet skiing?"

"I did. It was fun. I love it!!"

"That's cool. I've only done it a few times but I had a good time each time."

"That's good. I would think if you live here you would do it more often if you could."

"Yes, but local people don't really go to the beach that often because this is every day to them."

"I guess you are right. I just know that if I lived somewhere that looks like this I would go to the beach quite a bit.

"I can understand. Well listen, I am getting ready to head home and do some things before tonight. Can I have your number so I can let you know when I am on my way?"

"Sure you can," Kia gives him the number and tells him she will see him later. Kia chills for a few minutes before Javel catches up to her.

"Hey, so how did you like that?" he asks her.

"Oh man, it was wonderful! Better than I could imagine. We went far down the coast too!!"

"Well, I am glad you enjoyed it. And yes we did go far down the coast. Think about it, going for 15 minutes non-stop on a jet ski will take you a long ways."

"Yea, it will. I had fun though. I really enjoyed it."

"Well, I am glad you did. If you come back tomorrow I will take you out again."

"That sounds like a plan. It is my intention to come back."

"Cool. I would like that," he smiles.

"So, how much do I owe you for this day?" Kia asks.

"Just your phone number so I can keep in touch with you," he smiles.

Chapter 20

Kia returns from her massage feeling relaxed but looking like an oil slick. She can barely walk back from the spa because her feet are sliding so in her shoes. Since she took a shower before she left, she just wipes some of the greasiness off with a towel. She decides to keep on the same dress that she wore for the massage to wear tonight with Amani. She is relieved to be going out and doing something different to keep her distracted from thoughts of Levy.

Her phone startles her when it rings. It was Amani.

"Hello?"

"Hey, are you ready? This is Amani."

"Yes I'm ready."

"Ok good. I'm outside."

"What?! I thought you were going to call me when you were on your way."

"I forgot and before I knew it I was here. But I'm calling now," he says in an attempt to make light of the fact he forgot to call.

Kia was not amused. "Ok, I'm coming out."

Kia is annoyed because this is not what they agreed on. She intentionally takes her time gathering her things and leaving out of the door. When she opens the door she can see him standing next to his vehicle in the middle of the driveway area. He greets her with a hug and she half reciprocates it. She is still annoyed but she quickly gets over it because she is taking a risk getting in the car with him on this island. He is virtually a stranger, and he can do anything to her. She realizes that, so she prays for her safety.

"So, where are we going to go this evening?" Kia asks.

"Well I said I would take you to the boardwalk. So we can start there and then see what else we may want to do. I know what I want to do."

"And what might that be?" Kia asks with a slight attitude because she feels where this is going.

"I want to make you feel good and help take your mind off of your situation."

"That's nice, but that is not what I want. I want to have a good time and see this boardwalk. I have heard it goes a long way."

"It does go quite a ways. We are going to go over by The Gap."

Kia was a little relieved to hear they are going by The Gap because this is somewhere she is familiar with. It takes them no time to get there from where she is staying. Before she knows it they are turning by Café Sol. There is a little bit of traffic on The Gap but not much. It feels awkward to Kia riding in a car back here because she is normally walking along this road.

"So, how often do you come back here?" she asks.

"Well, when I'm here I come every now and then. Not that often though."

"Oh, ok. So when was the last time you were here for work prior to this time?"

"Last year. I pretty much work the Caribbean."

"Well, that's what's up then. I would love to have a job like that!!"

"Yea, it's pretty cool."

They arrive at the parking lot where they are going to park. As they pull in, Kia hears some god awful singing, and she figures they are doing karaoke. When she gets out of the car, she can see that is exactly what is going on. As they are walking up, Amani reaches out and grabs her hand to hold it as if they were a couple. There is no way in hell Kia is having that. She does not want to hold his hand. She doesn't jerk it away right away because she doesn't want to embarrass him because people are looking at them as they walk up, so she switches her bag to the other shoulder so she would have to let his hand go. He tries to get it back but Kia clutched to the strap of her bag.

"You don't want to hold my hand?" he asks.

"No. I don't know you like that and besides we are not a couple."

"Aww, come on. Don't make me look bad out here," he tells her as they are looking for somewhere to sit.

Kia couldn't tell if he is playing or if he is serious so she takes it for serious. "You are looking the best out here just because I am with you. Don't get it twisted now," she quips.

As they are walking along, she is noticing there seems to be nothing but couples out here. They decide to go and walk along the beach even though it is dark. They pass a couple on the deck doing everything but having intercourse, and Kia is amazed at their lack of regard for the other people around them or for themselves for that matter.

"Well damn, I guess they don't care," Kia comments.

"Oh no, you will see all kinds of shit out here. It goes down on the Boardwalk, all along the Boardwalk," he informs her.

"I can see that. Is that why you wanted to bring me out here?"

"No. Of course it is not. I wanted to bring you out here so you could see it and we can relax for a bit. Maybe you might even let me rub you down."

"I just had a rub down. I'm good," Kia is trying to keep from going off.

All of the lounge chairs are chained up by the tree but there is one on the very top that is free. Amani manages to get it down so they can have somewhere to sit.

"So, how are you enjoying being out here with me?" he asks her.

"It's okay. I just have a lot on my mind you know."

"I can understand. Like I told you earlier, I have been through this before so I know what it's like. When my girl left me, I was devastated and heartbroken. I basically had to cut all communications with her to get over it. It helped that there was somebody there to help me pick up the pieces. That girl would come over and cook for me and massage me and give me head. That would help ease mind. Then I would fuck the shit out of her. Pardon my words. But that is what helped me, and I want to help you."

Kia held it for as long as she could. "Look, it is awful that she left you and you were heartbroken, and I'm glad that you had someone there to help you move on and pick up the pieces, but that is not what I need. Throughout this entire time you have not once asked me what it is I need or want. Instead, you are trying to make me feel better the way you want to. That is not what I need. I don't know how many times I have said that but not one time have you heard me because you keep telling me about what you want to do for me. Or should I say what you want to do to me. What about what I need?"

"You're right," he said without hesitation. "What is it that you need?"

"Right now I need a pineapple soda, and I need this. To get out, to do something different, to sit here and listen to the ocean at night and hope the crabs don't bite me. This is what I need."

"Well, ok then. That's what we will do. We will sit here and enjoy the night breeze coming off the water. How's that?"

"That sounds just fine, but umm, I still need that pineapple soda too!!"

"We will get your pineapple soda on the way back."

"Sounds like a plan," Kia says to him.

The two of them sit there for a little while longer engaging in casual conversation. They even snap a few pictures, hoping the flash worked good on the camera being they were in darkness. They decide to walk down the beach a little ways before going back to the car. As promised on the way back to the room, they stop at a petro station for Kia's pineapple soda.

"Hey, do you have some change because the smallest I have is a $50?" Amani asks as he pulls out a Ziploc bag full of money from under the seat.

Kia is trying really hard not to be annoyed at him in this moment, but she can't help it. She looks at him and rolls her eyes. "No I don't have any change, but this is a gas station, they should have some."

"Oh, you're right, you're right. They should."

Kia knows this is his way of showing her he has some money, but she doesn't give a shit about him or his money at this point. She really wants to just ditch him at the gas station and go to the Subway across the parking lot to get a snack. But she doesn't. He goes in to get her soda and comes out with something for himself as well.

Suddenly Single

"Thank you," Kia says as she cracks open the bottle and takes a long swig while they are backing out. "This really hits the spot."

"You're welcome. You know I would love to take you to Cabo San Lucas one weekend."

Kia almost spit soda all on her lap. "What?" she says shocked.

"Yea, I would love to just buy you a ticket and have you meet me in Cabo one weekend."

"That sounds nice, but I don't even know you."

"I know we don't know each other but after we get to know each other maybe this will be something that we can do."

"Maybe," Kia says as she looks out the window into the darkness. She knows damn good and well she is not going to Cabo with him not now, not ever. She is not attracted to him, and for a trip like that, she would have to give it up. She just doesn't want to with him.

In no time at all, they were back at the place where she is staying. When they pull up, Kia barely lets the car stop before flinging open the door to get out. He comes around to her side of the car and attempts to walk her to the door but she is already there. She tells him good night and thanks again for the outing and the soda before going in.

"You're welcome. I will call you tomorrow," he tells her.

"Ok," she says as she closes the door. She has never been so happy to be back in this 700 square foot space. Amani just did not rub her right way. She looks at her phone and realizes the whole day has passed and -- *incoming call from Levy*-- she had not heard from Levy. "Hmmph, speak of the devil. Hello?" she answers.

"Hey. How are you?"

"I'm fine Levy. How are you?"

"I'm ok. Listen do you want to hang out tomorrow? I will have a little bit of time, and I can take you around."

Kia knows she should probably not even talk to Levy much less entertain the thought of hanging out with him, but she did still love him. "Umm, I guess so Levy. What time will you pick me up?"

"I will get you in the morning around 9:30-10:00. Is that okay?"

"That's fine. I will be ready."

"Ok. Have a good night."

"Thanks. You too," she tells him.

She has told Levy good night a thousand times before over the phone; however this time felt strange because they are on the same island only a few miles apart. They are so close yet so far.

"Who is it?" Kia asks knowing it was Levy.

"It's me," he says.

Kia opens the door to let him in. "Good morning, how are you?"

"I'm fine," he says as he walks in. "You've been smoking in here?" he asks.

"I did last night but not today. Are you ready?" she was ready to leave because if they would've lingered in there she couldn't trust herself to not try and make a move on him.

"Yes, we can go."

They get in the car and start off down the road. "So, what made you want to see me today Levy?"

"Well, I miss you, and I wanted to see you. I have some time today and I want to spend it with you."

"I see. Okay." Kia couldn't help but feel a little mushy inside. She does still love this man and wants to be with him. "Well, for what it's worth, I'm glad you did call me. So, where are we headed to?"

"I'm just going to take you around to some scenic spots today."

"That sounds cool. I'm excited."

"Me too, I'm glad you said yes," he tells her as he reaches over and rubs her thigh under her short skirt.

The two drive for what seems like forever. Clearly they are on a side of the island in which Kia has never seen. They stop at a gas station to get some drinks to have on hand in case they get thirsty. "Do you have everything you need?" Levy asks.

"I do," Kia says as she gets in the car.

"Good," he says as he looks at her. She catches his gaze and she gets caught up in the moment and just like a scene from a movie the two engage in a passionate embrace. It is like they have not seen each other in 10 months. This is the embrace Kia was expecting at the airport when she arrived. She is breathless when they finish kissing; her hot spot is throbbing and her legs are shaking. Levy had a rush of blood that caused a bulge in his pants, and Kia couldn't help but grab it. "You better stop before we give the people a show."

"I don't care about giving them a show because they don't know me, and I won't see them again," Kia says as she starts kissing his neck.

They kiss again before Levy finally declares they have to keep moving if they are going to see some more of this island. Kia agrees, and she straightens up in her seat and puts on her seatbelt. As they turn out of the gas station and onto the road, Kia notices that this part of the island looks deserted compared to the area where she is staying.

She and Levy are chatting about different things. Kia does not want to bring down the mood by talking about the break up. She just wants to enjoy spending time with her man....well ex-man. Just as she is taking in the view of the water in the distance, they make a right turn into what looks like the middle of a field. The road is just a path through the field.

"Umm Levy, where are we going?"

"You will see. I promise you will like it."

"But Levy we turned into the middle of a field!"

Levy laughs at Kia because he knows while this does indeed look like a field they are actually on a road. "Kia relax. I promise you will like it." Just as he said that, the road veered to the left and Kia is met with an absolutely breathtaking view. Before them is a narrow tree lined path where the tree limbs meet in the middle and the turquoise blue water is in the distance.

"Awww," Kia gasps. "Levy, this is beautiful!!!"

"I told you that you would like it."

"You were right. I do like it! It is absolutely gorgeous. What is it called?"

"This is Foul Bay."

"Oh, ok. This is nice!"

The two drive down to the end of the path and they make a left turn down another little path that leads them to a tree lined beach. They are the only people out there besides one local man that looks as if he is washing something in the water. There is an overturned row boat out there that complimented the picturesque beauty. Kia steals a kiss from Levy before getting out of the car to soak up this area. Her mind has plummeted right to the gutter because she sees nothing but opportunity for a naughty romp. It doesn't help that Levy has pulled out his log and is relieving himself on the side of the car.

"You want me to hold that for you?" Kia asks with a devilish smirk.

"I don't think you have enough hands," Levy chuckles.

"Uhh, I think two is enough!" Kia laughs.

The two walk down towards the water out from under the trees but they don't go too far because Kia does not want to get too much sand in her shoes and feet. She stands silently looking at the sheer beauty of each turquoise colored wave as it comes crashing on the shore. Levy stands behind her and puts his hand on her shoulders and kisses her on the neck not saying a word. Kia starts pulsating in that spot between her thighs, and she can feel Levy poking her with something other than his hands because they are on her shoulders.

She reaches back and begins to rub on his thigh until she finds the thing that is poking her. She strokes it up and down as she is trying to undo his zipper. He gently pulls her and they walk backwards until they reach the overturned boat. He faces her towards the boat and places her hands on the top of it. He spreads her legs then he raises her skirt and much to his surprise she is not wearing any panties. "MMMM," he moans as he slides one of his fingers into her slippery threshold. "Ahh," she gasps as he works the finger back and forth making the come here motion inside of her. She can't help but let out a loud moan. He kisses the back of her neck and then each of her ears. As he is doing this he is unzipping his pants and before she knows it he has replaced his finger with his manhood and Kia melts right on top of him. She slides down onto him so there is no space between their two middle sections.

Neither one of them say a word. The sound of their love fills the air. Kia reaches her goal first and then shortly thereafter Levy reaches his. The two of them somewhat collapse on the boat. They look at each other in the eyes lovingly and Levy breaks the silence. "I love you Kia."

"I love you too Levy."

Before leaving Foul Bay, the two take several pics together and some individually. Kia wants to capture this moment in her life.

"So, where to now?" Kia asks.

"Well, I know you wanted to see where The Crane is so we will drive by there and I can show you where Crane Beach is as well."

"Sounds like a plan!"

They drive a little further up the road making a couple of turns. It is not much on this side of the island at all. The only eating spot Kia sees is a little deli seemingly in the middle of nowhere. There are no clubs or restaurants on this side at all. They turn into a non-descript driveway where they are met by a guard in a guard shack. After a little chat, he lets them drive through The Crane even though they are not staying on the property. Kia is surprised to see that this hotel is virtually in the midst of nowhere on the island. It is not close to anything. It is very beautiful from what she can see from the car. The lawn is manicured to perfection.

After they leave out of The Crane a little further down the road, they turn down a rather narrow street that almost looks like an alley of trees. Levy parallel parks the car, and they get out and head towards the water which Kia can see in the distance. Levy leads her by the hand down a little path of rocks in which they have to go down and then back up. When they reach the top of the rocks, there is nothing but water straight ahead as far as the eye can see.

"You see over here to the right is Crane Beach, and just beyond that is the hotel."

"I see. So that is the famed Crane Beach." Kia snaps a couple of pics of the beach so she could show her co-worker who came here on her first honeymoon. "What beach is this over here?" she says looking to her left.

"This is just another beach. I don't know if it has a name."

Kia's mind plummets a little bit because it is nobody on this beach and part of it is under a cliff but it is still open where you can see. She wouldn't mind another round with Levy but this area is more out in the open. The two take a few pictures on top of the rocks where they are standing before making their way back to the car hand in hand.

"That was fun. I had a good time," Kia tells Levy.

"I had fun too!"

"So, where are we headed now?" Kia asks.

"Well, I have to do some work on my auntie's house so I figure we could go over there."

"Ok, cool. What are you doing to her house?"

"Building her a new one on the lot in front of her old one."

Kia is instantly turned on again because a man that is good with his hands is sexy to her. As they drive, they are engaging in lighthearted conversation, and Kia can't help but be a little sad. She is leaving in 2 days, and she is leaving without the official proposal she came for. She tries not to think about it too much because if she does she will start to cry, and she did not want to ruin this day with tears of sadness.

They twist and turn through the streets of the south coast of Barbados until they reach his aunt's house. Almost immediately, he starts fussing and complaining as soon as they pull up in the yard.

"What's wrong?" Kia asks.

"I told Ian to start mixing the concrete so it would be ready when we got here, and he has not started yet. Ian!!" he yells as he walks up to the door.

Ian opens the door and the two exchange some heated words that Kia cannot understand because they both are talking fast and in the local dialect. Kia stands there looking at the two of them. She wants to laugh, but she doesn't. Instead she just watches them and shook her head.

"I'm sorry about that Kia. How are you? Good to see you again."

"I'm okay Ian. How are you?"

"I'm doing okay. How is my cousin treating you?"

Kia wants to tell him the truth that he had broken up with her 3 days ago and shattered her heart in a million pieces but instead she puts on her game face. "He's treating me fine." She looks over at Levy, and he looks relieved that she did not make a smart comment or let on that they broke up.

Levy shows her around the work that he had completed and tells her what he will be working on while they are here today. Kia is impressed that he is literally building the house from the ground up. He finds an old car seat for her to sit on, and he gets a towel from inside the house to cover it so she won't get dirty. He makes sure she is squared away before he begins mixing the concrete. This is boring as hell to Kia, but she doesn't mind because she is with Levy.

She checks her phone for a Wi-Fi signal, but there is not one in this part of the island so she can't get on Facebook. She just decides to sit and watch Levy and Ian work. While she is watching them work, she gets turned on thinking about their unplanned tryst earlier. Thankfully Levy's aunt comes home, and it snaps her out of the naughty thoughts she is thinking.

"Kia come meet my aunt." Levy tells her as he is walking over to help her up from her seat.

"Hello. I'm Kia," she says as she extends her arm to shake her hand.

"Nice to meet you Kia. I am Aileen. I am Levy's mother's sister."

Kia assumed she is his mother's sister because she looks just like Naomi and besides he does not really know his father. "Oh, ok well, it is very nice to meet you," Kia says.

"How has my nephew been treating you?" she asks.

What is it with that question? Kia wonders. *He has been treating me fine. Just fine*, she smiles knowing that is a half-truth.

"That's good because he talks about you all the time," she reveals.

"Does he now?" Kia says sounding shocked.

"Yes, he does." She tells her as the two of them go back over to where Kia was sitting. Aileen sits on a couple of cinder blocks that are stacked up there next to where Kia is resting. The two ladies engage in friendly conversation. Kia learns that Aileen works at a chicken processing plant there on the island, and she invites her to come and take a tour to see how they actually kill the chickens. Kia passes but tells her she will consider it for her next trip.

After a few minutes of the two ladies talking, Kia decides to send Levy a text: `Come over here and kiss me...`

She sees him pull out his phone and read the text. He doesn't even look at her, rather he puts the phone back in his pocket and walks straight over to her and plants a big one on her lips, right there in front of everybody. She is a little shocked that he does this, but she is happy he did.

They stay out there until they run out of supplies, which is another couple of hours. Levy makes some progress on the wall he is constructing, and the house is really starting to take shape. As they are leaving, Kia gives Aileen a hug and tells her it was nice to meet her and she hopes to see her again.

"So, where are we off to now?" Kia asks as they get in the car.

"Well, I need to stop by Pearl Gardens to check on the pool. Then we can go to the store to get the seasoning for you to take back."

"Cool. At least I will get to see the lights in the pool if they are working."

"Yep, and they should be working."

It takes them a little bit of time to get to Pearl Gardens because traffic has started to pick up, and the fact that most of their route is only two lanes does not help the situation. That is fine with Kia though because this gave her more time with Levy. At this point, she does not care that they are no longer together officially. She still wants to be with him, and for right now, she is.

When they arrive at Pearl Gardens, they look at each other and indulge in a kiss that made Kia's toes curl. She is thinking they can go in the house and go for what they know, or they can stay out here because there is not anyone back here and it is privately fenced off from the neighbors. She resists temptation and lets Levy do what he came here to do.

He goes in the house and pulls the chair for her to sit in if she so chooses. At this moment, she decides to stand for a while and watch him. She walks around the property and finds some shells that would look great as a necklace. She decides to take them so her friend Liz who makes jewelry can put them together for her.

Levy finishes the work he is doing and he goes to the shed and flips the switch to cut on the lights in the pool. It is getting dark so Kia is able to see the full effect. They change colors every few seconds creating a sea of changing colors. The purple was her favorite.

"You like it?" Levy asks.

"I do! It is very pretty. I could definitely see having a pool party or something out here."

"Yea, that would be cool, but this is the pool for all six houses here. It doesn't belong to just one person you know."

"Yea, I know but it would still be the perfect setting for a party."

"Well we better get going."

"Ok," Kia says solemnly. She does not want this day to end. She has enjoyed every minute of it.

"What's the matter?" he asks her.

"I just don't want the day to end," she says as she is choking back tears. Levy can sense she is about to cry.

"Don't cry. You're going to mess up that pretty face of yours," he says as he kisses her on the forehead.

This makes a tear fall which opens the flood gates. Levy grabs her and puts his arms around her and holds her close until she can get herself together. "Are you ready to go get some seasoning?" he teases.

"I'm ready. I'm sorry for crying it's just that this day has been amazing and I don't want it to come to an end especially knowing that you are going home to another woman and that I am leaving here in a couple of days without you and without the future we used to talk about."

"Listen, I told you I am not giving up on us. I am going to get myself together so we can be together."

"Ok, Levy," she sniffs.

The pair get in the car, *her car,* and head off towards the grocery store. They stop at the store they went to before in Oistins. Kia almost starts crying again thinking about the first time they came in here, but she holds it together. He takes her to get the seasoning she needs and wants. They get some wet seasonings and plenty of dry ones. They pay for them and head back to the car.

When they arrive back at Kia's room, Levy walks her to the door. She opens the door and he follows her in to make sure there is no one in the room, and that it is safe.

"Thank you for today," she tells him.

"You're more than welcome. Thank you for agreeing to come. I enjoyed it."

"Levy, do you have to go? Don't you want a repeat of earlier?"

He looks at her deeply in her eyes almost piercing her soul, "I would love to have a repeat of earlier, but I have to go." He gives her a deep kiss then turns and walks towards the door. "I will call you tomorrow."

Suddenly Single

Kia is crushed, but she knows this is what has to be done.

Chapter 21

Kia awakes to a new day. She follows her same morning routine as she has in the days prior to this one. When she gets to the beach, she looks for Javel the lifeguard but does not see him. Maybe he is off today. She isn't sure, but she isn't going to let that stop her from having a good day.

As she is getting settled under her same umbrella, her phone rings before she could even turn on some music.

"Hello?"

"Good morning, sleepy head. How are you?"

"Levy, you are two hours late. I have been up!" she jokingly snaps.

"I figured so. What are you doing? Are you at the beach?"

"Yes, I am. Can't you hear the waves?"

"Yes, I can. Listen, I was calling to see what time your flight leaves tomorrow," he asks.

"It leaves at 3 something. I don't know the exact time off hand. Why?"

"Well, I was going to take you to the airport. So I guess you would need to be there about 1:00 then."

"Yes, that would be about right."

"Ok, well I will be there to get you at 12:45. Ok?"

"Ok. I will be ready."

Suddenly Single

"Cool, well I will talk to you later then, ok? If for some reason I don't speak to you again today, just know that I will be there to get you tomorrow."

"Ok, Levy. Thank you but I hope I get to talk to you again."

"I know. I will try. Bye."

"Bye."

Kia hangs up her phone and proceeds with getting settled. To kick off her musical interlude today, she chooses *Don't Disturb This Groove* by The System. She follows this song with *Heaven Help Me* by Deon Estus featuring George Michael. She has to listen to these two songs back to back. She has them on a CD like that and ever since then, she has to listen to them together.

Kia is enjoying the music and the scenery. She is still a little sore from all of the swimming the day before yesterday. She decides to take a dip in the water because it is too inviting. Besides, she has to make up for not getting in the water yesterday. For the first time since she has been here, she gets in the water and is not interrupted by anybody trying to talk to her. She enjoys this and takes advantage of the time by reflecting on her trip here.

She still cannot believe that she took a trip this far by herself and that she in fact ended up by herself. She is grateful for the people she has met but she is hurt by the ultimate outcome of her visit. This is not how it was supposed to be. She should be getting ready to leave tomorrow with a ring on her finger and a completed Form I-129F in hand. Instead, she is leaving with a broken heart.

She stays in the water until she is wrinkled before deciding to get out. Once back in her lounge chair, she lights up one of her last cigarettes and flags down the guy to order a drink. This time she orders a piña colada. She looks at her phone and she does not have any missed calls, then she remembers that Phillip was supposed to be calling her to take her around the island. She decides to give him a call because it is getting late in the afternoon, and if they are going anywhere, then she needs time to get ready.

"Hello, good afternoon?"

"Good afternoon Phillip, how are you?"

"Not so good."

"What's wrong?" Kia asks out of genuine concern.

"Well, I was not able to rent the car. Then my son was having some problems with his class enrollment at school so I am up here now trying to get that straightened out. I'm just frustrated."

"Well, I can understand. Try not to be frustrated. I just thought I would check on you because I haven't heard from you, and I know that is not like you. I know you are a man of your word."

"I hear you. I'm trying not to be frustrated, but I really wanted to take you around."

"It's okay Phillip. Maybe the next time I come here you can take me."

"That sounds like a plan to me," he seemed to perk up just a bit. "Listen, will you need a ride to the airport tomorrow?"

"No, I have a ride to the airport but I thank you, and I appreciate you for being willing to help me out."

"Well, you know I will do anything for you," he tells her.

"I know Phillip, and I appreciate that. Thank you. Well listen, I will let you go so you can handle your business. Call me when you can."

"I will do that. Goodbye now."

"Goodbye."

Well, Kia was not going to get to tour any more of the island so she relaxes and enjoys the rest of her day at the beach.

It is about 7:30 when Kia wakes up from her nap. She had a long day at the beach trying to make up for the day before and subconsciously trying to soothe her hurt soul. The water was her elixir. She is feeling a little hungry so she decides to go down to Jus Grillin and get some of the chicken and potatoes she had before. She decides to try and eat well tonight because she leaves tomorrow and she does not eat big on the days she travels.

While she is eating she decides to call Javel. She was hoping he was at the beach today, but she did not see him.

"Hello, good night," he answers on the second ring.

"Good night. This is Kia, from the beach, how are you?"

"I know who you are. I locked your number in my phone. I am doing good this evening, how are you?"

"I'm okay. I'm just eating my dinner here at Jus Grillin," she says in between bites.

"Oh, okay. So what are you going to do when you leave there?"

"Just go back to the room and pack and get ready to leave tomorrow."

"Ok. Well maybe I can come and help you pack. I would like to see you before you go."

"Ok, well that will be fine. I should be back in about 15-20 minutes or so."

"Ok, that's perfect. I will be there in about 30-40 minutes."

"Do you remember where I'm staying?" she asks.

"Yes, I remember."

"Ok, cool. I'm in number 23. See you in a few then."

"Ok, then. Goodbye."

Kia hangs up her phone and almost as soon as she does it rings again. "Hello?"

"What up wit' it?" Mack says on the other end.

"Not too much just finishing up dinner. I'm a little sad to be leaving tomorrow, but at the same time, I can't wait to get back."

"I can dig it. I was just checking on you to make sure you are ok. I intended to call you before now, but I've been busy."

"I can understand that. How are the kids?" she asks.

"They are good, getting ready for school tomorrow."

"Ok, cool. Well kiss them for me."

"Will do. Will do. Well okay I will let you go. Have a safe trip tomorrow, and holla at me when you get back."

"I definitely will. Thank you for checking on me."

"No problem. I told you, you my girl," he reassures.

"I know. Thank you."

"Alright, I will talk to you later."

"Bye."

This made Kia feel good. It's good to know that she has friends that care about her and her well-being. She finishes her food and gathers her things to head back to her room. She wants to see Javel, but she hopes he does not try anything because she really is not in the mood for it.

She makes it back to her room and waits for Javel to arrive. She turns on the TV and starts packing while she waits for him. She looks at each of her pretty lacy panties that she bought to wear for Levy that she never got to wear because of what happened. She is glad the truth came out but part of her wishes he would've spared her the pain. She is not ready to let go of the happiness that he made her feel. She is able to pack up most of her belongings before there is a knock at the door.

"Who is it?" she asks.

"Javel."

"Good evening," she says as she opens the door to let him in. She is a little taken back because he looks different in his street clothes...better...but he still looks older to her. He says he is 42 but she is not so sure he is telling the truth. She does recognize the fact that he spends most of his days in the sun and that can take a toll on your skin.

"Good evening. How are you this evening?" he says once he is inside.

"I'm doing good. Have a seat."

He takes a seat on the futon and she sits on the bed.

"So, how have you been?" he asks her. "I looked for you at the beach on Monday but I didn't see you."

"I've been okay. Yea, I didn't come to the beach on Monday. I looked for you today, but I didn't see you."

"No, I was off today. I was hoping to see you again because I was going to take you back out snorkeling."

"Aww, I hate I missed it. But thank you though."

"It's no problem, anything for you," he winks.

Kia ignores the wink because she does not feel like engaging in anything remotely sexual unless it is with Levy. The two sit and talk about all sorts of things from stretching your back out to the differences of swimming in the ocean and a pool. He stays for about an hour before getting up to leave.

"Thank you for coming to see me tonight," Kia tells him as she walks him to the door.

"Thank you for letting me come."

"You are welcome. I wanted to see you."

"I'm glad because I wanted to see you too. Listen, don't be a stranger now," he tells her as he gives her a hug.

"I won't. I promise."

"I'm going to hold you to that. Have a safe trip tomorrow."

"I will. Thank you. Bye," she says as she waves at him.

"Bye."

Suddenly Single

Kia retreats back into her room and makes a sweep of the room packing the last of her items with the exception of the things she will need in the morning. This is bittersweet for her. She is getting ready to leave this beautiful island, and she is definitely not leaving the same way she came.

Chapter 22

Kia wakes up early. She can't slack today because this is her last day in paradise, and she wants to take advantage of every minute. She puts on her swimsuit and cover up and quickly heads off to breakfast. For the last time on this trip she orders the same breakfast as she has had each morning. This time she decides to spring for two fruit punches instead of one since refills are not free.

Once she finishes breakfast she heads across the street to the beach. She makes it there so early that the chair guy has not even begun to put out the chairs. She sits her bag down where "her" chair would be and she disrobes down to her swimsuit. She walks towards the water expecting it to be chilly since it is still early morning but much to her surprise it is quite warm.

She wades out knee deep, then waist deep, then chest deep. She soaks up each gentle wave as it hits her body. She does not want to leave her island paradise but she needs to get home so she can start to heal and process what has happened here.

She only stays in the water about 30 minutes before getting out. As she is drying off, she decides to snap a few photos to capture her last day at the beach. She does not do any selfies because she looks too bad having just gotten out of the water. When completely dry and clothed, she stops and takes one last long look at the sugar white sand and rolling turquoise waves before making her way back across the street.

She gets in the room and she hangs up her swimsuit for it to dry as much as possible before putting it in her suitcase. She takes a shower and packs up the last of her toiletries and puts on her clothes when finished. She looks at the time and sees that she has a little while before Levy picks her up so she decides to walk out back and take some more pictures. There is a tree in the back that looks like a big Christmas tree that is leaning. She snaps a picture of that and some of the flowers that were in pots by the back door. She also takes some of the water in the distance so she can remember how close she was to the beach.

When she finishes taking the pictures she goes back inside and watches a little TV to kill the rest of time before Levy gets there. *Excuse me boss you have a text message*: Hey Babe, I am on my way to get you.

Kia replies: Ok, I am ready.

About 20 minutes later there is a knock at the door.

"Who is it?" she figures it is Levy, but she asks anyway.

"Levy."

"Hey good afternoon," she says as she is opening the door.

"Good afternoon," he says before kissing her on the lips. Kia notices that he is dressed in the outfit she brought for him. As she suspected, the pants are a little bit long on him, but he looks nice in it none-the-less. "Are you ready?" he asks her.

"I am. My suitcase is here with my purse and my bag," she says pointing to the table where they are laying.

"You know I came right on time because if I would have come early we would have been doing it," he tells her as he is walking closer and closer towards her. He is so close she can smell his breath. Thank God, it smells fresh.

"I know," she says kissing him, "but you know we could still do it. My plane does not leave until 3:40 so we have some time," she says in between kisses.

"Are you sure you want to?"

"How is this for sure?" Kia says as she takes off her panties and skirt all in one fair swoop.

"Wow. I guess you are ready," he says as his pants drop to the floor.

"I stay ready." And with that their bodies collide in a fast and furious yet rhythmic motion much like the waves crashing out on the shore. With each stroke Kia can feel every inch of Levy and the passion between them is radiating off of their skin.

Before turning Kia over on her stomach Levy whispers, "I left the car in the middle of the driveway. No other cars can get by."

"Let them go around," she can barely get the words out because she is practically breathless.

Once on her stomach it was not too much longer before Levy reached the goal ahead of her. She isn't surprised because it takes longer than 10 minutes to really get her going. Levy wipes off and redresses immediately then runs out to check on the car.

"Give me 5 minutes Levy; I just need to clean up really fast."

"Ok, but we should get going."

Kia cleans herself up in record time before taking one last sweep around the room to make sure she has not forgotten anything. She even calls in Levy to look around. As instructed, she leaves the key in the drawer and locks the door knob lock before walking out. If she left anything, it's too late now.

Levy has loaded up her luggage in the trunk and Kia gets in the car. She is overwhelmingly sad. Part of her wants to go, but the other part wants to stay, not because this is like heaven on earth but because she does not want to leave Levy, not like this anyway. As they are enroute to the airport, Levy breaks the silence. "So, where do we stand?"

"What do you mean where do we stand?" Kia asked sounding perplexed.

"You know what I mean Kia. C'mon."

"Levy look, as far as I'm concerned, we are broken up. I am a single woman. You need to get yourself together and when you do, look me up."

"So, you are just giving up on us like that?"

"What do you mean giving up on us? You gave up on us the second you decided not to tell me the truth about your situation. I do love you because love does not die in a day, and I sincerely hope you get yourself together. This is not what I wanted. I want us to be together, but we cannot do that as long as you are in her house."

"Fair enough, but I love you, and I want to be with you."

"Well, get yourself together then, Levy."

"So what are you going to tell your friends? You can tell them I had a little dick or something so you broke up with me."

"I will tell them nothing of the sort. I'm going to tell them we broke up. What does it matter anyway because we are not together?"

"You're right, but I just don't want them to think badly of me."

"Levy, why do you care what they think? Those are *my* friends."

"Yes, but you never know one day we may end up back together."

"Hmmm....Ok."

The two ride along in silence. Kia knows she will be on the verge of tears once they get ready to say goodbye. She tries to think happy thoughts like getting back to her family and seeing her dog, Sisi. She looks at the scenery and tries to etch it permanently in her mind because she does not know when she will be back to this beautiful place. As they turn in the airport, she feels the lump in her throat forming and tries with all her might to choke it down.

"What time does your plane leave?"

"At 3:40 so they will probably start to board a little after 3:00."

Levy looks at the time and sees that it is only 1:20. "Ok. Well since you have a while and I have a little time, I will sit with you before you go in if that is ok."

"I would like that," this helps Kia to swallow that lump a little easier.

They pull up into the airport, and Kia gets out of the car. Levy gets her luggage out and tells her that he is going to park the car. Kia checks in her luggage and takes a seat on a bench. Eventually, she sees Levy walking back across the parking lot.

"Hey, sorry it took so long but I had to find somewhere cheap to park."

"It's okay. Do you want to sit at those tables over there?"

"That's fine. I want to go in Chefette and get a Roti first. Do you want anything?"

"No, thank you. I will go find a table for us to sit at while you are doing that."

"Ok."

Kia and Levy walk over to towards the food court, and Kia finds a table while Levy is getting his food. Kia looks around at the people sitting here, and they all look like they are ready to go. She is definitely sad to be going back to reality especially since this is not the new reality she had envisioned for herself. It is no time before Levy is walking up to the table with his food. He sits across from Kia and the two engage in meaningless conversation while he is eating, but all she could think about is leaving. Before Kia knew it, her face is wet with tears. Levy comes over and sits next to her and puts his arm around her so she can lean her head on his chest.

"Kia, why are you crying?"

"Because I don't want to leave," she sniffs. "I don't want to leave you. I love you, and I want us to be together."

"I love you too!" he says kissing her on her forehead. "And I want us to be together too. I believe our paths crossed for a reason and I will work hard to get myself together so that we can be together. I want to spend the rest of my life with you raising our son," he tells her as he rubs her stomach.

"Who says we are having a boy?" she jokes feeling a little better but not enough to stop the tears from flowing.

"You know I want a son," he chuckles.

"Well, it's up to you to send over the right chromosome to make a boy you know."

"I suppose it is," he stops and looks at her.

"What is it?" she asks him.

"You are so beautiful," he admires her.

"Thank you. We should take a couple of pics before I leave."

So Kia pulls out her phone and she and Levy snap a couple of selfies. They look at the pics and he just stares at her again before gently grabbing her face and pulling it close to his. He very slowly begins to kiss her like he is not going to see her again. Kia's eyes are swollen with tears and her face is flushed from being drained of all fluid through her eyes. When the kiss is over, Kia quickly grabs a napkin to soak up the tears from her face and neck before they stain her clothes.

"Kia, you are going to mess up your pretty face. Look at me." Kia looks up at him.

"I know I must look like a wreck out here in the airport. I know the people around us are wondering what the hell is going on."

"I don't care about them. I only care about you," he says as he kisses her again on the forehead. "Listen, I'm going to leave because I have to go pick up Ian so we can do some work on the house. Sit here for a few minutes and get yourself together. Then go to the bathroom and put some water on your face because you have tissue stuck under those pretty eyes of yours."

"No, Levy I cannot sit here and watch you walk away. We will leave together. I will go my way, and you will go yours."

"Ok. If that is what you want we can do that."

The two get up from the table and walk down to the edge of the sidewalk in front of Chefette.

"Well, I guess this is it," Kia says still with what seems like and endless flow of tears running down her face.

"I guess it is," Levy says as he puts his arms around her giving her one last hug.

After they break from the hug, Kia has a hard time swallowing the fact that this might be the last time she sees him and asks for one more hug which he gives her. This time they stand there for a minute letting it all sink in.

When they finally pull apart, they look deeply into each other's eyes. Levy kisses her on the nose. "I love you."

"I love you too, Levy."

And with that he turns and walks away. Kia, not bearing to see him walk away, turns the opposite direction and walks towards the door to security. She glances back just once to see that he had made it almost all the way across the parking lot and what she really hopes is not out of her life forever.

Chapter 23

Kia feels overwhelmed at the whirlwind she was caught in while in Barbados. When she is on her flight home she cries most of the way back to the United States. She is eventually able to make it through the day without crying. Breaking up with Levy is like mourning a death. In a way it is a death, the death of her relationship, the death of her happiness, and the death to the future she wanted with him.

Kia resumed writing in her journal she started when she first met Levy. This helps her channel her emotions and get them out. She intended to give it to him when she went but she forgot it at home which is fine because she will pick up where she left off and give it to him at some point in the future.

> **September 15, 2013**
> *Hey Levy. I hope all is well with you. A LOT has happened since I last wrote you 6 months ago. I just wanted to tell you that even though we are "not together" anymore, I really miss you. You know, I get it. I get that you had to self-preserve. Nobody wants to be homeless especially when their nearest preferred second option is 2554 miles away. I just wish you would've been upfront with me and told me the truth from the beginning. It makes me question everything that you have told me, every "I love you"...every "I miss you"...every "I want to see you"....the marriage proposal....the plans for our future. It makes me wonder was it all lies. I don't want to be a fool or be made a fool of. You hurt me Levy. You said things that were hurtful. When I left Barbados, we left with the understanding that you will get your life in order then contact me (and of course we would talk in between time). I sincerely hope that you get yourself together and start living the life you desire. I love you Levy and I want us to be together.*

Kia gets a call from Jordyn who was checking on her, "Dawg, I know you just left Barbados but I want you to come back with me in December."

"Week 50?" Kia confirms.

"Week 50."

"Let me think a minute because that is another major trip in just a few months and I don't know if I can afford that."

"Listen, I will buy your ticket, just pay me back half."

"Ahh man, you don't have to do that."

"Dawg, it's okay. I know you have been through a lot. Besides you are only paying me back half for the ticket and we are staying at the timeshare so you won't have to pay for lodging. What's there to think about?"

"You're right. Ok, I'm in!"

Kia is excited because she is going back even though her last trip was heartbreak in paradise.

September 15, 2013 - Part 2
Well, it is official. I will be back in Barbados on December 13, 2013. I can't wait to see you. Hopefully, we will have the chance to spend some time together and even have another tryst in Foul Bay. Anyway, it is my sincere hope that you have made some progress towards getting yourself together by then. That is if you want to be with me. Anyway, I'm sleepy and need to go to sleep. I will talk with you or write you tomorrow. XOXO

September 16, 2013
Good evening babe. I hope all is well with you. Listen, I talked with you this morning and told you that I hope you get yourself together because I really want to be with you but we can't be together as long as you are with her and living in her house. I

will be honest; it hurts me to know that right now you are probably laid up with her while my heart aches for you. I wish I could make all of your troubles go away but I don't have a magic wand. All I can do is pray for you, me and us. I guess I need to make sure you want to be with me and not her. I guess proof of that will come in time. The only thing I ask is that if at some point you decide you don't want to be with me, let me know and let me go, and I will do the same. As you said before I left, you believe our paths crossed for a reason and I believe the same. I believe <u>we</u> were meant to be together. I love you....

September 19, 2013
Levy I really want to talk to you because I need to make sure that you want to be with me. I know what you say, but now the trust is gone. It can be rebuilt but that takes time. I just want to make sure because I don't have time to play games in life. Levy I am mad as hell that you played with my emotions for the last 9 ½ months. I LOVE YOU!!!! We talked about a future together and it absolutely tears me apart to know that at night you are sleeping WITH HER, but yet during the day you are telling ME you love ME. I should just walk away now, but something inside of me won't let me give up on US. I refuse to believe that the words you told me (you don't crave me....and this does not feel right) are true. I believe you tried to use them as a way to escape from telling me the truth about your situation. I could be wrong, but I pray that I am not. Dammit Levy!!!! Why couldn't you have told me the truth??!!! SHIT!!!!! I mean why take me through this? Did you tell her you proposed to me? You couldn't have. You just don't know I always referred to you as MY HUSBAND. When I returned I was going to file your visa papers on October 1, I was going to tell my family we were getting married and start planning our wedding....Finally, I would officially be on the way to being Mrs. Brathwaite that I referred to myself as. I guess the hardest part is that I told you my deepest and darkest secret, and you came back the next day and did not judge me or leave me, but yet you couldn't be honest and upfront with me. Oh Levy...I don't know what to do.....I do know that I love you.

September 23, 2013
Levy, oh Levy. I don't even know what to say. As you know, I love you, but it hurts me to know that you are with her. This morning when you called me you told me you would call me later because you were going to be with her all day. While I VERY MUCH APPRECIATE your honesty, I was hurt. Like right now it is midnight in Barbados, and it tears me up to know that you are with her in her bed. I really would like it if you move out. *PERIOD* I know it would be unfair of me to ask you to move out now knowing you probably don't have anywhere to go. HOWEVER, I feel like if you really wanted to be with me, you would do what you have to do. Now, I know you say you are in the process of getting yourself together and I believe you but what is going to happen when it comes time to move out? The more time you spend with a woman the stronger her feelings grow. So again I ask, what is going to happen when it comes time for you to move out? Did you tell her that you want to be with me and are getting your life together to be with me? Of course you didn't because you are still with her or did you tell her and you are playing both of us? IDK....I really hope that is not the case. I do love you and I want us to be together FOREVER!!!

September 27, 2013
Levy do you realize today is the first day in the 286 days that I have known you that I did not call you? There have been days that we have not talked but I have called you every single one of them. Yesterday, when you told me about the ultimatum she gave you and your decision, you asked me to let you call me first from now on until things settle down. So I did that, and you did not call me. I don't know why you didn't call me. You said you would keep credit on your phone to call me. I try not to worry about you, but I do. Levy, dammit; pick me, choose me, love me!!!!! What gets me is that it's almost like I am supposed to roll over and take this shit. I can't do that. I need you to know that my heart hurts. I don't want to put added pressure on you, but look it's time to put up or shut up!! Meaning, stop talking about getting yourself together, and GET yourself together!!! *PERIOD* I really believe that when your

situation became what it is, you thought you would have it resolved before you saw me again, so you wouldn't have to tell me about it. What you didn't count on was me coming back when I did. So you had to come clean with me because I was going to want to see where you live, etc...and I wanted you to stay with me while I was there. But then you had to come clean with her because there was no way you could explain staying with me for 9 nights, or you would be homeless. Levy, my love, you are truly caught between a rock and a hard place especially if you want to be with me.

One Sunday afternoon in early October, Kia talks to Levy as she had most Sunday afternoons and almost every day in between since she has been back. "So how are you?" she asks.

"I'm okay, just missing you."

"I miss you too, Levy. So, are you any closer to getting things together for yourself?" What Levy didn't know is that Kia has already made up in her mind that she will give him until his 33rd birthday which is in May to get himself together. In the meantime, she will date other people if the opportunity comes about but that is not going to be her focus. She certainly is not going to get into another relationship with anybody.

"Yes, I have some things in the works that should help."

"Ok. That's cool. So how long do you think you need to get yourself together?" she asks.

"Until the end of the year," he responds.

This is a lot quicker than Kia had expected, and she is glad about it. "End of the year? Ok that's cool. But when I say get yourself together I mean move out into your own place." She wants to make it very clear what she is talking about.

Suddenly Single

"I know what you mean, and if everything goes according to plan, then yes by the end of the year I should be moved out."

"Ok Levy. I just want to make sure you know what I'm talking about."

"I do, and I love you."

"I love you too. Talk to you later."

Kia had conversations of this sort pretty much every day with Levy. It is almost as if they are still together.

> **October 7, 2013**
> *You sent me a text today that said you feel I want you to get put out. How could you say that? Why would you say that? Because I called you? Of course I want you out of her house BUT 1) I don't want to see you homeless and 2) I want you to want to leave her house and leave on your own free will NOT because you got put out. Now I have been nice the last few days and have obliged your request not to call you first but damn Levy, I feel like you are putting me in a box with communicating with you. What about me Levy? I feel like I am the one having to sacrifice. I want the freedom to talk to you when I want to...when I need to. You always tell me I don't understand the pressure you are under, but I can't if you don't tell me......*

October 14, 2013 - Kia is at work and she gets a message on Facebook from Levy:

Hi

          Hey Babe!! How are you?

I want to talk to you for a minute

          Ok...Cool

This is not Levy

Kia's heart stopped.

>Who is this?

My name is Chevelle, Levy lives with me but we are not a full fledge couple. He told me about you. But I believe most of what he told me is lies.

>What did he tell you?

He told me that he met you in December and that you guys were in communication and you surprised him and came to Barbados. He also told me you guys had sex three times.

>Why do you think that is lies?

Not that part

>What part then?

Give me a minute. A day you called him and asked him if he was crying right?

>???

Kia recalls the day she is referencing, but she wants to see where Chevelle is going with this.

I was right next to him, and I had just told him that I don't want him. He cried and begged me for days. I told him he could stay but just as a friend.

When he went with you on the Monday that you came, I told he to go and be happy, however 2 days later he calls and tells

Suddenly Single

me that he is with you but can't stop thinking about me. He came back, and we talked all night and he told me that he is ready to be the man that I am looking for and that he will go and tell you his feelings.

Kia's heart is on the ground. She can't believe what she is reading. She walks around to her friend Kimi's desk for support because she is at a loss for words. She is livid.

> I'm a little confused as to why you are sharing this with me if you all are not a full fledge couple and you don't want him......

He is kind, but he lies sooooooo much. That night when he came from by you he told me that he was prepared to change and do anything to be with me. He said he wants to be an open book and gave me his Facebook and e-mail passwords to prove that he was no longer communicating with you.

This confirms it for Kia. When Levy left that Wednesday night, he left to be with her. What Chevelle didn't know is that Kia has the Facebook and e-mail passwords too. She isn't going to tell her because that is not something she needs to know.

And that is where I saw the pictures of you and him kiss and with my car in the background. Those were the very same days and nights he was begging me to be with him and telling me that you don't mean nothing to him.

Kia is about to explode. She is furious!!

He said that the second night you were together he didn't have sex with you because all he could think about was me and that you begged him for sex.

He is right here saying that is not true that he does not call you ever, that you call him.

> He is lying. Check the call log. I just talked to Levy last night...and HE CALLS ME EVERYDAY...Every morning... And I call him in the afternoons

I will. He said that you call him crying and begging.

> Chevelle, let me tell you something: First of all Levy knew I was coming there...I bought my ticket 63 days out...If you look on his page I made a post to that effect. Right before I came he asked me to send him a text saying I got two weeks off work and I am coming to Barbados so he could show off to his "cousin". So he knew damn well I was coming. In retrospect, he probably did that to try and make it look like I was surprising him...Bastard... And let me be clear about something, I was not begging for anything. Crying yes because I get emotional about the people I love. But begging...hell no!

I know that the stories he has been telling me can't be true. They don't make sense.

> When I was there he did not tell me about you until the 5th day....when he broke up with me...We were supposed to get married next year. He proposed to me "unofficially" on January 23rd of this year.

He only slept away from home 2 nights. He told me that it was you that asked he to get married before you leave after he broke up with you.

> I know he only he stayed 2 nights with me because he picked a fight with me to leave on the third night...I later asked him did he leave because he HAD to leave and he said yes...meaning he HAD to leave and come be with you. He asked me to marry him......I came with the documentation for the fiancé visa

> so we could speed up the process...after the breakup he asked me if I could hold papers for 6 months. I told him I could but I wasn't....in an effort to save my relationship I did say let's just go to the magistrate there but then he told me it was not that easy.

Wow, you would not believe how this boy begs me, does anything I ask him.

> I believe it....he painted the picture for me as if you were a place to stay for him. I knew that if it was a roommate type of situation with you then he could've stayed all 9 nights that I was there so I knew it had to be more to it than that.

He told me you met last year but did not have sex.

> That is true. We did not have sex until I came back.

Is it true that you only had sex three times?

> Yes that is true 3 times in 10 days.

Kia is really furious at this point because he has told this woman the most intimate details of their relationship. There is no way she could have known this unless he told her.

This boy is a piece of work. Right this minute he is kneeling at the bottom of my bed begging telling me that you are lying, and that he doesn't know why you would lie. I know that it is him that is lying. He said that you are desperate to be with him that way he is desperate to be with me.

> Levy is lying...He tells me he loves me every day!! He told me just yesterday that I am a wonderful and special woman...I feel like he is begging you because he does not want you to put him out...

I agree. I shouldn't even say this but when we do have sex he licks EVERY part of me telling me that I am the only one he ever did that to because he loves me so much and would do anything on earth to be with me. He said that he told you that you are a wonderful person but not that he loves you.

> Lies he is telling.

He has somewhere that he can go

> Well maybe he should go.

Yes he should, he just left and came back inside crying.

> Because this what happens when you lie...I don't know if he told you but I am coming back in December with a friend of mine... Tell him don't bother calling me. This is a fucked up situation but I thank you for sharing this information with me.

Ok same here. You can call me when you get to Barbados 234-5678.

Kia is speechless. She is at a loss for what to say or what to do, but in a strange way she is relieved. Kia asked God three times if Levy was the one for her and to please let her know and show her if he isn't. Each time the response was a little greater but this time it is like He slapped her on the face to make sure she didn't miss it. This is the most powerful and impactful response that she got. There is no way she could ignore this. Equally, there is no way she can wait until she got to Barbados to call Chevelle. When she returned from lunch, she dialed her number.

"Yes, hello?"

"Chevelle?"

"Yes, this is she."

"Hi, good afternoon, this is Kia. How are you?"

"Aww Kia. I'm doing well thank you. Thank you for asking."

"Listen, I decided to go ahead and call you to talk to you about our conversation earlier. So, how long have you known Levy?"

"I've known Levy for about 12 years. He and I have dated off and on during that time and currently we are not together. Levy is sweet as pie but he lies so much for no reason, and I can't take that."

"So, how did he come about living with you?"

"He lives with me yes, but we have a lease agreement. He has his own room that he pays me rent for. See my sister rented out rooms in her home, and Levy lived there. Then she decided to move so I decided to rent a room in my home, and that is when he came to live with me."

"So, how long has he lived with you?"

"Since right before Christmas last year."

"Oh, ok then so more or less around the time that we met."

"Yes that would be correct."

Kia is taking mental notes because she remembers Levy moving but it wasn't until around April. "Really? Huh. Ok and you say he pays you rent?"

"Yes he does. Listen, Levy does nothing but make it easy for me. I own an ice cream shop and sometimes in exchange for using my car he will open the shop for me and run errands that need to be ran for the shop. He's a good guy, but he just lies so much. This is not the Levy that I met 12 years ago. When he told me about you, I told him to go and be happy. We are not together. Then he told me that he did not want to be with you anymore that he wanted to be with me. I told him by the looks of the pics on Facebook he did not look too unhappy. You two looked very happy together. And he told me that he only took those pics to look happy for you and your friends. He just lies so much. Then I saw the one with my car in the background and you know how he got my car that day?"

"No, tell me."

"I am having a house built not too far from where you guys were in Foul Bay and he told me that he was going to do some work on my house that day because he is helping to build it."

"He did do some work on a house that day but he said it was for his aunt."

"Yes, she is getting a house built too, and he is doing most of the construction on it. I just don't know what to do with him. He was crying and begging me earlier not to put him out and to give him until the end of the year to get himself together before I decide if I want to be with him or not because he is ready to be the man I want and that he really wants to be with me."

"Until the end of the year? That's funny because just a few days ago I asked him how long he needed to get himself together and he told me until the end of the year. So, I guess whether or not he would 'have himself together' depended on what your response to him was going to be."

"Yes, he told me that he was going to string you along as plan B in case I didn't take him back."

"He said what? That muthafucka! Huh uh…. Let me just tell you Chevelle that I am nobody's plan B! And I damn sure am not now or not ever the gullible and desperate soul he made me out to be. I love Levy, but I refuse to let him do me that way or paint me in a horrible light. So can I ask you how old are you?"

"The same as you."

"39?"

"Yes."

"So damn he told you everything then. That just pisses me off."

"He did. He claims he was trying to be transparent with me and tell me everything so I would know that he was not hiding anything from me. Oh and another thing…where you were staying by the Chefette is maybe a 5 minute walk from my house, 1 minute by car."

Kia is flabbergasted. So on the night he left, even though he made it to Chevelle's house in less than 10 minutes, he did not let her know he made it home until a couple of hours later, sneaky bastard.

"Well, he must really want to be with you because he has told me nothing about you other than the fact that it was your idea for him to break up with me. Then he made you out to be crazy and as if you would kick him out if you found out we are still together. I just can't believe this. Well listen, I'm sure we can go on all day about Levy said this and Levy said that, but I need to go back to work. I thank you for this information."

"You are welcome. I just wanted you to know what was going on because as a woman, I would want to know."

"Well, I appreciate it. Take Care."

"You take care as well, and call me when you get to Barbados if you want."

"Will do, bye now."

Kia is once again overwhelmed by what she has just learned. It is no way in hell Levy is the one for her. "I get it God. Thank you for showing me!!!"

Chapter 24

The day after her conversation with Chevelle, Kia's phone rings at approximately 5:20 AM.

"Hello?"

"Good morning. Can you call me back?"

"No, Levy, I cannot. What is it?"

"Are you happy for what you did yesterday?"

"What?! Hello?? Hello?? Did this muthafucka hang up on me?!?!"

Now Kia is pissed that Levy called her so early in the morning, interrupting her sleep with this bullshit. She tries to go back to sleep, and she manages to right before her alarm goes off. Kia doesn't have time for these types of games. On her way to work she is thinking about everything that has occurred, and be quick to forgive is dropped in her spirit. She does not want to walk around harboring anger and bitterness, so she decides to call him.

"Hello?"

"Levy listen, I only have 5 minutes credit, and I'm not adding more so listen up. It was fucked up what you did you to me, but I do not want there to be any bitterness between us so I forgive you. I know you have said in the past that talking to me has helped you through difficult times and if this is true then you can still call me from time to time if you need to."

"Ok. Thank you. I have to go."

"Ok, bye!"

Later that night Kia gets a message on Facebook from Levy or so she thought.

```
Hi this is Chevelle. Just thought I'd log into Levy's
account to see how you were doing. Are you alright?
```

```
                    Yes Chevelle I am doing fine. Thank you for
                    asking…How are you?
```

Kia is a little perplexed as to why Chevelle is checking on her. She figures Levy must've told her she called him this morning since he tells her everything.

```
Good he told me that he called you and asked you to
call him back and you didn't.  He said he wanted to
apologize to you.  I told him that he owes you an
apology.
```

```
                    He definitely does but I do not want it if
                    it is not genuine. He did call me at 5:20
                    this morning. In my slumber it sounded like
                    he was trying to blame me for what
                    happened, and I couldn't talk to him at
                    that moment if that was the case.
```

```
Blame you for what? You didn't do anything wrong.
```

```
                    I know that and you know that, but I was
                    not sure if he knew that.
```

```
Hmmm…. I don't know.  We are not together. He is still
here, but I haven't seen him that much. When I saw him
last night, he did ask me if I could do two things for
him and that is 1)forgive him and 2)don't give up on
giving him the opportunity to prove himself to me. I
told him that I had 0 trust in him.
```

Suddenly Single

> So he is still trying to get you after all of this…smh… I did call him this morning to tell him that I don't want there to be any bitterness between us and that he can call me from time to time… I wouldn't trust him either.

You are strong. I would be fuming if I were you and came all the way to Barbados. But you are right, we have to forgive if we expect to be forgiven but forgetting is another thing. And yes, he is absolutely still trying to get with me. He tells me every time we see or speak to each other, but I think I've had enough of him and his promising to get his act together.

Think? Kia scratches her head on this one.

> Don't get me wrong, I was fuming! But that takes too much energy. I do miss Levy…he was an integral part of my daily life so not talking to him multiple times a day is hard for me…I love him but I love me more…and I REFUSE to let him play me any further. It is rather clear to me that he does not want me and that is okay…I don't blame you for being tired of dealing with him and his promises…He is a grown man and it is time for him to act like it.

Well said.

> Thank you ☺

I'm glad that you are okay. I am too. He is the one that shouldn't be ok with all that he has done. If he realized the chemistry wasn't there, he should have been 100% honest with you and when he came to me that night at 1 in the morning begging to be with me, he should have told me the whole truth and not just the parts he wanted me to hear. He messed up all the way around.

> Yes he did mess up…hopefully he will learn from this and learn that honesty is always the best. I feel like he lied to me twice. Once for not telling me the situation then again for not telling what the situation really is or was.

He said you never cussed him out or told him off for what he did, well let me tell you I did it enough for the both of us. I cussed him out good and proper. Told him some pretty mean things. I told him he was a boy and a coward. He got told OFF.

> LOL. He deserved it. Thank you. I didn't cuss him out because that is not me. I'm very laid back plus it is harder to be mad at someone who is keeping calm. Don't get me wrong now, I do get upset and you will get told but I have to be pushed to the limit.

I have to run but it was nice chatting with you and take care.

> It was nice chatting with you as well…take care.

Kia shakes her head and chuckles. She loves Levy, but she knows it's time to move on from him. The easiest way for her to do that is to stop all communication with him, and she hopes that she can do that. She has a tendency for having weak moments, but it helps that Javel has sent her a rather delightful photo of himself. All of a sudden, Kia sees him in a whole different light.

October 15, 2013
Yesterday I get a Facebook message from Chevelle. Imagine my surprise…She basically laid it on the line for me and told me some truths about you. What got me was the fact that this woman that I have never met told me the intimate details of our relationship down to the number of times we had sex and on what days. She also told me that you have your own room in her house and you pay her rent. So if this is true then I could have stayed with you or at the very least have seen where you live. But being that did not happen lets me know that at least in your mind you held her in a higher regard, meaning you at least thought you and her had more of a relationship than what we did, and that you thought you had more of a relationship with her than what you actually did. What Chevelle basically clarified for me was that 1) you really want to be with her 2) she doesn't want to be with you and 3) you were stalling me and keeping me as your "Plan B" in case she wouldn't take you back or if she decided not to be with you at the end of this year. Then you call me early this morning and have the unmitigated gall to blame me for yesterday. Are you fucking kidding me?!? Get the fuck outta here with that bullshit. Part of me wants to wake up from this nightmare but the other part of me knows this is my painful reality. I'm not going to lie, this is hard on me because you were an integral part of my life and I don't deal well with change. I love you but I love me more and I'll be damned if I am going to be anybody's PLAN B!!! In the off chance we were meant for each other, just not at this time, then our paths will cross again. If it is meant to be it will be….

Over the next couple of days, Kia talks to one of her closest and dearest friends that happens to also be a marriage and family therapist. He reassures her that the feelings she is having and the emotions of it all are okay. She tells him that she has been journaling and he encourages her to keep it up.

Kia still talks to Levy periodically because it is hard for her to cut him loose cold turkey but after today's conversation she believes she is at that point.

October 20, 2013

*FUCK YOU LEVY!!! YOU TOLD ME TODAY THAT EVERY "I LOVE YOU", EVERY "I MISS YOU", EVERY "I WANT TO BE WITH YOU" WAS A **LIE**!!! FUCK YOU!!! YOU DON'T DO THAT TO PEOPLE. YOU DON'T STRING PEOPLE ALONG FOR 10 MONTHS AND THEN TELL THEM IT WAS ALL A LIE. YOU BETTER HOPE YOU DON'T GET WHAT YOU DESERVE. YOU BETTER HOPE GOD EXTENDS HIS MERCY AND GRACE TO YOU. YOU DON'T WANT TO TALK TO ME ANYMORE BECAUSE YOU ARE TRYING TO WORK IT OUT WITH CHEVELLE...WAKE UP LEVY SHE DOESN'T WANT YOU!! BUT GOOD LUCK ON TRYING TO GET HER. MAYBE IF SHE STRINGS YOU ALONG YOU WILL GET A TASTE OF HOW I FELT. BUT IF NOT THAT'S OKAY BECAUSE YOU REAP WHAT YOU SOW, AND IF YOU SOW SEEDS OF LIES, DECIET, HURT AND DISTRUST THEN THAT IS WHAT YOU WILL GET IN RETURN. I HATE IT HAD TO END THIS WAY BUT FUCK YOU!!!!*

Chapter 25

Kia struggles from time to time with not talking to Levy anymore. She is pissed at him so that makes it a little easier to deal with; however, it is still difficult and takes time to detach emotionally from somebody that you cared so deeply about. It definitely helps that Kia and Javel have maintained constant communication since she has been gone and they have become quite good friends. She sees him in a totally different light than before. She is in a different place emotionally than from when they met, and she is able to see him for what he is....intelligent, sincere, and not to mention extremely sexy. When she returns in a few weeks, she definitely plans to see him and spend some time with him.

Kia is sitting at her desk daydreaming of Barbados and how she can't wait to get there when she is interrupted by her phone vibrating.

Incoming call from Javel McClain

"Hey babes, good morning."

"Good morning, how are you this morning?" Kia asks.

"I'm doing ok, just thinking about you while I'm sitting out here on the beach, so I figured I would give you a shout."

"Awww, that's sweet. Thank you. That makes me feel good. I can't wait to see you when I get there in a few days."

"I can't wait either," he tells her. "I miss you and I can't wait to kiss your lips...both sets."

Kia is blushing because she can't wait either and she can only imagine what he is going to feel like because he is definitely blessed on so many levels. "Oooh wee, you got me hot and bothered just thinking about it. Damn!"

"Because you are a naughty girl," he chuckles. "I will talk to you later ok? Have a good day."

"Ok, I will talk to you later. You have a good day as well."

Talking to Javel always makes Kia feel good inside. It has been a big distraction from the break up with Levy. Kia still thinks about him almost every day but her longing to be with him has diminished.

The day has finally come for Kia to return to Barbados with Jordyn. Kia is a bundle of nerves, and she is contemplating whether or not she will even call Levy. She has made a conscience effort not to forget the journal because she really wants him to have it, but she doesn't necessarily want to see him because she does not want to stir up any residual feelings she may have for him. She has been so stressed about this that she has made herself sick these last few days. She cannot seem to hold down any food and she feels lightheaded most of the time. She pulls herself together because she does not want anything to ruin her vacation.

She has made it through this flight with no problems and is waiting to meet Jordyn in the Miami International Airport. Luckily, she does not have to wait too long before Jordyn lands and while she is waiting she decides that she will go ahead and call Levy because she really does want to give him this journal. While it cannot change what has happened, she wants him to see on paper and be reminded of what he took her through emotionally. She wants him to somehow feel her pain.

Suddenly Single

Jordyn and Kia arrive in Barbados and get checked in to their hotel. Since they arrive a couple of days ahead of when the timeshare starts, they stay at the Hilton Barbados the extra two days and absolutely fall in love with it. Once settled in the room, Kia calls Levy to try and get in touch with him, but there is no answer.

"Dawg, why are you trying to call him? Can't you just leave him alone?" Jordyn inquires.

"I want him to have this journal. He needs to really understand what he did to me. I don't want him back or anything like that. I just want him to know."

"I guess."

Kia tries a couple of hours later to reach him, and there is still no answer. *Could he be avoiding me?* she thinks to herself. Fed up with him not answering the phone because she feels he is dodging her, she decides to try another approach.

> Hi Chevelle, this is Kia. I made it to Barbados and I just wanted to tell you thank you again for all of the information that you shared with me. It really helped me to see Levy for who he is. Listen, I need a favor: I have something for Levy and I really want him to have it, do you mind passing the message on to him?

Excuse me Boss you have a text message: Hi Kia. I'm glad you reached the island. Sure, I do not mind passing along the message. But may I ask why not just call him directly yourself?

> I tried calling him twice and for some reason he is not answering my calls. I know he listens to you so I figured I would ask you to relay the message if you don't mind.

Excuse me boss you have a text message: Oh ok. I see. It's no problem. He said he does not want whatever you have but knowing him he will probably contact you later to pick it up.

```
I doubt it, but thank you for passing along the message
and thank you again for everything.
```

Excuse me boss you have a text message: `You're welcome.  Enjoy your time here on the island.`

Kia is not satisfied with this response but she lets it ride for now. She just got here, and she wants to relax and start her vacation on a good note. In between calls to Levy and texts to Chevelle, she gets in touch with Javel and they agree to meet later that evening. He will pick her up from the hotel and they will go from there. She is excited because they have done some heavy flirting the last couple of months, and Kia is ready to see if he can back up everything he said. In the meantime, she and Jordyn explore the resort in search of some nourishment.

"How do I look?" Kia asks Jordyn. She wants to make sure she is looking right for Javel.

"You look fine!! Does it matter anyway? He is only going to see your dress for a few minutes before taking it off," she laughs.

"Says who?" Kia says with her jaw dropped to the ground, appalled at the thought that she would dare show him what is under her dress. "You're right!!" she laughs. She knows good and well it's not really the dress she has on that has to be right but more so the bra and panties she has on underneath. She has on her favorite pair of black thong panties with a black strapless bra to match.

She finishes primping and gives Jordyn all of Javel's phone numbers because she does not know exactly what the night has in store, and she needs for Jordyn to be able to tell the police who she was with in case she didn't come back.

Suddenly Single

Kia heads for the lobby to wait on him to get her. He called her a few minutes ago saying he is on his way. While she is waiting she can't help but to think about Levy and how he brushed her off. She tries not to let this anger her because she wants to have a good time tonight and not let thoughts of Levy ruin her evening.

Javel finally arrives. He took a little longer that what Kia expected, but it is worth it to see him again.

"Hi good night!!" he says as he is walking over to her to give her a hug.

"Heeeyyy, how are you?" she says squeezing him as hard as she can. She can't help but be taken in by his masculine scent. She is excited already.

"So how was your flight in?"

"It was ok, uneventful. I guess that's good when it comes to flights."

"Yes I suppose you are right," he says as he looks at her and starts rubbing on her leg.

She instantly starts to tingle on the inside. It's like he has awoken a sleeping beast in her with a single touch. She can't help but look at him for most of the way to his house. She can't believe she didn't see his sex appeal before. She is so consumed with Javel that all thoughts of Levy have vacated Kia's mind and have been replaced with nervous excitement of what the night has in store.

When they reach Javel's home, he gives her a quick tour then she takes her seat on the couch.

"Would you like something to drink?"

"Sure, what do you have?"

"I have some lemonade I made this morning."

"That sounds perfect. Yes I will take some."

He brings her the lemonade and she takes a sip. "Oh my God this is good!!! How did you make it?"

"It's the secret ingredient that makes it good," he laughs.

"Well, what is that?" she asks as she takes another sip.

"It's a secret. If I tell you I might have to spank you if you let it slip."

"I might like that. You never know," she smirks.

"You're a naughty girl, and I like it!" he says as he walks over to her and bends down and kisses her sending pulses of energy to that spot between her legs. He tells her to move over to the chair and when she does he kneels down in front of her and traces the outline of her thighs with his tongue until he reaches the top of her panties in which he takes off in one slow motion. He raises her dress to get a closer look at the prize, and he tells her to scoot closer to the edge of the chair. She slides down and she is almost flat in the chair, just her shoulders and neck are touching the back of it.

He puts her legs over his shoulders and he dives in face first tasting every fold from the top to the bottom. Kia instantly starts to moan in ecstasy. She couldn't fool herself any longer; this is what she has been waiting for, the chance for him to prove he can back up everything he has told her over the last couple of months.

Kia is so enthralled with how this man is tasting her very essence, she didn't even realize the front door is wide open and she is sitting right in front of it. She doesn't care. He manages to find the key to unlock the flood gates contained within her lower half. She couldn't help but release her nectar in his mouth. When he comes up for air she tastes herself on his lips, and she tastes sweet. He closes the door and ushers Kia to the bedroom. He slowly pulls off her dress pulling down each strap one at a time licking every inch of exposed skin in the process until the dress falls to the ground. He disrobes and Kia couldn't help but reach out and stroke his massive erection.

"Oh my God," she whisper moans.

"What is it? Not enough for you?" he whispers in her ear.

"On the contrary," she manages to say in between kisses to his lips and neck.

"Lay down."

Kia complies. She lies down on the bed on her back. He spreads her legs apart holding one in each hand and he proceeds to flick the bundle of nerves hidden within her lower lips with his tongue. She couldn't help but let out a loud moan as she is already sensitive in this area. Just when she is at the point where she can't take anymore, he replaces his tongue with that massive erection and Kia almost chokes. She gasps for air because he takes up every inch of her wet spot. He touches her in places and in ways she has not been touched before.

About an hour later Kia sends Jordyn a quick text letting her know she is ok and she will be back in the morning. After Jordyn responds, Kia puts up her phone and retreats to the bed. She does not want to lie in the wet spot but that is difficult because it extends to both sides of the bed. Javel spreads a towel for them to lie on because he is too tired to change the sheets, and more than likely, there will be another session either before they go to sleep or in the morning or both.

Javel returns Kia back to the hotel early the next morning before he goes to work, and they agree to meet again that evening. Kia slips in the room and tries not to disturb Jordyn because she knows she is a light sleeper. She takes a shower and gets in the bed and tries to get some sleep seeing as how she only got about an hour's worth of sleep the night before.

After sleeping a good little while, Jordyn wakes Kia to see if she wants to go to breakfast, and of course, Kia does not miss any meals. She puts on some clothes and meets Jordyn downstairs at the restaurant. The ladies order their breakfast and are engaging in hearty conversation. They are glad the clouds have parted the sky and the sun is out. Kia gets up to go to the bathroom and when she returns she stands there a minute.

"Dawg what is wrong with you? Why don't you sit down?"

"I can't," Kia says with her voice shaking a little.

"What's wrong?"

"Ummm, I'm really sore if you know what I mean. Like it hurts to really even stand here much less sit. I think my shit is swollen."

"Got damn!!!! That's what I'm talking about!! He put it on you like that?!?! Ooooh wee!! Yea, take your time sitting. I understand completely."

Kia couldn't help but laugh. She is indeed hurting and he did indeed put it on her like that. She briefly reconsiders tonight's meeting but quickly banishes the thought. She is only on this island for a few days and she intends to take full advantage.

"So what's on the agenda for today?" Kia asks trying to take her mind off of the throbbing between her legs as she sits down.

"I say go to the beach. Either one of them around here is fine."

"That's what I was thinking too. I need to soak in the sea. That natural salt should be like Epsom salt I guess."

Jordyn couldn't help but laugh. "The beach it is then."

Later that afternoon as the women are leaving the beach, Kia sees a pay phone and she decides to attempt to call Levy. Maybe he will be more apt to pick up the phone since it will be coming from a local number and not her number. She puts in the change and dials his number but again it just rings and rings. Kia tries not to grow frustrated, but she really wants him to have this journal. She leaves it alone for now and goes to the room to get cleaned up and prepare herself for tonight's meeting with Javel.

After she gets dressed she decides to make one last attempt to contact Levy so she sends a text: Levy, I have something for you. It is not something bad, but it is something that I want you to have. If you don't want to see me that is fine, I can leave it at the front desk of the Hilton for you but before I do that let me know if this is what you want me to do. Thanks

Kia waits and waits but Levy never responds. She is pissed that he is ignoring her but resigns to the fact that he will not see the last entry which is perhaps the most important in the journal.

    December 13, 2013
    I'm pregnant.

Acknowledgements

M. Sherrer would like to thank:

My Family:
Thank you for always being supportive in anything that I do,
and especially to my mother and sister for always taking care of my baby when
I'm off on an adventure.

And to the Lord God Almighty Himself:
Thank you for answering prayers!!! Thank you for dropping this book in my
spirit and seeing me through until the end. You placed the right people in my
life at the right time to make this possible and for that I am grateful.

Dark Diamond Publishing, LLC.

Check us out and follow us at

www.darkdiamondbooks.com
www.facebook.com/DarkDiamondPublishing
www.twitter.com/dd_publishing

Read excerpts and subscribe to the newsletter. Stay tuned for future developments from M. Sherrer and Dark Diamond Publishing

About M. Sherrer

M. Sherrer makes her writing debut with Suddenly Single: Heartbreak in Paradise. Hailing from Houston, TX, she enjoys escaping to the Caribbean and unofficially claims Barbados as her second home. Her host of life experiences and her love for adventure will aid her in future works.

Learn more about M. Sherrer at
www.darkdiamondbooks.com/author_msherrer.html

www.ingramcontent.com/pod-product-compliance
Lightning Source LLC
Chambersburg PA
CBHW061630040426
42446CB00010B/1344